AF557793

MIDDLE CLASS INDIA

MIDDLE CLASS INDIA

Driving Change in the 21st Century

MANISHA PANDE

ALEPH

ALEPH BOOK COMPANY
An independent publishing firm
promoted by ***Rupa Publications India***

First published in India in 2024
by Aleph Book Company
7/16 Ansari Road, Daryaganj
New Delhi 110 002

ISBN: 978-81-19635-46-7

1 3 5 7 9 10 8 6 4 2

Printed in India

Dedicated to
Ma and Babu

∽

Contents

PART III

FROM LIBERALIZATION TO THE PRESENT

(1991 Onwards)

Introduction

Globally, India is in a unique position today. With a population of about 1.4 billion, it is the most populated country in the world; it is the world's largest democracy; and, as per the World GDP Ranking 2024 list, it is the fifth largest economy. The biggest factor behind India's increasing influence has been its middle class, which has seen unprecedented growth since the economic liberalization in 1991. Between 1995 and 2021, the middle class, which is an eclectic mix of social identities, grew at a rate of 6.3 per cent per year. Currently, it constitutes 31 per cent of the population, when using a higher income band (approximately $17–100 per day[1]), and is expected to hit the 60 per cent mark by 2047.[2] The highlight of the Indian growth story is that, according to a recent UNFPA report, 24 per cent of the middle-class population falls in the age bracket of 0–14 and the segment aged 10–24 constitutes 26 per cent.[3] Thus, India has a fairly young middle class, as compared to the ageing middle class of China.

An expanding middle class scripts progress for a country because it increases consumption, which drives the economy. The rapidly expanding Indian middle class, despite broad variations in income between its sub-classes, presents a promising consumer market to the world. India is now recognized as one of the fastest growing economies in the world, second only to China. The growth of the Asian middle class has reshaped the global consumption market, with the balance shifting to the emerging markets of Asia. And since the growth rate is faster than its western counterparts, it holds sway over decisions related to product and service development. According to World Bank estimates, by 2030, both India and China will constitute roughly two-thirds of the global middle-class population and 59 per cent of middle-class consumption that is expected to tally $64 trillion by 2030. Which means that middle-class spending in both countries will exceed the combined middle-class spending in Europe and the US in 2015. And though by then 70 per cent of the Chinese population would have entered the middle-class bracket, India is expected to surpass both China and the US due to its sheer bulk.[4]

The journey of this class from a somewhat subdued presence to being the main driving force of the country needs to be studied to understand how it came to acquire such power as to influence political decisions and economic trends, and dictate social norms. It is equally important to comprehend the challenges it faces from its heterogenous existence and how they can impact the country's progress in the future. As India completes seventy-seven years of independence, it is only befitting to acknowledge the role of its most socially and politically ambulant class—the middle class—in shaping the country. The very nature of this class makes it the main driving force of India's economy. It is ambitious, upwardly mobile, imaginative and innovative, ruthless in pursuing its goals, and it adapts to changes easily. In a sense, it is the foundation on which India's dream of becoming a $5 trillion economy is built.

Much has been written about this class, about its role in politics, economy, society, about its ideologies and its various identities, and about its beliefs and value systems. Still, there are certain aspects that could do with reviewing as they change over time. For example, scholars are now exploring the concept of 'rewealthization' and its impact on the middle classes of the West. In the case of India, too, the story of the middle class needs to be seen from a new perspective, an Indian perspective. This is what this book aims to do: provide a fresh perspective on the middle class and its development in the light of sociological, political, economic, religious, and psychological developments that have taken place in Indian society.

Giving a definitive explanation of what constitutes the middle class is perhaps one of the most difficult tasks as there are no set criteria to arrive at a definition. Over the years, the term has become subjective and can be approached from various angles, each presenting a set of characteristics that, although similar on most counts, differ from each other drastically in some perspectives. Economists, for example, describe the middle class as an 'economic strata that falls between the working class and the upper class'. They base the distinction mainly on income or wealth. Sociologists, on the other hand, define it as 'a class of people intermediate between the classes of higher and lower social rank or standing', the emphasis being on social status, although the markers remain the same, that is, education, occupation, income, etc.[5] Anthropologists define the middle class in terms of culture. The focus, in this case, shifts to lifestyle, attitude, and self-assessment. Thus, although the markers that determine the middle class remain more or less the same, their context and perceptions change according to the theme of the argument.

Also, what needs to be understood is that the definition of middle class changed from time to time, as new parameters were added to it. It began with a simple segregation of a class of people falling between the upper strata and the working class. From there on, at every turn of development, be it social, economic, or political, additional markers were added to its definition, making it extremely broad-based. Today, a certain lifestyle and mindset are enough for someone to 'feel' middle class.

The multiple approaches to studying middle classes have, on the one hand, highlighted the various parameters being used to distinguish these classes from the upper and lower classes. On the other hand, they have made its categorization extremely fluid, thereby presenting a kaleidoscope of definitions from 'a wholly subjective set of aspirations to a highly specific measure of household income'.[6]

However, after much deliberation, scholars have finally concluded that middle class definitions can be segregated into three broad categories: economic resources; education and occupation status; and attitudes, self-perception, and mindset. Hence, all three categories need to be considered to judge whether one belongs to the middle-class bracket.

Class, as a concept, was first introduced by German philosopher, sociologist, and political theorist Karl Marx in the mid-nineteenth century in his book *Das Kapital.*

Marx distinguishes societies into two groups based on their 'modes of production' (i.e., the nature of its technology and division of labour): the bourgeoise, who owned the means of production; and the proletariat, who did not own any means of production but sold their labour power. This, according to him, creates a distinct social structure in which an individual's position is determined by the role he plays in the production process, and his political and ideological beliefs are shaped by his class position.

Marx could not clearly define middle class. He had written only a page-and-a-half of the chapter on classes before he passed away, leading many sociologists and anthropologists to conclude that the Marxist theory on class remains incomplete. Also, Marx was unwilling to categorize the middle class as a 'class' because he believed that with the growth of capitalism, this 'class' would eventually split, with the more successful members merging with the bourgeoisie while those remaining unsuccessful would form a part of the working class.

While there are instances of middle-class people falling back into the fold of the lower class due to high inflation and other contributing factors, there does not seem to be any long-term trend indicating a decline of the middle class. Also, while there has been polarization of classes, one sees a simultaneous formation of new middle-income groups.

The Marxist theory can be challenged on the grounds that Marx did not take into account the '"fallible and sinful"[7] nature of man and "seriously underrated"[8] an individual's ability to adjust to inequality'.[9] This is why, scholars argue, modern societies have not turned out as Marx predicted they would.

In contrast to the Marxist theory of social division are the functionalist theories of social divisions.

The first to contest Marx was another German philosopher

and sociologist, Max Weber. Although he, too, defined class in terms of ownership of property, Weber disagreed with the Marxist classification of society into two simple groups. He maintained that, similar to economic factors, non-economic factors, too, were important criteria for social stratification. He identified these factors as status and power.

Weber categorizes society into three types of classes: property classes, commercial classes, and social classes. People coming from the same class situation, based on their possession of goods or their social status, belong to the same class. He doesn't clearly distinguish between property classes and commercial classes but mentions the presence of a middle class in each.[10] As per Weberian theory, class organization can happen in all class situations, but class consciousness and class action happen only under certain conditions.

Weber also stressed on social mobility and explained it through the concept of 'life chances'. There are many factors affecting the life chances of an individual ranging from the class he is born into to geographical location, access to social privileges, race, gender, ethnicity, etc.

French sociologist Émile Durkheim had a different perspective on social stratification and social behaviour. He emphasized the interconnectivity of all the elements comprising a social class. He introduced modern concepts of collective conscience, mechanical solidarity, and organic solidarity to the study of sociology. He characterizes pre-industrial societies as exhibiting mechanical solidarity, 'a type of social order maintained by the collective consciousness of a culture'. After industrialization, this system was replaced with organic solidarity wherein the social order was based on the 'acceptance of economic and social differences'.

In essence, Durkheim takes a somewhat holistic view on social stratification by talking about external and internal inequalities within societies through the concepts of mechanical and organic solidarity. As per Durkheim, moral values play an important role in class distinction. While expounding his theory on social stratification in his book *The Division of Labour in Society*, first published in 1893, he concludes: It is not a simple juxtaposition of individuals who bring an intrinsic morality with them, but rather man is a moral being only because he lives in society, since morality consists in being solidary with a group and varying with this solidarity.[11] Thus, according to him, morality differs from society to society. It exists, 'in all its forms'[12], only in society and varies depending on social conditions. This is the reason why moral values differ from country to country and region to region.

Thus, the middle class came to be defined in terms of economy, social status, power, and moral values.

Today, the definition has expanded to incorporate additional parameters such as national/racial, cultural, and religious identities, and marginal groups between classes. These parameters differ from country to country, thereby giving the global middle class a highly heterogenous existence. As British sociologist Anthony Giddens says, the middle class is a 'heterogeneous environment, the mixture of highly unstable (fluent) "old middle class" and somewhat more stable but less numerous, called "modern middle class".'[13]

In the Indian context, however, the concept of middle class changes altogether. Since ancient times, Indian society has been segregated into four social groups (jatis): Brahmin, Kshatriya, Vaishya, and Shudra. Each social group was linked to a particular occupation. For instance, the role of the Brahmin was to impart knowledge and perform religious activities; Kshatriyas were warriors and belonged to the ruling class; Vaishyas were engaged in commerce; and Shudras formed the bulk of the population, which was the labour class engaged in farming and other professions that required labour. A fifth group was made up of those who were considered outside of the caste system.

Thus, the Indian subcontinent had an existing stratified society based on occupation, which created a power structure defining the status of each social group in the caste system and their corresponding social values. This system continued till the advent of the British in the eighteenth century, and thereafter, it incorporated the modern social, economic, and political parameters of class as was defined by the West. Class in India is, therefore, an amalgamation of ancient Indian 'class within caste' system and the new middle class that was created under British rule.

The first comprehensive work on the Indian middle class was by B. B. Misra. His book, *The Indian Middle Classes: Their Growth in Modern Times,* published in 1961, is a detailed account of the rise and growth of the middle class in India, from the beginning of the eighteenth century till 1905. Although, in his 1948 book, *Social Background of Indian Nationalism*, sociologist A. R. Desai did write about the rise of new social groups as a result of British policies, he made only a passing reference to the class of absentee landlords, who were essentially 'moneylenders, merchants and people who had amassed great wealth in urban vocations', and the rise of bourgeoisie and proletariats in modern Indian capitalist society.[14] While he was heavily influenced by Marxist thought, Misra toed the Weberian line, and both strongly believe that the middle class was a result of British rule in India.

There have been many more books on the Indian middle class since, but most authors hold a similar view.

Author Pavan K. Verma's *The Great Indian Middle Class*, published in 1998, also presupposes that the Indian middle class was a product of British imperialism. Says he, 'The creation of a native elite in its own image was the most spectacular and enduring achievement of British colonialism in India.'[15] Verma gives a splendid account of the changes this class has undergone since the eighteenth century. He traces the journey of the middle class that emerged under the British, its mobilization during the national movement, its progress in the decades following Independence, the transformation in its size and character in late sixties, and its changing attitudes and behaviour post liberalization. However, he, too, adheres to the belief that the middle class was a creation of the British.

Anthropologist Imtiaz Ahmad echoes a similar sentiment. In the book *Middle Class Values in India and Western Europe* (2001), he says: 'British rule produced a revolution in social relations and class structures in India. A class of intermediaries emerged that served as a link between the people and the new rulers... It was only after the advent of the British rule in India that the ideas and institutions of a middle-class social order were imported to India.'[16]

Rajesh Misra, who taught Sociology in Lucknow University says that the middle class in India is not 'a' class but 'many' classes. 'And here we should examine the concept of old middle class and new middle class.'[17]

The old middle class, as per sociologists, emerged in the old system and included petty shopkeepers, small producers, contractors, those who did not have educationally acquired intelligence or knowledge but contributed to the economy in a different capacity and stayed in the middle. People who got professional training from educational institutes formed the new middle class. These were the technologists, professionals, scientists, teachers, doctors.

Professor S. C. Mohapatra, a professor of Sociology in Delhi University, believes there was no concept of 'middle class' (in terms of terminology) in India prior to the British. For him, middle class as a Western concept was applied to map society and social transformation in India.

He defines the term 'middle class' in the most intriguing way, calling it a perception. 'You cannot define middle class on the basis of income, occupation or lifestyle. Middle class is a kind of perception for those who believe that they belong to the middle class. So, when you talk about the middle class in the context of India, we have people from the tribal background joining the middle class, we have the Muslim middle class, we have rural middle class, we have urban middle class, we have women belonging to the middle class. Thus, the middle class is not a cohesive category. There are different interest groups in the middle class.'[18]

His observation is validated by a survey carried out in 2014 on self-perception by three Indian economists, Milan Vaishnav, Neelanjan Sircar, and Devesh Kapur. Most people self-identified as middle class, even those who, judging from the assets they owned, were clearly poor. This, say the economists, indicates that the middle class is an aspirational identity. But it is not just the poor who ascribe to this identity, surprisingly, even the rich call themselves middle class. This is because ascribing to the middle-class identity increases their cultural worth as the middle class is perceived as the custodian of Indian culture.

One important point highlighted by journalist Madhukar Upadhyay is that the middle classes in the West were 'economy driven' whereas in India they were 'social strata driven'. He maintains that in the chaturvarna system, 'the Brahmins and the Thakurs, Thakurs being the rulers and the Brahmins being the knowledge banks, were the upper class. The Shudras formed the lower class. And the middle comprised Vaishyas. That's how money got attached to middle class in India.'[19]

Sociologist G. S. Ghurye also presents this view in his book *Caste and Race in India*, remarking that the 'status of a person depended not on his wealth as in the classes of modern Europe, but on the traditional importance of the caste in which he had the luck of being born'.[20]

One major reason scholars have perhaps overlooked while identifying the middle class in India has been the Indian philosophy of Aparigraha or non-possession, which has had a deep impact on the masses. The philosophy is one of the central teachings of Patanjali's *Yoga Sutra*, written somewhere between 2 and 4 CE. It has been a part of people's lives since ancient times and defies the Western idea of accumulation. It preaches contentment. However, this does not mean that people were not in a position to aim higher or accumulate wealth. They chose not to do that.

All of this brings us to the question: How should one really define the middle class?

In simple terms, the middle class refers to a group of people who fall in the middle of a social hierarchy, often defined by occupation, income, lifestyle, education, or social status. There are certain traits associated with the middle class that distinguish them from the other two classes, namely, they are mostly engaged in white-collar jobs, are upwardly mobile, and aspirational; and perceive themselves as being middle class. Of course, the composition and components associated with it differ from region to region, and culture to culture.

That said, the various theories apropos the definition and composition of the middle class make two clear distinctions: *a)* the definition of middle class has been changing with time with the development of society, economy, and politics around the world; and *b)* the Indian middle class should not be studied using modern Western parameters. Instead, it should factor in Indian culture, philosophy, and ethos. The study of the Indian middle class should be seen in the context of the given time with contemporary social, political, and economic factors.

The purpose of this book is to view the Indian middle class considering all these factors. When we examine the history of ancient and mediaeval India, we realize that, contrary to popular belief, not only was there a middle class (though not too large), but it was socially upwardly mobile and fought for its rights whenever necessary.

 က

Though the middle class has always been in existence in India since ancient times, I decided to begin its study from the Battle of Plassey, 1757, for two reasons: first, the group underwent major transformation only in the eighteenth century; and second, there is not enough attitudinal and lifestyle variation among the Indian middle classes prior to the eighteenth century. It is only with the coming of the British that one sees major shifts in the attitude and composition of the traditional middle class and the rise of a new middle class that changed the future of India. But to understand the character of the contemporary middle class, it is important to study the salient features that contributed to its evolution, making it crucial to review the period between the Battle of Plassey and the Revolt of 1857.

Since the emergence of the new middle class in the mid-eighteenth century, after the battles of Plassey and Buxar laid the foundations for British rule in India, the Indian middle class has undergone significant transformation in terms of size, composition, and complexity. Starting with a traditional middle class and a small class of individuals largely restricted to the presidency capitals of Calcutta, Delhi, and Madras under the British Raj, in its nascent stage, to its polymorphous state today, the growth of the middle class in India can be categorized into three noteworthy phases: pre-Independence (1757–1947), post-Independence (1947–1991), and post-liberalization (1991–present). What makes these periods significant is the outcome one sees at the end of each phase and the role the middle class played during these phases. Each phase was characterized by a distinct thought that brought in critical changes in the economic as well as socio-political framework of the country.

Middle Class in the Pre-Independence Era

From Plassey in 1757 to the turning point of the Uprising in 1857 to the Quit India Movement between 1942 and 1945, this section traces the journey of the middle class from being traditionally apolitical to becoming the leader of the national movement.

There are two important takeaways in this time period.

Most scholars and historians believe that the Indian middle class was a British creation, and that the introduction of modern education, the rise of capitalism, and the development of the market economy resulted in the upward mobility of the existing social classes and created a new class with traits similar to those of the middle classes in the West. Instead, we see from several examples in ancient texts and from studies by eminent historians and scholars that there was indeed a thriving middle class in the mediaeval as well as ancient Indian societies.

The second point challenges the popular belief that the middle class did not participate in the Revolt of 1857.

Most scholars and historians hold the view that the revolt was essentially a rebellion by the feudal classes and the army against the British, and that the middle class had no role to play in it.

The book presents documented evidence to disprove this general view. While it is true that in most areas the middle class abstained from participating in the revolt, especially in Bengal, where the bhadralok remained completely aloof, there is no denying the fact that in Oudh (Awadh), which became the epicentre of the revolt, not only did the middle class side with the rebels, but actively participated in it too.

Tracing the evolution of the new middle class and the changes taking place in the socio-political set-up of this newly formed country, this section also highlights the different trends impacting the emerging new middle class, namely: the influence of Western education on youth; the confluence of tradition and modernity and its impact on the emerging middle class, which was developing a Western social outlook that challenged its own identities in multiple ways; the growth of feminism, which prompted women to come forward and fight for independence as well as their own rights; and the politicization of the religious identities of the middle classes that eventually led to the partition of the subcontinent.

The chapter on the middle classes of the West explores the causes that led to their rise and the role the group played in defining the politics of the region.

From Independence to Liberalization

The period between Independence and liberalization can be defined as a transitional phase for the Indian middle class, during which it underwent several changes to emerge as a powerful social order having considerable influence on the politics of the country.

In this section we examine the transformation that the middle class underwent in terms of ideology, social composition, and political affiliations.

The first few decades saw policies being drafted for the development of the country. The focus was on education, economy, and the building of a scientific temper. The middle class was expanding, resulting in the formation of additional groups and sub-groups, giving it a more complex structure. While they all were aspiring and upwardly mobile, these groups differed in their social and political preferences.

The middle class was politically most active during this phase. Deepening impact of education on an expanding population combined with state policies resulted in an exponential growth of the middle class. It became more varied as individuals from ethnic and tribal backgrounds, rural areas and lower castes, from different linguistic groups, joined ranks with it. Its impact can be seen in the number of movements this period witnessed, which were spearheaded by the middle class. And it is not that the middle class fought for its own interests, it also became a part of the workers' union, thereby standing up with the working class. The highlight of this period, as Rajesh Misra points out, was the number of tribal, ethnic, state, and language movements that attracted middle-class youth into their folds. For instance, the language movements of the seventies, especially the Hindi and Tamil movements, which ran counter to each other, were greatly supported by the middle class. Another significant development, according to Misra, was 'the women's liberation movement'.[21] The middle class associated with this movement was well-educated and, most importantly, gender-specific, that is, the movement was initiated and carried forward by women. Also, it was limited in numbers and only restricted to some urban areas like Pune, Mumbai, and Delhi. The Chipko Movement started with lower-class and lower-middle-class rural women, but later on, when the Uttarakhand Sangharsh Palika was created, people from the middle class joined in.

The most notable factor of this period is the transformation in the consciousness of the middle class which happened over a span of three decades. From a nationalistic orientation in the fifties, one sees it moving towards sectarianism, resulting in different ethnic movements that started in various parts of the country. Maharashtra's Dalit Panther movement, for example, created a counter culture and separate identity for the Dalits, bringing caste consciousness among Dalit youth and providing them with political representation. Cult politics saw its origin in this period as Prime Minister Indira Gandhi emerged as a cult figure in Indian politics, the only Indian woman in this position so far.

As socialism slowly gave way to capitalism, middle class consumption patterns and aspirations also started changing, and along with that, new middle-class markers came into existence. Electronic goods like televisions, refrigerators, and mixer-grinders became the new status symbols for the middle class.

Economic Liberalization to the Present

The period of economic liberalization saw the complete dismantling of socialism and the rise of capitalism, although many economists consider it crony capitalism. With the end of the Licence Raj and introduction of several reforms, the private sector got a much-needed boost. New and better prospects saw middle class fortunes rise. Innovations and entrepreneurship became the norm for the middle class which was getting exceedingly ambitious.

This new class became highly consumerist and extremely conscious of its new-found power. There have been many significant developments since in the nature and attitude of the middle class which are highlighted in the chapters constituting this section.

One of the defining characteristics of the current middle class is its diversity. This diversity acts as a driving factor for different social groups to gain recognition in society through economic progress. However, it also stops it from being a composite unit, which affects its interests at the macro level. This is most evident in politics. A report in the *Sunday Guardian* notes that 'since it is politically amorphous, and has not organized itself into a pressure group, even political leaders who have emerged from this segment have not focused on it. As a thumb rule, most of India's politicians who achieved success either came from the wealthy/dominant classes or conversely the poorest of poor'.[22]

Which is why, perhaps, when the Aam Aadmi Party was launched, it received immense support from the people as it originated from the middle class, having 'a relatively young, articulate, educated leadership, mostly self-made', and focused on issues like education, healthcare, and water and power distribution.

Identity is another major factor influencing middle class behaviour. The confluence of caste and class, combined with a multitude of languages and religions, has created a multi-layered society in India, of which the middle class is an integral and important part. Traditional social elites don't seem too bothered about identities for the simple reason that they don't need social recognition, for they already enjoy a high social status, wield enormous economic power, and have access to the corridors of political power. The middle class, on the other hand, craves social recognition, which makes it more conscious of its social identity.

The question of identity is not limited to caste or religion, it extends to gender as well. This section also focuses on the hardships faced by the LGBTQA+ community despite the repeal of Article 377 which de-criminalized homosexuality.

The Middle Class through the Years

To gauge the overall progress of the middle class, it is important to do a comparative analysis of all three phases. It will not only trace its growth pattern but will also highlight the changing mindset of the middle class and its implications for society and the politics of the country. In a world that is getting smaller and more competitive by the day, knowing where India stands is important to expedite progress.

The section on comparative analysis evaluates the progress the middle class has made in different sectors since pre-Independence. While on education and economy fronts the progress has been tremendous, one finds it lacking on social and political fronts. It is the 'why' that this section dwells on.

The seventies and eighties saw the introduction of various women-specific laws and bills related to education, right to property, etc. And after 1991, women, especially in the middle class, emerged as a big contributor to the country's GDP. While progress has been made in this segment, not all have fared well.

When we analyse the three periods, we realize that on the social scale we have actually regressed, with far reaching consequences. It has affected not only the unity of the country but has compromised economic growth as well.

Another aspect worth analysing is the political and perception quotient of the middle class. It started off as the 'thinking class'—studying new trends, making use of opportunities arising from them, and promoting new thought. By the eighties, though still under the influence of socialism, it had started shifting towards the extreme right. In 1952 the Rashtriya Swayamsevak Sangh (RSS) established its first school, Saraswati Shishu Mandir, and it has been working at the grassroots ever since to expand its base in the country, and it has been successful in doing so. For instance, in the seventies, there were more than 500 RSS schools in the country with approximately 20,000 students. The RSS propagated its Hindutva doctrine through these education centres. Today, there are 12,828 schools with approximately 3.4 million students enrolled in them. The RSS also runs more than 6,400 informal education centres.[23] The definition of nationalism has also undergone a significant change, it has become narrow and rigid. Liberalization itself has led to rising consumerism and promotion of selfish interests over that of the nation as a whole. So, we find degression in this aspect as well.

The other most significant factor influencing the middle class has been generational change, which has led to sweeping changes in its value system. It is significant because it is the middle class where the change is most visible. The lower classes, though at times seen to be emulating the behaviours and attitudes of the middle classes, are restricted by their socio-economic environment and, hence, have not undergone these changes. For example, most urban upper-middle class youngsters are more globalized in their outlook because of their exposure to the world, as opposed to the lower class, which can barely afford higher education. The upper class, on the other hand, is not bound by any value system. It is not that they don't have a value system in place, but the fact that they are not restrained by it.

The creation of new social identities has increased the challenges faced by the middle class, as it has pitted one generation against the other, leading to social disturbances, even violence—honour killing being a prime example of that.

In conclusion mediaeval Indian society was far more developed than Western societies of the time—a fact endorsed by British historian Alex Von Tunzelmann. The opening paragraph of her book, *Indian Summer: The Secret History of the End of An Empire*, begins thus:

> In the beginning, there were two nations. One was a vast, mighty and magnificent empire, brilliantly organised and culturally unified, which dominated a massive swathe of the earth. The other was an undeveloped, semi-feudal realm, riven by religious factionalism and barely able to feed its illiterate, diseased and stinking masses. The first nation was India. The second was England.[24]

In such a thriving society, it's not possible that the middle class was absent. It was not politically active, of course, but as far as social and economic spaces were concerned, its presence cannot be denied.

As for the changing middle class behaviour, especially in view of the ongoing battle of majority vs minority, one needs to factor in the lack of common goal. The contemporary middle class is highly pluralistic in nature and each social group comes with its own set of aspirations and goals. For instance, the Dalit community, the OBC community, the LGBTQA+ community—all have different interests and are in pursuit of different goals, which may or may not clash with each other. The only common feature is upward mobility, but the processes to achieve that differ considerably.

The only way in which the Indian middle class can fight its way out of the quagmire is to aim for social harmony and peace. That is the only way forward, and the only way one can become a $5-trillion economy.

PART I

The Middle Class in Pre-Independent India

(1757–1947)

1

The Middle Class Before the British

The most perfect political community is one in which the middle class is in control, and outnumbers both of the other classes.

—ARISTOTLE

The Greek philosopher is quite categorical. According to him, the best scenario is one where the middle class forms the majority of society and is larger and stronger than both the other classes, namely the rich and the poor, and prevents either of them from becoming too assertive or dominating. This kind of middle class that Aristotle described in 350 BCE came into prominence in Europe only in the eighteenth century. It is not that Europe did not have a middle class in ancient or mediaeval times. But it neither outnumbered the other two classes nor was it powerful enough to keep them in check. This was true of the Indian middle class as well. Here, too, it was inconsequential in terms of numbers. However, in terms of power, one finds that the traders and merchants of India were in a better position than their Western counterparts—they were able to fight for their rights. Kautilya's *Arthashastra* mentions that guilds, at the time, were great military powers. The book mentions srenivala, a class of fighters, which was used for both offensive and defensive purposes. He also refers to a class of Kshatriya guilds.[1]

Ancient Indian societies had organized trade and artisan guilds that formed their own laws and, the 'king (was) to consult guild representatives while dealing with matters related to the guilds', as per the diktats of the Gautama Dharmasutra, writes historian K. K. Thapliyal. He further states that, 'perhaps the punch-marked coins in earlier stages were issued by rich merchants and guilds, may be with the permission of the state'. In the West, in the Roman Empire, for instance, one does not find any reference to guilds. The state exercised great control over trade and commerce, though free trade also existed. The state also 'taxed the movement of goods between provinces and also controlled many local markets'.[2]

Historian Irfan Habib states that, during the reign of Alauddin Khalji, Hindu merchants of Daulatabad worked in the form of a corporation, much along the lines of the Akarim or Karim of Egypt. The Indian mercantile system was way ahead of its European counterpart in the pre-British era.

The scientific and technological developments in Europe, after the Industrial Revolution (1760–1860), led to large-scale production of goods, especially cloth, which, in turn, created a need for a continuous supply of raw material and markets to sell the surplus produce, and for the promotion of trade and commerce.

Starting from England, countries across Europe witnessed rapid urbanization as peasants moved to cities in large numbers to work in factories. This migration necessitated the need for improved public works, such as good hospitals, schools, housing, financial services, etc. Thus, we witness the emergence of a new class and a new system associated with it in Europe, which was remarkably different from the old feudal set-up. As it became economically strong, this class created unions to protect its interests from feudal lords, and over time became powerful enough to play a defining role in state polity—the East India Company (EIC) being an exemplary example of that.

The situation in India was drastically different. Here, society was already categorized into four sections via the varna system. India had flourishing trade and commerce that required the presence of professionals to take care of business and finance, accounts, and other related activities. Most historians and scholars have, however, by and large, overlooked this section of society that was middle class by nature. Their contention has been that the Indian middle class is a British creation.

The first to propagate this thought was historian B. B. Misra, who in his book *The Indian Middle Classes: Their Growth in*

Modern Times (1961), wrote that the middle class in India was more a consequence of 'changes in the system of law and public administration than in economic development, and they mainly belonged to the learned professions'. This, he pointed out, was contrary to the West where the growth of the middle classes was a result of economic and technological changes. In his book, which presents a historical survey of the class, its composition, character, and role in defining India, Misra acknowledges that there was a conducive environment for the development of the middle class in India, yet, according to him, the political and social systems of the country prevented its formation. He bases his argument partly on Max Weber's observation that 'modern capitalism did not develop indigenously before or during the English rule. It was taken over as a finished artifact without autonomous beginnings',[3] and that modern capitalism could never have originated in India from its 'completely traditionalist Indian trades'.[4]

However, Weber's theory suggests that the British introduced capitalism as a well-developed system with a one-point agenda—to create a market for British manufactured goods and tap into India's resources to sustain and expand their industrial growth. But this suggestion overlooks many other aspects of the existing Indian socio-political system. For instance, despite an extremely rigid caste system, there was social mobility in Indian society, as British writer Sir William Wilson Hunter notes in *The Indian Empire*:

> On the one hand there has been a tendency to erect every separate employment in each separate province into a distinct caste. On the other hand there has been a practice (which the European observers are apt to overlook) of the lower castes changing their occupation, and in some cases deliberately raising themselves in the social scale. Thus, the Vaisya caste was in ancient times the tillers of the soil. They have abandoned this laborious occupation to the Shudras and the mixed castes, and are now the merchants and bankers of India.[5]

The movement of castes, upward or downward, in local hierarchy has also been noted by eminent anthropologist M. N. Srinivas. Srinivas maintains that though Indian society was stationary, fluidity of the political system made mobility of castes possible. He backs his argument by quoting several scholars and numerous examples from ancient as well mediaeval history. The mediaeval Pala dynasty of Bengal, for instance, was Shudra in origin.[6] In fact, Panikkar has stated that since the fifth century BCE, from the times of Mahapadma Nanda, most royal families came from a non-Kshatriya caste.[7]

Also, connecting the middle class only with modern capitalism would be a mistake in the case of India, which already had a society segregated on the basis of caste, with class infused in that.

The definition of the middle class has changed from time to time. As societies developed as a result of technological developments and a changing world social order, the middle classes acquired new characteristics and came to be seen in a new light. Added to this were regional factors that played a significant role in defining the middle class of a particular area. Keeping all this in mind, it would be incorrect to assume that there was no middle class in Indian society prior to the coming of the British.

Moreover, the argument that the middle class could not evolve because of lack of social mobility is also incorrect. No society can remain static, even in a traditional set-up. Social mobility is inevitable in societies based on class and caste structures. Srinivas cites two important factors which resulted in the social mobility of castes in an otherwise rigid caste system. First was the 'fluidity of the political system', which enabled people from the lower castes to become powerful in regions they dominated and assume the status of Kshatriyas. The other was the availability of marginal land (which is land that has very little agricultural and industrial value) that could be brought under cultivation. It is on the basis of these two factors that dominant castes such as Reddys in the south and Marathas in the west could seize political power and claim Kshatriya status. 'When the leader of a dominant caste escalated [to] the rank of raja or king, it became a source of mobility for the other members and this was strengthened by adoption of practices and lifestyles of the upper castes,' writes Srinivas.[8]

Thus the perception that Indian society in the ancient and mediaeval times was static and rigid is incorrect as it is based solely on the continuity of the caste system. It fails to take into account the changes and adjustments that societies underwent with the incoming groups. At times these changes were quite revolutionary and led to the creation of sub-castes, indicating a continuous process of change in the social, political, and economic systems.

Another crucial aspect worth exploring is the concept of a 'unified' or 'unitary' middle social segment in terms of class. According to Misra, the middle-class elements in Indian society remained segregated and could not unite to form a 'unitary middle class social order' as was the case in the West. This argument is often presented by historians and scholars who view class formations as described by Karl Marx and relate class with capitalism because, as historian Sucheta Mahajan states, it signifies the 'coming together of a nation'.[9] What it means, essentially, is that when we talk about a particular class, it pre-supposes its presence across the country, for instance the peasant class, or the working class.

However, such an argument ignores two important details: first, the caste system was followed throughout the Indian subcontinent in the ancient as well as mediaeval periods. And since class was very much inherent in caste, we cannot negate the presence of the middle class in India.

The second, and perhaps the most crucial factor, was urbanization, which is thought to be an essential pre-requisite for the growth of middle class. The Indian subcontinent witnessed urbanization as early as sixth century BCE. The early Pali literature lists sixteen mahajanapadas (multi-city kingdoms) extending from northwest Pakistan to east Bihar and sub-montane regions in the north down to the Godavari in the south.[10] Despite political fragmentation, there was socio-cultural and economic continuity in the different kingdoms in the subcontinent. As Chaturvedi points out, in economic continuity, every urban centre had a group of small businessmen, performing artistes, and artisans who had attained a certain degree of financial autonomy. These groups were not part of the elite or the lower classes. They constituted the middle class both in economic as well as social terms.

Misra further states that despite a highly developed cottage industry and specialization of work, an accomplished class of merchants (with trade links to countries like China, Sri Lanka, and empires like Rome, etc.), presence of guilds, a kind of banking system, agents working as middlemen for mercantile and business houses, and a developed money economy, India did not have a middle class because, 'modern capitalism did not develop indigenously before or during the English rule. It was taken over as a finished artifact without autonomous beginnings'.[11]

Also, despite the presence of 'commercial and professional elements capable of growing into a middle class', an autocratic political system, disintegrated social order, and a monopolist economy did not let the same flourish. 'The introduction of Western science and technology thus involved the task of creating through English education a middle class who might act as an agency of imperialist economy and administration'.[12]

Though Misra presents a fairly vibrant picture of nineteenth-century Indian society, with an exhaustive account of the socio-political background against which this class emerged, his analysis overlooks two crucial factors which point to the pre-existence of such a class in pre-colonial India. First, he takes a very narrow view of the middle class, relating it solely to a capitalist society, a term advocated by Scottish economist and philosopher Adam Smith only in 1776; and second, in a bid to segregate Indian society on the basis of 'class', he too has largely ignored the already existing caste-based division, which was also based on economic activities.

To trace the social history of the middle class, one needs to delve into the early history, economics, and sociology of India.

Misra's own admission that he has 'some knowledge of the first, but not of the remaining two' makes his analysis of middle-class history incomplete.

Indian society was very different from that of the West. Here, society was already segregated on the basis of economic activity, which in due course led to specialization in various fields. The description of society in Hindu religious texts like the Ramayana and Upanishads indicates a well-developed society with highly specialized groups of people who were involved in occupations other than agriculture. There were jewellers, gem cutters, weavers, chariot makers, potters, ivory workers, etc., and artisans had their own guilds. According to historian Santosh Kumar Das, 'artisans enjoyed special privileges and some of the higher craftsmen, especially those engaged in the canons of the rituals of the Silpasutras, brief scriptures found in Hinduism, Buddhism, and Jainism...enjoyed a high social status. Similarly, those engaged in irrigation works and the preparations of public buildings enjoyed high privileges.'[13]

European society in the sixteenth and seventeenth centuries was feudal in character. In terms of economy, following the commercial revolution, which began in the eleventh century and ended with the Industrial Revolution, there existed a putting-out system. This meant that merchant-employers put out material to the producers who worked either at home or in workshops and returned the finished product to the merchant in exchange for wages. As production was not mechanized, manufacturing was done manually. The presence of a middle segment of people—tradesmen, merchants, and craftsmen, who had some wealth but did not own any means of production yet—that were not part of the upper class indicates the existence of the middle class in the European society.

Around the same time, similar conditions existed in India—a highly feudal society and a thriving international trade. Misra talks of the emergence of traders in England in the fourteenth century as an independent class. He acknowledges that this category formed the 'first step in the rise of a middle class'. Yet, he overlooks the same in the case of India. The Hundred Years' War ushered in major socio-political changes in England and France. Its most lasting impact was, perhaps, the unfolding of a sense of patriotism and national identity in England.[14] The war resulted in creation of personal wealth and the development of several industries, such as textile and armaments. As Misra points out, this period saw the emergence of a trading class, which had segregated itself from well-to-do craftsmen. This new merchant capitalist class monopolized specific areas of trade and organized their associations that dominated local government. They also financed craftsmen, supplied raw materials, and marketed produced goods.[15]

Thus, Misra associates the English 'merchant capitalists' of the fifteenth and sixteenth centuries with the middle class as they had 'control over the municipal governments', whereas in India, he maintains, the guilds had only 'money power' and were not 'supported by any authority'.

Indigenous and foreign writers have made several references to the existence of a middle class in India as far back as 500 BCE. The earliest record establishing this is the *Gautama Dharmasutra*, written sometime in 500 BCE.[16]

The *Dharmasutra* mentions that 'cultivators, traders, herdsmen, moneylenders, and artisans have authority to lay down rules for their respective classes', and the king was to consult their representatives while dealing with matters relating to them. The Jataka tales refer to eighteen guilds, to their heads, to localization of industry and to the hereditary nature of professions.

This indicates that though the traders and merchants did not have control over the king, they did have the freedom and authority to conduct their business the way they wished. This system was certainly beyond the comprehension of Weber.

Historian K. K. Thapliyal gives examples of the epigraphs from Sanchi, Bharhut, Bodh Gaya, Mathura, and sites of western Deccan (200 BCE–300 CE) that refer to 'donations made by different craftsmen and traders'. Thapliyal divides the history of the guilds into four-time brackets: 1) the Vedic period; 2) the Buddhist/Jain periods; 3) the Mauryan period and; 4) the post-Mauryan period. Some of the guilds mentioned in the epigraphs are potters, oil millers, weavers, and manufacturers of hydraulic engines. According to Thapliyal, the guilds had their own set of laws, recognized by the state, which dealt with the organization of guilds, the manufacturing of goods, and fixing of commodity prices. The laws probably differed from guild to guild as they were based on the customs followed by each of them. The objective was to provide protection against state oppression and interference. 'The *Gautama Dharmasutra* (written around c. 6 BCE) enjoins upon the king "to consult guild representatives while dealing with matters concerning guilds".'[17]

In 1869, Scottish historian and member of the Indian Civil Services, William Wilson Hunter, was tasked with writing the *Imperial Gazetteer of India*, wherein he stated that the word 'caste, which had obtained such a wide currency in literature of sociology, comes from the Portuguese adventurers who followed Vasco da Gama to the western coast of India'.[18] He wrote, 'Each caste is a trade guild, mutual assurance society or a religious sect. Caste division brings specialization. As a trade, the castes insist upon proper training of the youths of its crafts, regulate the wages of its members and deal with delinquents and promote good fellowship.'[19]

Traders did have the power to influence the ruling class whether directly or indirectly. It was essentially because the authorities understood the relevance of this class in furthering their own interests and, hence, were not indifferent to them.

In 1668, baniyas of Surat called a 'strike' to protest 'against forced conversion to Islam by Muslim rulers. How much influence the merchants could exert over imperial policy was shown clearly in 1619 when the Surat traders resisted English attempts to buy textiles for the Red Sea market and were fully supported by the emperor and his officials. The fact that the English encroachment on the Red Sea market would have adversely affected the amirs' commercial interests was no doubt partly responsible for this unanimity'.[20]

Several accounts of the mediaeval period reveal that India's economy was far ahead of that of Europe. Apart from well-developed and extensive trade and commerce, there was rapid urbanization too, as great cities, like Surat, flourished along its trade routes and ports. Portuguese writer Barbosa gives a detailed account of inland, coastal, and overseas trade carried out by the ports of Gujarat, Deccan Malabar, and Bengal, dealing in a variety of merchandise. With such extensive trade, there was bound to be a capitalist class, so the presence of a somewhat 'modern-day' class structure cannot be ruled out. Till the eighteenth century, Indian mercantile groups were way ahead of their Western counterparts in trade practices. By the close of the sixteenth century, increasing foreign trade and money economy had led to the emergence of merchant capitalism.[21] French writer Abbe Raynal comments in his 1784 book *Philosophical and Political History of the European Settlements* that 'we hardly suspected that there was such a thing as commercial principles, yet they were already known and practised in this part of Asia'.[22]

The second reason, cited by Misra, that prevented the growth of the Indian middle class, was the stringency of the inherent caste system. Undoubtedly, the caste system was (and still remains) a rigid social order. However, there was scope for mobility within a caste or a community. This, he simply overlooks.

Even Hunter, in his research, asserts that the European observers were 'apt to overlook' the fact that there existed the practice among the lower castes to change their occupation in order to climb up the social order. He quotes many such instances where a particular caste gave up its traditional occupation to become merchants and bankers. 'There is, therefore, a plasticity as well as rigidity in caste,' he notes. 'It (is this) plasticity that has enabled the caste to adapt itself to widely separated stages of social progress, and to incorporate the various ethnical elements which make up the Indian people.'[23]

Compared to caste, class is fairly a new concept, and although both have distinct characteristics, they overlap considerably. As S. C. Mohapatra, professor of Sociology in Delhi University puts it,

'Where there is a class, there will be a middle rank, and where there's a middle rank there will be middle class.' The question one could ask then, is whether there is an inherent middle class within each caste.

'I will not say that each caste has middle class,' says Mohapatra, 'but within the system of caste, you find the class is primarily entangled. For example, a rich Brahmin will never have alliance with a rich non-Brahmin family. Caste matters. But at the same time, a rich Brahmin will not have an alliance with a poor Brahmin family, unless the boy is a civil servant or a professor or an entrepreneur. There also, within the caste, class matters. So, he will not agree on class when marriage is inter-caste and he will, probably, not agree to marriage within the caste unless class matches. Therefore, class matters. Within the class and between the caste.'[24]

Class has always existed even in the times of land economy,[25] though it became more evident post-Industrial Revolution. But it's not that class comes in only with industrial development. In the agrarian sector, too, according to Ivan John, professor of Sociology at Sophia College, one witnesses different classes making up the rural population[26]—for instance, the land-owning classes, landless labourers, and intermediary classes, which were not rich enough to be included in the elite nor too poor. These classes were always trying to align themselves with the rich. Here, caste also played a major role in establishing the middle class.

Another thought-provoking argument presented by John is that generally it was either the 'downtrodden' or the 'exploiters' that were talked about, or written about. The focus was all on the rich and the poor. The middle class played a subservient role and aligned with either according to convenience. 'I would say, the middle class was perhaps not visible, not loud, not open about their concerns because the focus invariably went to the two extreme categories.'

Hunter was right in saying that it was difficult for a westerner to understand the Indian caste system. In India, the stratification of society was occupation-based, unlike the rest of the world where it was based on money. Money was secondary in the case of India. 'So, it was very difficult to identify the middle class in India because the westerners could think only on monetary terms,' says Delhi-based journalist and author Madhukar Upadhyay. 'Under the chaturvarna system, Brahmins and Thakurs constituted the upper class while Shudras were the lower class. Vaishyas formed the middle class, and that's how money got attached to the middle class in India.'[27]

Contemporary accounts mainly from the sixteenth and seventeenth centuries speak of merchants transporting goods from Bengal to Surat and vice versa, and down south for trading. This indicates that there was a class of people, engaged in such activities throughout the subcontinent, which does give it a kind of uniformity in terms of occupation. Also, there is ample reference to the 'professional classes' engaged in different pursuits at the time.

Historian Irfan Habib states that 'the intelligentsia, including the professional classes, was not an extensive body in Mughal India. A fair part of it was directly patronized by the emperor, rajas, and nobles. [François] Bernier was misled by the absence of European-type 'academies and colleges' in India into concluding that a universal ignorance was the natural consequence of the Mughal tyranny which precluded the 'benefices, the employments, the offices of trust and dignity, that require ability and science'. Poets, scholars, artists, musicians, calligraphists, physicians and the like were all beneficiaries of imperial or aristocratic munificence. Together, they constituted a fair proportion of the middle class. More important, the peasant's surplus was very usefully at work here, helping to create and continue significant cultural forms, the rich tapestry of Indo-Mughal civilization.'[28]

While describing the pre-industrial social organization, Misra, points out that, though the *Manusmriti* defines it in an altogether different light, Brahmins were, in reality, not on top either politically or economically. There were other classes, such as feudal lords, military officials, tradesmen, bureaucrats, etc., which were far stronger. 'When the Muslims came, especially the Mughals, the system got transformed. The dependency of the Mughals on Indian bureaucracy was immense. This, in sociological terms, is called oriental despotism. Tehsildar, kanungo, patwari…these terms were not coined by the British, nor are they modern terms. These terms were in use during Mughal rule. The tax system was run by these officials appointed by the emperor, who would collect taxes from the farmers. Later, the British amended it and brought it to the level of Collector. So, there was a system…through which the Mughals were ruling. And it is important to know this fact in order to understand the middle classes of India today. The rule of oriental despotism and colonialism was heavily dependent on this middle-class bureaucracy. And this formed the most powerful section of the middle class.'[29]

'Class as a category for me comes only with capitalism,' says Sucheta Mahajan. Though she does acknowledge that there were 'groups in society which occupied the middle rung, and they would be the people who were the traders and the merchants if we see in the context of the caste system, in a broad occupational kind of way, not in terms of rigid hierarchies. In occupational sense the Khatris and the Baniyas were groups which occupied the middle space,' she says.[30]

The India of today may not have existed, but there were large kingdoms, some extending from Afghanistan in the west to Burma in the east, and they were quite prosperous, with flourishing trade, a highly developed society, and a plethora of specialized jobs, all of which ensured the presence of a middle class. Though Mahajan considers class as a category related to capitalism, she does agree that, when seen in the regional context, one could say that there was a very thin layer of the middle class that existed prior to the British. Based on these arguments, it can be contended that when Misra talks of the emergence of the middle class in India under the British, he is referring to the new middle class, which was colonial in origin. A class that was the outcome of British policies and was drastically different from the traditional middle classes.

Yet, at the same time, there was an existing indigenous middle class too, the presence of which can be seen in the written records of various foreign travellers, indigenous writers, and British officers. In caste terms, they were Kayasthas and were affiliated with the princely states and the Mughal empire and had a whole system of administration in the states of Baroda, Mysore, Kolhapur, Malabar, Cochin, Darbhanga, and Jaipur.

Perhaps the most befitting explanation is by Anand Kumar, a retired professor of Sociology from Jawaharlal Nehru University, who rightly sums it up: The Mughal court and other smaller kingdoms had an administration system that led to the creation of a middle class. This system was not ruptured by the arrival of the British. In fact, there was a kind of integration that led to the creation of colonial bureaucracy, legal structure, and health system. And that, in turn, gave shape to a new middle class.[31]

2

Plassey, Buxar, and the British

When talking about the emergence of the new middle class that scripted the future of India, it becomes imperative to understand its backdrop first. The milestone was the Battle of Plassey in 1757. It was a significant turning point in the history of the subcontinent, one that changed its political as well as social course. This intriguing tale of unbridled ambition, blind faith, and wilful deception was, according to British soldier and military historian G. B. Malleson, an unfairly fought battle. Yet, it scripted one of the most defining moments in the history of India.

Politically, it signalled the beginning of the British rule in India which lasted for almost two centuries. Economically as well, for, to the victor belong the spoils. And the victory landed the British one of the most affluent provinces in Asia—Bengal. However, there is one other aspect, less discussed yet equally pertinent in bringing about the transformation of eighteenth-century Indian society, and that is its social aspect. The social fallout of the battle created a new middle class, which was ambitious, aspirational, and proved to be an ally of the British in expanding their control over the Indian subcontinent, as it gradually replaced the old middle class.

On 23 June 1757, the nawab of Bengal, Siraj-ud-Daula, faced his opponent Robert Clive, who was leading the British army near village Palashi on the banks of the river Bhagirathi. Little did the nawab know that three of his most trusted generals, who had pledged their loyalty and unwavering support as recently as a few hours ago, would promptly side with the enemy in his most crucial hour of need. They had urged the nawab to withdraw from the battlefield, leaving them in charge of the armies. As advised, the relatively young and inexperienced nawab (he was only twenty-three) climbed atop a camel and raced out of the battle ground with some 2,000 odd horsemen. This single act of resolute trust not only cost him his throne, but his life as well.

The events that followed have been well documented by both British as well as Indian historians. Many historical texts detail the events leading up to the battle, including the deception and treachery that led to the defeat of Siraj-ud-Daula and, ultimately, his execution by Miran, son of Mir Jafar. The battle resulted in two outcomes. First, it put an end to the French dream of establishing a base in Bengal, thereby eliminating competition; and second, by granting the British EIC zamindari rights to 24 Parganas, it gave them access to the richest treasury in the Indian subcontinent.

Close on the heels of Plassey came the Battle of Buxar. On 22 October 1764, the EIC, led by Hector Munro, defeated a confederate of armies of the nawabs of Bengal, Awadh, and the Mughal emperor at Buxar. The victory marked the beginning of the British conquest of India.

The economic destruction that followed not only crippled the economy but also contributed majorly to one of the worst famines in history to hit Bengal in 1770, which were preceded by harvest failures in 1768–69. A detailed statistical survey of the country was conducted between 1869 and 1881. The report published by *The Imperial Gazetteer of India* states: 'The first great famine of which we have any trustworthy record is that which devastated the lower valley of the Ganges in 1769–70. One-third of the population of Bengal is credibly reported to have perished. The previous season had been bad; and, as not uncommonly happens, the break-up of the drought was accompanied by disastrous floods. Beyond the importation into Calcutta and Murshidabad of a few thousand hundred weights of rice from the Districts of Bakarganj and Chittagong, it does not appear that any public measures for relief were taken or proposed.'[1] The *Gazetteer* volumes were published under the supervision of W. W. Hunter who joined the Indian Civil Service in 1862 and served as assistant magistrate and collector of Birbhum district in Bengal.

The irony was that reportedly, while almost a third of Bengal's population perished, plunging the province into the quagmire of poverty, Britain saw the birth of a new era brought on by technical advancement that resulted in the commencement of the Industrial Revolution, putting it way ahead in the race of modernization among its competitors.

American historian Brooks Adams gives the credit for this to the loot of Bengal by Clive and other Company officers. Writing in detail about the Company's activities in *The Law of Civilization and Decay*, he says, 'Very soon after Plassey the Bengal plunder began to arrive in London, and the effect appears to have been instantaneous, for all authorities agree that the "industrial revolution," the event which has divided the nineteenth century from all antecedent time, began with the year 1760. Plassey was fought in 1757, and probably nothing has ever equalled the rapidity of the change which followed.'[2]

This observation gives credence to the argument presented by renowned economist and Nobel Laureate Amartya Sen and historians William Dalrymple and Jon Wilson that 'the Bengal famine was caused by exploitation, mismanagement and the EIC's greed under Clive's leadership'.[3] The EIC remained at the helm of the affairs in the Indian subcontinent for almost a century. By 1857, owing to the policies adopted by Clive and his successors, British annexation of India was nearly complete, although the governing body continued to be the EIC.

The ease with which the British managed to take control of India prompts one to explore why there was no resistance to them socially. In the eighteenth century, India was faced with two major challenges: a highly volatile and violent political environment and a deeply fractured feudal society. Politically, the situation was advantageous for the British as they could offer their support to the rulers in lieu of trading rights as they did in Bengal. The EIC's superior European training and weaponry gave them an advantage over the Indian armies.

But it was not who ruled over the land rather how it was ruled that mattered to its people who had become accustomed to constant wars, battles, and foreign invasions after the death of Mughal emperor Aurangzeb in 1707. According to popular folklore, the last words of the eighty-eight-year-old weak, ailing, and battle-weary Aurangzeb, just before he died in his 'moving capital' Ahmednagar on 20 February, were 'Azma fasad baq!'(After me, the chaos!)

And chaos it was.

For none of his descendants had the vitality or the verve to hold together the great empire extending from Kabul in the north to Mysore in the south and Baluchistan in the west to Bengal in the east. And the once mighty empire gradually disintegrated into smaller kingdoms and states as one after the other weak successors ascended the throne. In the thirty-year rule of Mughal emperor Muhammad Shah (1719–1748), the provinces of Hyderabad, Awadh, Bengal, and Carnatic (the four most powerful and rich) became independent states ruled by Mughal nobles, now called 'nawabs'. The Marathas in Deccan, Sikhs in Punjab, and the Jats in areas around Delhi and Agra emerged as formidable forces, keen to expand their authority. Rajputs converted their watanjagirs into little kingdoms and were always looking for opportunities to extend their control over neighbouring areas. Then there were the British, French, and the Portuguese trading companies which were looking to expand their activities into the mainland.

The period between 1757 and 1857 saw two important developments: the growth of the British EIC from 'trade to territory'; and the rise of a new English-educated middle class under British rule.

After the treaty of Allahabad, the EIC got the diwani rights of the Bengal province. The British could now collect the revenues directly whereas the administration was left to the nizam who had to discharge his duties through the deputy nizam appointed by the British. Initially settling for dual administration, the British soon set out to expand their territory. Their tools of expansion were conquests and the Subsidiary Alliance System. By 1818, they had almost the entire southern, western, and eastern India under their control.

This is also the period that witnessed several peasant revolts and tribal uprisings, starting from the Fakir Revolution in 1763 which lasted till 1800. It was in response to the exploitative economic policies of the Company which had led to the great famine of Bengal. The British imposed restrictions on the movement of the pilgrims to holy places, who revolted and were joined by the poor peasants and dispossessed zamindars. Bengali writer Bankim Chandra Chatterjee's *Anand Math* is based on this historical event.

Between 1766 and 1771, Bengal witnessed a series of Chuar revolt, or peasant uprisings, which started from the Medinipur (or Midnapore) and spread to Jungle Mahals, covering the areas of Bankura, Purulia, and parts of eastern Bihar. The sequence of events has been recorded by British EIC administrator L. S. S. O'Malley in the *Bengal District Gazetteer*, Midnapore, 1911. Growing antagonism among the Chuars against the British and their persistent attacks on the Company strongholds forced the EIC to send an expedition in 1767 to the west and northwest of Midnapore to force them into submission and pay the revenue, and 'to capture and demolish as many of their strongholds as possible'. O'Malley mentions two more major revolts by the Chuars of the hills between Ghatsila and Barabhum, in December 1769 and November 1770. However, they did not attack Midnapore. 'In fact, most of the early depredations of the Chuars took place outside Midnapore district,' writes O'Malley.[4] Though the British authorities were successful in suppressing the rebellion, sporadic attempts continued till the first part of the nineteenth century.

Thus, resistance took place in small numbers, but one sees the absence of any mass opposition. In fact, Indian merchants and moneylenders, who constituted the traditional middle class, supported the British in their quest for political and economic control. Historical records provide a detailed account of the role that Jagat Seth* played in the conspiracy against Nawab Siraj-ud-Daula. The British spoke a different language, their culture, customs, and beliefs were drastically different from the natives and yet, their taking control of Bengal, Bihar, and Odisha was not perceived as a threat by the masses.

The sole reason the British could establish themselves in India, as mentioned by EIC administrator John Malcolm in his memoirs, was that the natives believed in their comparative superiority, 'in wisdom and strength, to their own rulers'. 'The want of union of the natives appears one of the strongest foundations of our power, it has certainly contributed, beyond all others, to its establishment. But when we trace this cause, we find it to have originated in the condition in which we found India, and the line we adopted towards its inhabitants'.[5]

The 'line' Malcolm was talking about was the consideration shown by the British towards the habits, institutions, superstitions, and religion of the natives. He writes, 'Our power has hitherto owed much to a contrast with misrule and oppression; but this strength we are daily losing—we have also been indebted to an indefinite impression of our resources, originating in ignorance of their real extent; knowledge will bring this feeling to a reduced standard. We are supported by the good opinion of the lower and middling classes, to whom our government is indulgent; but it has received the rudest shocks from an impression that our system of rule is at variance with the permanent continuance of rank, authority, and distinction in any Native of India.'

Mahajan cites a different reason. She points out that there was 'no nation then. When we say "Indian people", there is no sense that the people of India are being exploited by colonialism, by the Company.... It is regional and local, by local I mean group identities. So, the raja of Vizianagaram may revolt or peasants in

---

*Jagat Seth was a title conferred by Mughal Emperor Muhammad Shah on Fateh Chand, a powerful Marwari moneylender, who looked after the mint and treasury accounts of the nawab of Bengal.

Pabna may revolt, but these will be few and far between because there is no sense of India yet. Even in 1857, according to me, there is not yet a sense of nationalism.'

Sociologist Anand Kumar presents a similar viewpoint. He also highlights the fact that there was no 'interaction' of the British with the masses. 'The EIC was an invisible hand which expanded its territory through wars—the Mysore wars, Maratha wars, Sikh wars, and worked through the logic of the ruling elite in which the masses didn't play any role.'[6]

There was, perhaps, a psychological angle too, for the masses to be as 'tolerant' of the British as they were of the other outsiders. Barring a few, most outsiders who came to India stayed and became a part of the society. The Mughals are one such example. They did not pose a threat to the socio-cultural ethos of the natives.

Mohapatra agrees, 'Since the tenth century, you find different people coming to the subcontinent, either as invaders or rulers, settling down here and bringing their own culture into Indian society. [In] India...people lived in villages, having their own culture and lifestyle. They were, more or less, self-sufficient. There was not much movement of people. Occasionally, they would go on a pilgrimage or to the marketplace. In all, people didn't really bother about who was controlling power at the centre. Also, most of these invaders didn't change the way of life of the people at the grassroots. To initiate a movement, you require participation of the people. When their land tenure system is not changing, their rituals are not changing, their interpersonal social relationship are not changing, then why will they bother? People didn't realize that the presence of British would lead to monumental changes in the social structure shortly.'[7]

Perhaps the most surprising explanation is given by Scottish historian Jon E. Wilson, who hypothesizes that there was no outrage against the British because they 'did not intend to rule over India, initially' and that there was no 'civilizing mission' either. Wilson's comments are contradictory to Rudyard Kipling's 'The White Man's

Burden' published in 1899, which justifies colonialism. Wilson argues that the purpose of wresting power was to defend the British presence in India, that the East was seen as a career opportunity, and that the British were not interested in engaging with the locals. He argues that 'revolutionary ideology or the desire for military authority' were not the reasons behind the transformation of the Indian society in parts conquered by the British. He says, 'Social change was wrought instead by forms of government that anxious East India Company's officials used to defend their new position.'[8]

The EIC was a trading syndicate whose sole aim was to establish trade links, generate profit, and protect its commercial interests by brute force, if need be. Clive's policy of dual governance sought to achieve this goal by keeping diwani rights with the Company and giving nizamat, or administrative rights to the nawab appointed by Company officials, which meant that the nitty-gritties of ruling a province was left to the Indian rulers while financial affairs were controlled by the British. However, this division of authority was brought to an end in 1784 by Prime Minister William Pitt.

Historian V. P. S. Raghuvanshi views the political resistance to the British as a conflict between two social systems 'different in political consciousness, legal conceptions, and economic structure'. In the sixteenth and seventeenth centuries, Europe was going through an Age of Exploration brought on by commercial capitalism, whereas, Indian society was still being ruled by decadent feudal lords. It was a 'triumph of European capitalism over Indian feudalism'. The success of a handful of British merchants against the massive armies of the kings and nawabs highlighted the stagnant and 'unprogressive character' of the highly stratified society at large in the face of a more aggressive and dynamic Western society.

One crucial factor highlighted by Raghuvanshi is the heterogenous nature of Indian society that helped the British. 'The consummation of the British rule through stages of development through the second half of the eighteenth century is an inevitable historical phenomenon. It overtook the feudal state system of the country, which was too heterogenous in the class composition to offer vigorous resistance to the foreigners. It led to the disintegration of a society which had suffered from acute divisions, along caste and religious lines, and was demoralized into inertia by an orthodox reactionary priestly community and degenerate aristocracy.'[9]

One can, therefore, summarize that the middle class, in a way, was passively involved in establishing British rule in India. Of course, they could not foresee the extent of the damage this would lead to. 'And when the East India Company decided to open educational institutes in India,' comments Misra, 'the Allahabad college in the 1830s or the universities in Bombay, Madras, and Calcutta, introducing Western education, they became the production houses of the (new) middle class, where the children of Indian feudal lords were studying and getting converted into the educated middle class.'

3

Bengal Renaissance and the Revolt of 1857

The two most significant developments in eighteenth-century India were the creation of a form of capitalist society and the formation of India the nation as we know it today: with a defined territory, a common central governmental authority, and development of a certain degree of nationalism associated with a mental image of the nation in the minds of the individuals, which grew over time to take the form of the national movement. How these changes came about and the impact they had on the traditional middle class as well as the emerging new middle class can be understood by studying the administrative initiatives taken by the EIC.

The battles of Plassey and Buxar were pivotal for Britain as well India. The power shift in Bengal had a far-reaching effect on the subcontinent. From being a mere trading company, the British now controlled the provinces of Bengal, Bihar, and Odisha. It was the first decisive win on their way to gaining sovereignty over the entire subcontinent. For India, it marked the beginning of a long journey towards the formation of a unified nation and the creation of nationalist sentiment. And the development of new port cities such as Calcutta, Bombay, and Madras promoted a composite culture based on both Eastern and Western philosophies.

Much has been written about the Company rule and how it differed from the monarchical rule in India. 'In the absence of an adequate political and economic system,' writes B. B. Misra, 'they transplanted into India their own form and principles of government and economic organisation which they modified only to suit local conditions.'[1] It was, however, the same model of governance that was disintegrating in England that was introduced here by the British. They created the landlord class (zamindari) and ownership of private property (ryotwari). The ideas and institutions of the middle class social order did not originate from within; they were implanted in India without corresponding developments in its social and economic institutions.

After securing territorial rights, Clive and then Warren Hastings, the first governor general of Bengal, set out to introduce administrative, judiciary, and military reforms. 'The first point in politics which I offer to your consideration,' wrote Clive to the Select Committee in 1767, 'is the form of government. We are sensible that since the acquisition of the Dewanee, the power formerly belonging to the Soubah of these provinces is totally, in fact, vested in the East India Company.'

As per Clive's proposition, in the new scheme of things, the nawab was to remain the titular head of the province and protect the Company's interests by quashing any encroachment attempt made by foreign powers. He also had to shoulder administrative responsibilities and ensure people's grievances were redressed. 'Be it, therefore, always remembered that there is a Soubah and that though the revenues belong to the Company, the territorial jurisdiction must still rest in the chiefs of the country, acting under him, and thus presiding in conjunction.'[2]

But this model of governance failed miserably and was abolished in 1772. Rising corruption and misgovernance led to decline in revenues. 'There was no responsibility and no control.'[3] The Company's tax and revenue policies combined with natural disasters, as we saw (drought for two consecutive years followed by crop failure), resulted in what has been one of the most tragic moments in Indian history—the Great Bengal Famine of 1770. And so, in 1772, the dual system of governance was abolished.

Though the EIC had become the de facto ruler of the Bengal province, it was primarily a trading corporation whose sole intent was to earn profit. Company rule, therefore, was influenced by its commercial interests, which hindered the growth of fair and just administrative machinery. Which is why, perhaps, in the initial years, the EIC superimposed its capitalistic policies over the existing feudal model of governance, leading to 'colonial capitalism'. Clive's model of dual governance was the start of this colonial capitalism.

'For the first time, a new class of landlords was created which was the mirror-image of the feudal lords,' explains Sucheta Mahajan. 'They were only revenue collectors...these zamindars (not to be confused with the landowning zamindars). Many of the bhadralok* or certain class from Bengal, who were doing well and who took to the English, the ancestors of Tagore and others, not only made money by being zamindars of the new kind, but also benefitted from the rule of the Company. They became agents of the Company.'[4]

To further their capitalistic goals, it was necessary to replace the feudal order by capitalist forms in India as well. But it was to be a milder, modified version of the capitalist society, as a capitalist society is 'socially, politically, economically, and culturally stronger than a feudal people'.[5]

Sociologist Desai draws attention to the fact that India's conquest was by a modern England, which had vanquished feudalism in its own territory. Feudalism leads to a fractured society unlike capitalism which unites people politically as well as economically. Hence, the version of the capitalist society promoted in India was vastly different from that of England. Still, Indian society was changing, but unlike its counterpart in England, which switched from feudalism to capitalism, it transitioned from feudalism to colonial capitalism.

The British landed gentry were the outcome of private ownership of land. In the Indian economy, however, the concept of private ownership of land was missing. It was the economic policy of the EIC, brought into effect by Lord Cornwallis in 1793 in the form

*This was the new educated and upwardly mobile middle class that originated in Bengal in the early nineteenth century.

of Permanent Settlement* that led to the creation of the zamindars and peasant proprietors in India. This class creation fulfilled two basic requirements of the British: first, they did not have to bother with the management of their territories, it was the job of the zamindar to collect revenue and take care of the administration of the zamindari; second, they had the support of a local and loyal new class, which owed its existence to the British rule.

'If security was wanting against extensive popular tumult or revolution, I should say that the Permanent Settlement, although a failure in many other respects and in its most important essentials, has this great advantage at least of having created a vast body of rich landed proprietors deeply interested in the continuance of the British dominion and having complete command over the mass of the people,' wrote Governor General of India William Bentinck (1828–35).[6]

While on the one hand, the Permanent Settlement led to the commercialization of land as well as agriculture, on the other, it created a new ruling class comprising moneylenders, merchants, and urban people who had amassed great wealth. They did not have any direct connection with their land and managed it through managers. Just like the old zamindar class, they too displayed very little interest in the development of their farmland. Hence, observes Desai, the Indian zamindars never rose to the level of their Western counterparts.[7]

The other major change that swept across society in eighteenth-century India, land reforms being the beginning of this change, was in education. The Indian education system lagged far behind that of the West, which had undergone major scientific and technological developments at this time. India, on the other hand, was still struggling with limited education, technological backwardness,

*The Permanent Settlement was an agreement between the East India Company and the zamindars to fix the land revenue. The zamindars were given ownership rights over the land and had to pay 89% tax to the EIC, while keeping the remaining 11% for themselves.

and a land economy that was obstructive to the socio-economic development of the subcontinent. The need for a new education policy was felt by the British as well as Indians. The British needed an educated class to help them rule over their newly acquired territories, and the new Indian middle class saw it as an opportunity for their social and economic advancement.

The subtle changes that had been taking place socially after the British established themselves in Bengal, Bombay, and Madras became more prominent with the Charter Act of 1813 which was passed after much deliberation. Clause 43 of the Act empowered the governor general to 'appropriate a sum of not less than one lakh of rupees in each year out of the surplus territorial revenue for the revival and improvement of literature and the encouragement of the learned natives of India, and for the introduction and promotion of a knowledge of the sciences among the inhabitants of the British territories in India'.[8]

This led to a generation of Indians educated in British style. But the educated middle classes were more concerned about their status than being agents of social and economic change. As part of their educational policy, the British tried to establish a class which was 'comparable to their own' in order to help in the country's administration and in the development of 'its internal resources', which were required for the imports of British manufactures that were on the rise. 'In Macaulay's words, this was to be a "class, Indian in blood and colour, but English in tastes, in opinions, in morals and intellect".'[9]

In the context of India, Misra and Desai lament the lack of a stratified social order* and an under-developed economy, the two prerequisites for the creation of a middle class, prior to the advent of the British. Both believe that it was the rigidity of the Indian society[10] and the self-sufficient nature of the village[11] that

---

*Social stratification refers to a society's categorization of its people into rankings based on factors like wealth, income, education, family background, and power.

prevented the rise of the middle class in India. However, both, like many others after them, seem to have ignored the social mobility of people within and outside the confines of a particular caste. For instance, some carpenters in Bengal and Bihar hired workers while they themselves supervised. Similarly, in the Kashmir shawl industry, large workshops containing close to 300 looms were owned by master craftsmen. Thus, one can say that the emergence of artisans as capitalist entrepreneurs was not missing from the Indian scene.[12]

Also, equating India with any other nation would be incorrect because of the diversity of language, culture, and religion it embodies. So, development of a united and homogenous class was not possible (and is not even today). But there was a pre-existing extensive trading system, and a big industry, though not mechanized, that catered to the local demand and produced for the world market. With such an elaborate system of commerce and production, the presence of a middle class cannot be ruled out.

Nevertheless, the nineteenth century brought in its wake the crucial changes that set the future course of the country. These were the Bengal Renaissance and the Revolt of 1857. While one appealed to the philosophical and psychological sensitivities of the masses, the other strived to reassert the authority of the Indian ruling class by challenging the control of the EIC. This period of Indian history is of immense importance not just politically but socially as well, for it saw the emergence of new practices and development of new perspectives. India under the British was now open to changes in its polity and economy and that change, over time, pervaded the social space creating in its wake a class that was traditional in sensibilities and modern in outlook.

The Bengal Renaissance

In the time of Rammohun Roy the West had come to the East with a shock that caused panic in the heart of India. The natural cry was exclusion. But this was the cry of fear, the cry of weakness, the cry of dwarf. Through the great mind of Rammohun Roy the true spirit of India asserted itself and accepted the West, not by the rejection of the soul of India, but by the comprehension of the soul of the West.

—RABINDRANATH TAGORE[13]

Historian David Kopf views the Bengal Renaissance in the context of 'cultural continuity and change under British colonialism'. He divides the historiography of the renaissance between the advocates of 'British impact' and the 'Indian response'.[14]

Hence, the nature of the Renaissance depends on how one views it. If the emphasis is on British influence, then it is viewed as a harbinger of modernization, but if the stress is on response then it is taken as a 'reinterpretation' of tradition. More often than not, it is taken as a culmination of Eastern and Western philosophies.

India had an education system which catered to the needs of the masses. In the Rig Vedic age, education was not confined to any varna. According to the Rig Veda, non-Aryans, too, referred to as Pisacha, Asura, or Dasyu (later called Shudras) were entitled to education. The Adhikhand of *Padma Purana* gives a rather interesting definition of Shudras: 'one who is not capable of comprehending the meaning of the Vedas was considered a Shudra'.[15] However, it was more classical and spiritual than practical, though civil engineering, literature, medicine, and law also formed part of the syllabus. A study of the Brahmanas, Aranyakas, and Upanishads reveals that by the end of the Vedic era, Shudras had lost their right to the study of the Vedas and high military training. Still, all four castes had curricula aligned with their occupations and, for the better part of the later Vedic period, women's education remained the same as that of the Vedic era. It is only in the last leg of the later Vedic period, around 1000–500 BCE, that one witnesses a decline in women's education.[16] In fact, education in the field of Ayurveda was open to all the varnas.

Mughal emperor Akbar, during his reign, not only added courses such as agriculture, geography, and texts from other languages and religions to the syllabus, but also placed emphasis on writing and learning the script. The paathshalas, maktabs, and madrasas imparted knowledge in Sanskrit, Arabic, and Persian.

Baptist Missionary William Ward, who was based in Serampore after his arrival in Bengal in 1799, has commented in his writings that every village in the area had a school which taught reading, writing, and arithmetic.[17] A letter dated 3 June 1814, from the court of directors to the governor general in the Council of Bengal, mentions the subjects taught at the time. The medium of teaching was Sanskrit and the subjects ranged from ethics, law, botany, ayurveda, astronomy, and mathematics, including geometry and algebra.

Not wanting to interfere in local affairs, initially, the Orientalists in the EIC decided to support the existing education system. Politically, it was considered better to not get involved in the local affairs of the people for fear of retaliation by the upper castes. Warren Hastings founded the Calcutta madrasa in 1781, where Muslim law and related subjects were taught. Following this, in 1792, Jonathan Duncan laid the foundations of the Sanskrit college at Varanasi, where knowledge on Hindu law and philosophy was imparted.

The decision to implement the English education system was born out of convenience. By the end of the eighteenth century, it had become clear to the British that they needed a network of local people to carry out basic administrative duties to cut down on rising administrative expenses. The monopoly of the upper castes on education proved a hurdle in the scheme of things. Also, the British now wanted a uniform policy for the subcontinent.

There was an economic motive as well, as pointed out by Misra: 'The dress of the people and their mode of living had remained substantially unaltered for ages, and any attempt to modify these involved a clash with local custom and caste prejudice. Charles Grant, an evangelist who retired from Company service in 1790, was the first to realize that an English education would be the best means of changing old habits and values.

By the beginning of the nineteenth century, there were noticeable changes in the preferences of the Bengali bhadralok. According to an 1823 account by Bishop Heber, "Their progress in the imitation of our habits is very apparent, though still the difference is great. None of them adopt our dress. But their houses are adorned with verandas and Corinthian pillars; they have very handsome carriages, often built in England; they speak tolerable English and they show a considerable liking for European society. Few of them will however eat with us".'[18]

The upper middle-class of Calcutta, thus, was developing a taste for luxury. These people, according to Misra, constituted the new middle class; and though they were not class-conscious as yet, they did command wealth and influence, and 'supported English education in Bengal'.[19]

Then the Charter Act of 1813 was passed. Almost an immediate consequence of the Act was increased missionary activity in India. The missionaries opened charity schools which taught the Gospel translated into vernacular languages and conducted English classes for the locals. The Baptist Missionary Society founded the Serampore College in 1818, which imparted education in the arts and sciences of the West to Christians and non-Christians alike. The Missionary Society also obtained a Danish Charter in 1827 for conferring degrees.[20]

The second, and decidedly more significant impact was on the middle classes, which were beginning to crowd the capital cities of Calcutta, Bombay, and Madras by then. As the British territorial control and trade activities in India increased, more opportunities became available to the middle classes, who found the knowledge of the English language gainful.

'While ordinary men were concerned with the material benefits of the knowledge of English, some educated and liberal minded Indians, through their long interaction with the Europeans in Calcutta, had realized the futility of pursuing a system of exclusively classical education and the great possibilities which a knowledge of the language and literature of the West afforded,' comments Ghosh.[21]

The stage was set for one of the most crucial events of the century that would drastically change the socio-political as well as cultural ethos of India—the Bengal Renaissance.

The word 'Renaissance' originates from the Latin word 'renasci', which means 'be born again'. It describes the revivalist period of European history from the fourteenth to sixteenth centuries, when there was a resurgence of art and literature under classical models. Some would argue against the use of the term in the Indian context though, as the British introduced new concepts of nationhood and nationalism to the Indian polity and new trends of commercialization of land and agriculture, and market capitalism to the Indian economy.

How then, one would ask, can it be called a renaissance?

One could explain it in terms of revival of Hinduism that took place during this time.

Mimamsa or reflection had been at the very core of Vedic learning in India. Teachers would encourage their students to think, reason, and question, and then arrive at conclusion.*

This system of education came to be replaced by rote learning, and over time became stagnated. The middle classes followed the diktats of the Brahmins blindly, who interpreted the Vedas to suit their interests. The lower classes and women were barred from even listening to the Vedic mantras. The Bengal renaissance was an attempt to revive the true nature of Vedic learning, one that was based on reflection.

The founding of the Brahmo Samaj in 1828 in Calcutta by Raja Ram Mohan Roy marked the beginning of the Bengal Renaissance.

---

*The Upanishads mention three steps of education: Sravana, Manana, and Nididhyasana (Bri. Upanishad). Hearing texts and words uttered by the teacher is to be followed by the process of Mariana, deliberation, reflection on the topic taught, but it results only in an intellectual apprehension of its meaning. Therefore, there is the stage of learning, called Nididhyasana or Meditation, by which can be attained the realization of truth. See Radha Kumud Mookerji, *Ancient Indian Education (Brahmanical and Buddhist)*, London: Macmillan and Co., 1947, p. 31.

Roy came from a prosperous and orthodox upper caste Brahmin family and was, therefore, aware of the prevailing social iniquities. He was a well-read man and was proficient in several languages, including Bengali, Hindi, Persian, Arabic, Sanskrit, and English. 'He was also one of the first Indians whose thought and practice were not circumscribed by the constraints of kin, caste and religion.'[22] His exposure to the various languages and literatures, including the Vedas, Upanishads, Quran, and other Islamic texts, had a profound impact on his thinking and that led him to introduce many socio-religious reforms for which he faced severe criticism from orthodox Hindus.

However, his most debated achievement has been the introduction of the English education system in India. It was Roy's vision for a progressive India that made him push for it. In a letter to Lord William Pitt Amherst, who was the governor general of India between 1823 and 1828, Roy wrote on 11 December 1823:

> The Sanskrit system of education would be the best calculated to keep this country in darkness, if such had been the policy of the British legislature. But as the improvement of the native population is the object of the government, it will consequently promote a more liberal and enlightened system of instruction, embracing mathematics, natural philosophy, chemistry, anatomy, with other useful sciences, which may be accomplished with the sums proposed by employing a few gentlemen of talent and learning educated in Europe and providing a college furnished with necessary books, instruments and other apparatus.[23]

Roy has been criticized by politicians and scholars alike, even in present times, for his pro-British attitude. However, it's ludicrous to judge history in the present context. What Roy was aiming for was the establishment of institutes which would make modern education, and more so modern thought, available to the masses.

Also, as the British expanded their control over different territories, the demand for interpreters, agents, clerks, and copyists in the government as well as business houses grew. The familiarity of the emerging middle class with the English language presented them with an opportunity to be a part of the administration, which encouraged Bengali youth to opt for Western education.

Roy's denouncement of idolatry, superstition, and social practices such as polygamy, sati, and the caste system earned him the wrath of not only orthodox Hindus but his own family as well. However, his thoughts and teachings slowly, but surely, started bearing fruits.

In the beginning of 1820, Sophia Dobson Collet, in her book *Life and Letters of Raja Rammohun Roy* writes, 'A native called as a witness in a court of law refused to take the waters of Gunga. He declared himself a follower of Rammohun Roy, and consequently not a believer in the imagined sanctity of the river. He was allowed to affirm as Quakers do.'[24]

The introduction of English education system influenced the middle classes in two major ways: first, it was the only way the middle class could raise their status. The lower classes couldn't afford to send their wards to school. For them, it was more a question of survival. The elite were already sending their kids abroad for studies and were not really worried about jobs and careers. But for the middle class, this education was a means to an end. This emerging middle class was drastically different from the pre-existing traditional one. While the former was ready to adapt to the new culture and practices for socio-economic gains, the latter was orthodox and rigid in outlook. What the English education, so vehemently promoted by Ram Mohan Roy, sought to do was provide a different perspective to the middle-class mindset, one that was not limited to classical education but talked of new ideas and concepts that were shaping the world.

The need for trade and production resulted in the creation of employment; this in turn led to 'mobility virtually unprecedented in our history'.[25] People moved to cities in high numbers 'to seek careers in association with the British'.*

The second, and perhaps a more significant, influence was that it encouraged the masses to challenge and question existing social norms. It is generally believed that Roy became the first Brahmin to break the social taboo on crossing the seas. Brahmo Samaj worked a lot for the emancipation and upliftment of women. So taken were the youth with the teachings of the Samaj that, in defiance of the purdah system, they started taking their wives out publicly to dine with friends, dressed in an attire half-Indian and half-European in style as the 'customary female attire did not suit women going out publicly'. To lay emphasis on their commitment to widow remarriage, young men in Brahmo Samaj married widows.[26]

Thus, one finds the wheels of change churning Bengali society as the new middle class warmed up to the Western way of living. This also marked a sharp contrast between urban and rural middle classes as well as the traditional and new middle classes, leading to a clash of ideologies, identities, and cultural ethos. This clash was more evident during the Revolt of 1857 as the new educated middle class sided with the British in contrast to the old middle class, which extended its support to the rebels.

The Revolt of 1857

The Revolt of 1857 has elicited much interest among historians and scholars, who have presented different views, mostly contrasting, regarding its nature and the causes that led to the uprising. Hence, before ascertaining the role of the middle classes in this 'sepoy

*Although census data on the population of Calcutta in the eighteenth and nineteenth centuries are often unreliable, it is generally accepted that between 1821 and 1837, the population of the city grew by nearly 50,000. See A. E. Salahuddin Ahmed, *Social Ideas and Social Change in Bengal, 1818–1835,* Leiden: E. J. Brill, 1965, pp. 11–12. See also S. N. Mukherjee, 'Class, Caste, and Politics in India', in Edmund Leach and S. N. Mukheriee (eds.), *Elites in South Asia,* Cambridge: Cambridge University Press, 1970, pp. 36–38.

mutiny' and mass rebellion, there's a need to carefully study the behaviour patterns that the class displayed right from the beginning of the revolt to its end.

One of the dominant features of the middle class is that it always works towards securing its own interests. It is by no means egalitarian by nature. That's a class characteristic that differentiates it from the other two classes. For the upper class, in general, does not need to worry about protecting its interests. Being at the top of the social strata, they are able to exercise control over the means of production and use their wealth and relational capital to influence public policy; and for the lower class, equality is not merely a value but a support as well for their social, political, and economic existence.* However, the 1857 revolt brings to light the dual nature of the middle class.

The general view is that the middle classes did not play any role in the revolt. 'We don't have any evidence of the middle class taking part in this rebellion,' says Sucheta Mahajan. 'It was mainly a rebellion led by the feudal classes, the nobility, the landed elite, those kings and queens and princes who had been displaced by British rule. Policies like subsidiary alliance and doctrine of lapse, had affected them adversely, so rani of Jhansi and the peshwas, and Nana Saheb, led by the titular head, the ageing Mughal emperor Bahadur Shah Zafar II, rose up against the British. But there was no sign of the middle groups.'[27]

This is true to an extent. That the middle class was largely 'missing in action' during the revolt is clear from the personal accounts and letters, official reports as well as books on the chain of events that took place in 1857. The causes that led to the mutiny and the rebellion included discontented masses, especially in rural areas, which were burdened with taxes and high-handedness of the British agents; disgruntled sepoys, who demanded fair pay and

---

*Relational capital refers to people one knows and which have the potential for future value. See John Spacey, '15 Characteristics of the Upper Class', Simplicable.com, 6 March 2023.

were unwilling to cross the seas or use the 'infamous' cartridges due to religious reasons; and dispossessed zamindars, who lost their ancestral property in the auctions to 'strangers'. These were the classes that actively participated in the rebellion.

Nevertheless, this analysis of the revolt lacks certain crucial elements, like the urban merchant and trader classes, who formed the middle section of society. A study of the available material reveals great contradictions within the middle class as its attitude kept changing with the circumstances. Areas such as Awadh, which were the centre of the storm, saw participation (active as well as passive) from all classes, whereas in Bengal, the middle class, especially the English-educated bhadralok, remained either neutral or openly sided with the British.

Most of the studies focus on the causes leading up to the revolt, how the oppressive policies of the British and the socio-religious reforms culminated in a widespread, violent rebellion of the masses, led by dethroned kings and queens, that almost brought an end to the Company Raj, and the chronology of events, starting with the execution of Mangal Pandey in Barrackpore. However, there is hardly any reference made to the urban capitalist class or their involvement in the revolt.

Economic historian Tirthankar Roy raises this very issue and points out that not enough attention has been paid to the 'nature of capitalist contribution to the war'.[28]

Intelligence reports gathered by the British after they had defeated the rebels and re-established their authority over Benares, Mathura, Patna, Meerut, and the outskirts of Lucknow reveal that most of the prominent merchants and bankers in Lucknow were helping the rebel government. Chronicling the 1857 revolt, authors John William Kaye and G. B. Malleson mention that the efforts by the British to raise a public loan after they had reconquered Meerut in June 1857, failed because the 'local bankers did not respond'.[29] Another report states that 'until the winter of 1857, Lucknow traders refused to serve the British. Bairo Pershad and

Esree (Ishwar) Pershad, bankers of Benares, maintained a secret correspondence with the rebel government in Lucknow'.[30]

Since its annexation, many lower as well as upper-middle class people in Awadh, who served the crown and enjoyed royal patronage, suddenly found themselves jobless. The state of nobles and court officials was worse, stripped of their privileges and lucrative jobs, they were driven to destitution. A first-hand account illustrates how the 'native merchants, shopkeepers, and bankers, who, while Wajid Ali was on the throne, made large profits from supplying the luxurious want of the king (nawab), his courtiers and the wealthy ladies of the thronged harems, found no sale of their goods and the people in general, and especially the poor, were dissatisfied because they were taxed directly and indirectly in every way'.[31]

These incidents highlight the circumstances that motivated the middle class of Awadh to support the mutineers in any capacity they could. While talking about the punishment meted out to the prisoners or those who showed solidarity with the mutineers, which had become a rather routine act, British author L. E. Ruutz Rees mentions that 'among the prisoners, on that or other occasion, were also four banniahs (native shopkeepers), who were proved to have been agents of the mutineers of Benaras, and who had arrived here from that city in order to propagate rebellion at Lucknow'.[32] While on the one hand, the middle class helped the mutineers with money and information, on the other they stopped doing business with the Europeans as '...the mahajuns, and even the bank, had ceased to transact business. No drafts could be cashed or obtained, no loans were granted, no credit was given by natives to Europeans, and no purchases were made by merchants'.[33]

British historian Charles Ball describes the popularity of the revolt thus: 'In Oudh, the rebels could march without commissariat, for the people would always feed them. They could leave their luggage without guard because the people would not attack it. They were always certain of their position and that of the British, for, the people bought them hourly information.'[34]

Thus, it seems that the middle class favoured the rebels in areas that saw maximum action during the revolt, whereas in other parts of India, they were either neutral or in support of the British. For example, the zamindars in Bengal supported the British, so did the merchants and bankers in the coastal regions which were unaffected by the revolt. Punjab also remained loyal to the British.

The reason why the middle class backed the rebels in Awadh is two-fold: first, they had suffered huge losses after the annexation of Awadh by the Company. *Tilism*, an Urdu weekly started on 25 July 1856, edited and published by Muhammad Yaqub from Firangi Mahal in Lucknow, provides crucial information on the mismanagement of Awadh by the British and how it affected society, leading to an increase in crime and unemployment, which had a serious impact on the economy, particularly trade and commerce. Secondly, they did not want a face-off with the mutineers, and so, to protect their own interests, they sided with them.

But this participation was not uniform. In areas where the British were in a stronger position, such as Punjab, the middle class supported the British. In Bengal, too, the zamindars, the rural moneylenders, and baniyas, traders, and merchants, educated Indians and the intelligentsia sided with the British. In fact, one of the theories suggested by scholars subscribing to the Marxist viewpoint is that the 1857 revolt was also the result of a class conflict. In rural areas, peasants assaulted moneylenders and burned their account books along with property deeds.

In his account of the revolt, historian R. C. Majumdar comments that after the sepoys rebelled, other classes joined the fray to 'exploit the situation to their advantage'. 'The Zemindars and villagers took advantage of the general anarchy to obtain from Mahajans and Baneas their books of business and bond-debts etc.' The report of the Magistrate of Suharanpur, from which this sentence is taken, adds: 'It would appear as if the disturbances in the commencement were less directed against Govt, than against particular people and castes. When the fall of Delhi ceased to be looked upon as imminent, the agricultural communities began to turn their eyes towards the local treasuries and did not scruple to oppose themselves to government, officers and troops.'[35]

It was only natural, then, for these classes to turn to the British for protection.

What is most peculiar and confounding, perhaps, is the attitude of the Bengali bhadralok towards the rebels. They were completely apathetic to their cause. To say that they were loyal to the British, considering they owed their existence to them, would be incorrect. For they were learned men who were well acquainted with the concepts of freedom and liberty, and their role in society. Also, their allegiance to the British was conditional. So long as their interests were promoted by the British, they were loyal.

Historian Benoy Ghosh's analysis of the revolt brings a different picture to the fore with regard to Bengali intelligentsia's lack of support for the sepoy-peasant cause. The immediate cause of the revolt was religious in nature. The sepoys revolted because their religious sentiments were supposedly being hurt. 'The cry of religious interference was loudly raised by the sepoys just when the intelligentsia was fighting against that same cry of the orthodox Hindus in the city.'[36]

For the sepoys, it was a fight to safeguard their religion. However, the emerging educated middle class could not afford any association with religious fanaticism and orthodoxy as it would have compromised its situation. Thus, they had no other alternative but to remain neutral or side with the British.

Also, as these educated middle class Indians were fighting their ideological battles against orthodox Hindus with the support of the British, they had to stand with them (the British). Ghosh highlights another interesting point that by 'opposing the mutineers and their battle-cry of religious reaction' the Bengali intelligentsia was protesting the stance of the 'conservative' British rulers, who were condemning 'liberals among them for overdoing with social reforms and provoking the mutiny'.[37]

Ghosh also sees this opposition as a way of protecting the socio-economic interests of the emerging educated Indian middle class by the intelligentsia. He maintains that the middle class was more conscious of its role in the politics of the country, and that it did not want a resurrection of the old feudal order which the rebels were aiming for.

Mahajan provides another angle as to why the middle class did not participate in the revolt. She maintains that, considering the education policy was only about 15-20 years old, the creation of an informed middle class was hardly possible. 'If we are linking the rise of the middle class to education...then it has hardly been some 15-20 years since the education policy had been introduced. It's only after the 1857 revolt that the Hindus start to take to English education in a big way. As for the Muslims, they remained opposed to Western education and, consequently, did not progress.'

An interesting aspect about the revolt was the number of women participating in it, and not just the queens and the begums. These were ordinary Hindu, Muslim, and Sikh women, coming from middle, lower-middle, and Dalit backgrounds. One such example is Uda Devi. This fearless warrior from the Pasi community, whose statue still adorns the square outside Sikandar Bagh in Lucknow, killed a significant number of British soldiers in the battle of Sikandar Bagh, which was described at length in the memoirs of British commander William Forbes-Mitchel, who led the attack.

The action took place under a large peepul tree in the centre of the inner court of Sikandar Bagh. The tree was rather bushy and was surrounded by water pots at its base. After an intense battle that resulted in bloodshed, many of the soldiers proceeded towards the tree to take a short rest and quench their thirst. However, Captain Dawson later found a number of them dead, their wounds suggesting that they were shot from above. After the shooter was located [Quacker Wallace] fired on the sighted person and nobody could believe that, down fell a body dressed in a tight-fitting red jacket and tight-fitting rose-coloured silk trousers; and the breast of the jacket bursting open with the fall, showed that the wearer was a woman. She was armed with a pair of heavy old-pattern cavalry pistols, one of which was in her belt still loaded, and her pouch was still about half full of ammunition, while from her perch in the tree, which had been carefully prepared before the attack, she had killed more than half-a-dozen men.'[38]

Another fascinating character of the uprising was Azizun Bai. The courtesan of Kanpur joined the rebellion after being inspired by Nana Sahib. Historian Lata Singh writes: 'Azizun was very close to the sepoys of the 2nd cavalry, many of whom visited her house. She was particularly close to Shamsuddin Khan, the sepoy of the 2nd cavalry who played an active role in the Rebellion. ...Azizun's house was also the meeting point of sepoys. She had formed a group of women who went around fearlessly cheering the men in arms, attended to their wounds and distributed arms and ammunition. During the entire period of the siege of Wheeler's entrenchment, she was amidst soldiers. One of the eyewitnesses mentions that it was always possible to see her armed with pistols—in spite of the heavy firing—amongst her friends, who were the cavalrymen of the 2nd regiment.'[39]

Likewise, there are scores of prominent names such as Asghari Begum, Asha Devi, Inder Kaur, Bakhtawari, and Beebee who fought valiantly along with the insurgents and were shot, hanged, or burnt alive.

From these accounts, one can surmise that the middle class, in fact, played a crucial role in the Revolt of 1857, also called the First War of Independence by some. To deny any involvement of this old, traditional middle class in one of the highlights of nineteenth century India would be grossly incorrect. True, a majority were either aloof or sided with the British, but there was a segment, however marginal, that supported the cause.

4

Impact of the Revolt and the Swadeshi Movement

The Revolt of 1857 was an important juncture in Indian history. It occasioned a complete break from the past in more ways than one, as it brought about certain key changes in the socio-political fabric of the subcontinent. Foremost among them was the entry of the middle class into politics; the rise of a new, indigenous capitalist class; and building of a national character for India and its people. Quashing all hopes of a revival of the past,* the revolt led to the formation of a more Westernized social structure, which gradually replaced the traditional middle class with a new and aspiring middle class. A class that was ambitious, politically more aware, and that, over time, developed a strong sense of nationalism. It was this class, according to Rajesh Misra, that acted as a strong force in strengthening colonial rule in India.

The initiation of the middle class into politics started in Bengal, which had been the hub of activity since the British came to India. As British influence grew, Bengali society also underwent a transformation. The educated middle class had grown political ambitions too. It now wanted representation in administration, and that made it stay away from the mass uprising of 1857.

---

*The rebels wanted to restore dethroned rulers. Sir W. Russell, the famous correspondent of the *London Times* wrote: 'Here we had not only a servile war and a sort of Jacquerie combined, but we had a war of religion, a war of race, and a war of revenge, of hope, of national determination to shake off the yoke of a stranger and to re-establish the full power of native chiefs and the full sway of native religion.' See P. C. Joshi (ed.), *Rebellion 1857: A Symposium*, New Delhi: People's Publishing House, 1957, p. 122.

One important feature of this class was that it comprised those from an upper caste background. 'It was natural,' says Misra. 'Look at the leaders of the freedom movement, but for a few, all came from this background. This determines its social goal, and nature, and the differentiation among sections that was based on caste by birth. Even the Muslim middle class was the same.'

While the revolt was a lesson in diplomacy for the British, for the Indian middle class, it was an opportunity to realize their political ambitions. The 'mutiny', as the British called it, was a warning that had made it clear that the exploitative nature of the Company was detrimental to their rule and could cost them their most lucrative colony, and it almost did. So, with the Government of India Act, 1858, the British Parliament put India directly under the rule of the Crown. That the governance without the involvement, and consultation, of Indians was impossible had become clear. They needed people at the local administrative levels who could work as agents of British rule. By this time, Western education had taken root in a big way. The universities of Bombay, Calcutta and Madras had become production houses of middle class 'where children of big landlords and zamindars were studying and getting converted to middle class'.[1]

Thus, the Indian Councils Act 1861 marked the entry of Indians into the legislative assembly, though in a non-official capacity. The Act gave power to the governor general to appoint additional members to his council for 'better exercise of the power of making laws and regulations'. However, these appointees were allowed to sit and vote in only select meetings. Earlier, Indians were not allowed to sit for the civil services exam. But amendments in the Indian Civil Service Acts of 1861 and 1870 Indianized the civil service too. The first Indian to clear the civil service (1864) was Satyendranath Tagore, the elder brother of Rabindranath Tagore. By 1871, this number had increased to four, including Romesh Chandra Dutt, Bihari Lal Gupta, and Surendranath Banerjea (who was later dismissed dishonourably).

'By the middle of the 1880s, the Congress is formed and that does mark the entry of the educated middle classes into politics, in what we can call a modern way,' says Mahajan. 'These are not primitive rebellions, these are associations, which are again a modern concept. They are all coming after studying in the West, they are mostly English educated, they want a representation in the governance of the country, and they are willing to work for the reforms.'

The founding fathers of the Indian National Congress played a crucial role in formulating a vision for India. These moderates, as they were called then, were few in number and met only once a year, and their primary objective was to bind the people of India into a national entity. 'They were mostly lawyers. So, this social class and their form of protest is more about petitioning the government,' explains Mahajan. 'They are asking, "Why don't you make your rule in India as good as the rule back home?" Gandhi also believed in the basic good character and beneficence of the British rule. It is only later, after the Jallianwala Bagh incident, that the middle class starts getting disillusioned.'

The transformation in the attitude and nature of the middle class became more prominent after the 1857 revolt. The middle class forms the base of the establishment of rule, be it imperial rule or a democracy like today, and it is this base that one sees in the making post 1857. This new middle class was brought up on Western education; it had been a witness to two great revolutions of the modern world—the French revolution and the American revolution; and was well versed in the concepts of liberty, equality, and fraternity. In essence, it was not simply a 'safety valve', as described by certain historians and scholars, for the British against the colonized masses, but a catalyst of change that created a new civic culture by forming alliances, bringing out newspapers and periodicals, and taking social and political initiatives in which organizations such as the Brahmo Samaj, Adi Brahmo Samaj, and the Sadharan Brahmo Samaj took the lead.

One needs to understand that though this class was collaborating with the British, it was also, at the same time, propagating new thought that cut across social divisions. The pioneer in this was Raja Ram Mohan Roy who started his journey as a reformer as early as 1803. He sought to build a bridge between the East and the West by promoting Western education, with an emphasis on English, Science, technology and natural philosophy.

It was the vision of Ram Mohan Roy that revolutionized the thinking of the young, educated middle classes, and made them aware of their social and political rights. His Brahmo Samaj propagated the ideals of universal brotherhood at a time when the country was divided along caste and religious lines. And though, numerically, it did not achieve much success, a beginning had been made.

His greatest accomplishment, however, was the Bengal Sati Regulation Act which came into effect in 1829, making the practice of sati illegal in British India. Banning the heinous practice was just one legal aspect of the Act, its significance was much greater as it brought the issue of women's rights to the forefront. Issues such as women's education, their right to property, widow remarriage started getting discussed and fought for by men through institutions such as Brahmo Samaj. Most importantly, these men belonged to the middle and lower-middle classes.

The failure of the 1857 revolt had made it abundantly clear to the educated middle class that a direct clash with the British was futile till the time the masses remained uneducated and ignorant of the changes taking place around them in the world, and till they were socially divided. Thus, a process of enlightenment of the masses and their unification became the primary goal of the early liberals, which they deduced could be achieved only under the British rule. They were correct in this assumption as with the unified system of governance replacing the heterogenous political system, there emerged the concept of a nation. Hence, their attitude towards the British remained servile.

It was not easy for the middle class, though, to work for the British. As Mahajan points out, it was a very 'contradictory kind of a situation' for the rising middle class where, on the one hand, they were becoming a part of the system (members of the ICS) while on the other hand, there was a growing sense of nationalism, a loyalty factor, towards their motherland. 'It was a very genuine middle class…in the sense that the occupations are coming from education. And, of course, there's a very important segment that comes up by this time in the second half of the nineteenth century and that is what we call the capitalists.'

India did have a traditional capitalist class which took care of all the business activities. There were brokers, interpreters, financers, managers, accountants, etc. who facilitated trade and commerce, like the dubhashs in Madras, who were interpreters, the shroffs in Bengal, who dealt with money, or the paikars who were the middlemen. By the mid-nineteenth century, the traditional mercantile class was beginning to metamorphose into an industrial capitalist class which, though essentially mercantile in attitude, had acquired a corporate character. Indian merchant capitalists founded cotton mills in Bombay and Ahmedabad (Sir Dinshaw Maneckji Petit founded Maneckji Petit Spinning & Weaving Mills in Bombay in 1855) and slowly encroached upon other areas monopolized by Europeans.

Their opposition to imperialism came through legal and constitutional channels, for the simple reason that they were anti-imperialism, not anti-capitalism. This was also the reason why they did not go along with the mass Civil Disobedience Movement, as any hostility towards the British government, for any length of time, would have been detrimental to the nascent merchant capitalist class itself.

According to Mahajan, they did take advantage of the British policies at times, but mostly worked against them, trying to find loopholes in the system. Over time, they started replacing British capitalists in industries such as paper, silk, jute products, steel, etc. 'It's this capitalist class with its leaders and ideologues which has come up in quite a big way, and these people develop a very close association with the Indian National Congress.'[2]

Initially, Indian merchant capitalists actively supported the British hoping that they would help modernize India on the lines of Western countries. Historian Bipan Chandra notes that they even organized 'meetings in Bombay and Calcutta to pray for the success of the British' in the revolt. However, soon they realized that the country was regressing due to the negative impact of colonial rule. An analysis of the economic policies of the British revealed that, 'Colonialism no longer functioned through the crude tools of plunder and tribute and mercantilism but operated through the more disguised and complex mechanism of free trade and foreign capital investment.'

Any movement is successful only if the masses are involved with it. What makes the role of the Indian capitalists crucial at the beginning of the national movement is that they made the masses aware, through agitations, about the intent behind the economic policies of the British, which was to make the British economy grow at the cost of the Indian economy. For them the goal was to have an independent economy based on Indian capital. These nationalists concluded, says Chandra, that 'pro-Indian and developmental policies would be followed only by a regime in which Indians had control over political power. The result was that even though most of the early nationalist leaders were moderate in politics and political methods, and many of them still professed loyalty to British rule, they cut at the political roots of the empire and sowed in the land the seeds of disaffection and disloyalty and even sedition. This was one of the major reasons why the period 1875 to 1905 became a period of intellectual unrest and of spreading national consciousness—the seed-time of the modem Indian national movement.'[3]

Even Rabindranath Tagore believed that while the elite might be a small number, it is the educated community that 'shows the union of learning with feeling'. And it was this group that was capable of spreading awareness.[4]

This community that Tagore talks about comes from the middle classes, which was making inroads into the local administration, judiciary, and legislative councils, albeit in a subordinate capacity. And although it lent a sharp edge to the politics of the nation in general, and Bengal in particular, it had not yet become independent of imperial rule. Hence, it was not fully engaged with the idea of self-governance.

It was with the Swadeshi Movement that the middle class became more actively involved in the political affairs of the country.

The Swadeshi and Boycott Movement, which started in 1903, were in response to the British plan to divide the Bengal province. It started in 1903 with the moderates petitioning the government to drop the plan, however, their conventional methods proved futile as partition was enforced and in 1905 Bengal stood divided.

Contrary to other nationalists of the time, Surendranath Banerjea maintained that the movement was not 'anti-British in its origin'. His contention was that the boycott was a temporary measure to arrive at a particular goal, that of bringing the attention of the British public to the plight of Bengal; and that once partition was modified, the boycott was to be discontinued.

Banerjea's views on the Boycott Movement reveal the contradiction and hesitancy that existed among the Bengali middle class of the time. While the educated youth contemplated coupling the Swadeshi Movement, which had been gaining ground steadily, with the Boycott Movement to use it as a double-edged sword against the British, moderates like Banerjea were more concerned about its impact on their 'British friends' in Calcutta, who also disapproved of Partition and the manner in which it was being carried out. 'We were anxious that we should do nothing to alienate them, and that we should continue to receive their sympathy, which proved so helpful.... Thus the movement was not anti-British in its origin, nor even in its subsequent developments, though our official critics tried to make out that it was so...,' he wrote.[5]

The movement was as much a result of Bengal's partition as

it was of loss of faith in British governance. The heavy-handed repression of people plagued by famines and epidemics created a sense of hopelessness among the masses, especially the bhadralok, who held the British responsible for the increasing poverty of the Indian people.

There was also a purely economic angle. Since 1757, the British had systematically destroyed the indigenous industries in Bengal, and no attempt had been made towards industrialization. The educated Bengali youth was dependent on income from 'liberal professions', such as law, medicine, journalism, government service, education, etc., however, these jobs had become quite 'overcrowded'. This is evident in a speech delivered by a school teacher Kaliprasanna Dasgupta, in 1905, in which he exhorted students to look for jobs in industry and finance as there were 'far too many lawyers already and government jobs were both scanty and degrading'.[6]

The main feature of the movement was that it did not remain restricted to Bengal but evoked similar sentiments throughout India. In Punjab and other areas of North India, Lala Lajpat Rai and Ajit Singh promoted the idea of swadeshi; Lokmanya Tilak led the movement in Maharashtra; Syed Haider Raza took it to Delhi; and Chidambaram Pillai spearheaded the movement in the Madras presidency. In 1905, Gopal Krishna Gokhale, while presiding over the Benaras session of the Indian National Congress, officially launched the Swadeshi and Boycott Movement.

By the beginning of the twentieth century, many intellectuals, lawyers, academicians, journalists, and authors had joined Congress and were busy writing petitions, speeches, and memoranda. Even big landlords, who had supported the British until now, joined hands with the Congress once the partition proposals became public. This was done in the 'hope...that this would yield sufficient pressure to prevent this injustice from occurring'.[7] And in that respect, the movement turned out to be a failure.

It did, nevertheless, result in a mass movement, initiated by the middle class. People took to the streets, singing *Vande*

Mataram and tied rakhis to each other symbolizing unity. It was the first pre-Gandhian mass movement in which the middle class was heavily invested. Boycott did not remain limited to foreign goods; it developed into a form of passive resistance through non-cooperation. Students were encouraged to boycott government schools and colleges; appeals were made to people to resign from government services; students and women took part in picketing shops selling foreign goods; and women refused to wear foreign sarees and bangles.

The rise of this new nationalistic trend signifies the changing attitude of the middle class, especially the youth. After the mutiny, the British brought significant changes into the bureaucratic machinery. New municipalities were created, means of transportation (railways) and communication (posts and telegraph) were developed, and new courts were established to take care of land disputes, a number of schools, colleges, and universities were opened which imparted Western education. These measures opened new career options for the educated Indians. However, as historian Rajat Kanta Ray observes, the 'tightening grip of imperial rule pressed educated Indian society into a narrow administrative and professional mould. What the rulers needed was clerical skill, not entrepreneurial talent.'[8]

Exposure to Western education had given young Indians the confidence to demand what was rightfully theirs. From being unassuming they suddenly became self-assertive, so, when they found their entry banned into public and private enterprises, their discontent grew. And, as Ray suggests, when the newly-constructed class of educated Bengalis could not rise to top positions as expected despite collaborating with the British, they turned towards changing the system.[9]

Educated Bengalis had realized that the sycophancy of the moderates would not help their cause and a different approach was now required to get their demands of a larger representation of Indians in bureaucracy met. This middle class was more aware of its rights and sure of its wants and needs. Most importantly, access to British education had filled the Bengali bhadralok with confidence.[10] Thus, the new form of resistance suited its temperament. And owing to this temperament, they turned to 'political extremism' rather than 'constructive swadeshi'.

One rising trend that can be associated with the Swadeshi Movement was that it acquired religious overtones and, as a result, did not find favour with the Muslim youth. The first to move in this direction was Surendranath Banerjea, a nationalist leader and founding father of the Congress. He exhorted people to take swadeshi vows in temples. Thus, the swadeshi mood became 'closely linked with attempts to associate politics with religious revivalism. National education plans often had a strong revivalist content and "boycott" was sought to be enforced through traditional caste sanctions. Such aggressive Hinduism often got inextricably combined in the pages of *Bande Mataram*, *Sandhya* or *Yugantar* while Brahmo journals like *Sanjibani* or *Prabasi* were critical of this view.'[11]

This revivalism of Hindu practices coupled with the British 'propaganda' that the new province thus created would mean more job opportunities for Muslims, kept the majority of upper- and middle-class Muslims away from the movement. Led by Nawab Salimullah of Dacca, they supported the idea of partition thinking it would give them a Muslim-majority East Bengal. Though some prominent Muslim leaders like Barrister Abdul Rasul, Liaqat Hussain, Guzanvi, and Maulana Azad did participate, the Swadeshi Movement largely alienated the community from national politics. And that was its biggest failure.

As Anand Kumar states, till the Non-cooperation Movement, there was competition among all the layers of the middle class to get integrated into the system. The fight was not to separate, the fight was to participate in the bureaucracy and the army. In the army, the highest rank an Indian could reach was subedar major, similarly in judiciary they could get only the sub-divisional magistrate rank. 'Indians could enter the Indian civil service but on unequal terms.

Hence, there was a campaign for Indianization of bureaucracy, Indianization of army.'[12]

The mass involvement occurred after the Jallianwala Bagh tragedy in 1919, when the middle class became completely disillusioned with the British. The genocide that happened in Punjab shocked the nation, including British loyalists. 'It was not just what happened,' says Mahajan, 'but the fact that what was done was condoned and even celebrated by the British people. Dyer was given a sword of honour, and a purse was presented to him. This was absolutely shocking!'

The Jallianwala Bagh massacre changed the nature of the national movement altogether. The demand for home rule became stronger than ever, with people joining in from different strata of society. The assertive nationalism one witnessed during the Swadeshi Movement, at the helm of which was the triumvirate Lal-Bal-Pal (Lala Lajpat Rai, Bal Gangadhar Tilak, and Bipin Chandra Pal), had by now taken the form of militancy.

5

The National Movement (1920–1947)

'It is not the old India of romance and adventure with which we have to deal—the old India of magnificent emperors and marble palaces and jewelled gods. It is the new and commonplace India of our day where men are beginning to be moved by the same political aspirations, what have made England what she is…what has brought about this change in the India of our day? It is an uprising of the Indian intellect, an awakening of Indian thought and Indian aspiration, such as the world has not seen since the revival of learning in Europe,' wrote Sir W. W. Hunter, in his essay 'Popular Movements in India'.[1]

The uniqueness of the Indian national movement resides in the fact that it spanned almost a century and kept redefining itself in terms of character and pace periodically. To say that it was full of paradoxes would not be incorrect. Western education, which introduced the urban middle classes to the concepts of liberty and brotherhood and was understood to be the only path to freedom, in fact, distanced them from the rural masses. Similarly, despite the Congress's secular outlook, its leaders, in their quest to reach out to the masses, gave religious overtones to the movement which alienated the Muslim middle class. In terms of caste, too, the contradiction was very evident. Though the educated middle class, coming essentially from upper castes, had 'risen above' caste barriers, it had retained a superior social attitude. Author and political analyst Bidyut Chakrabarty presents the case of Subhash Chandra Bose as evidence. He maintains that despite his commitment to building an egalitarian society, 'he (Bose) referred to his high-caste affiliation' in his autobiography. 'In other words, though he was opposed to caste, he emphasized his own caste background to highlight his relatively higher position in the social hierarchy.'[2]

There are many views about the beginning of the movement itself. Some believe that it started with the Swadeshi and Boycott Movement, while others, such as V. D. Savarkar, have called the Revolt of 1857 the first war of Independence. 'I found, to my great surprise, the brilliance of a war of independence shining in the mutiny of 1857. The spirits of the dead seemed hallowed by martyrdom, and out of the heap of ashes appeared forth sparks of a fiery inspiration,' he writes in the introduction of his 1909 book titled *The Indian War of Independence of 1857*. In that respect, in the ninety years of its journey (1857–1947), one can see a significant transformation in the nature of the movement as well as people's participation in it, which was greatly influenced by the political, social, and economic changes taking place in the Indian landscape at the time. The most peculiar aspect of this movement was the Indian middle classes, which kept changing their stance as the movement progressed.

The Revolt of 1857, as we have seen earlier, was largely restricted to the north-central parts of India. It was essentially a revolt by the army, the princely states, and peasants. Middle-class participation was restricted to a few areas which came to be occupied by the rebels, for example, Awadh. By the time the Indian National Congress was formed, middle-class participation in the movement had increased significantly, and so had the demarcation between pro-British and the nationalists. The social groups who remained loyal to the British included the bureaucratic middle class, the Muslim middle class, and the princely states.

Even after the formation of the Congress, the tone of the nationalists remained suppliant. The change in the character of the national movement starts with the Swadeshi Movement, initiated by the educated urban middle class. One sees a different, more aggressive, approach towards politics with Tilak evocatively proclaiming in public: 'Swaraj is my birth right, and I shall have it.' This sloganeering is reflective of the revolutionary thinking of the middle class that had started replacing the more moderate approach of the Congressmen, who were essentially men of letters with a reconciliatory approach that was limited to petitions and memoranda. It also reveals that the educated middle class was becoming more aware of its political and civic rights. Thus, we have the emergence of new ways of protesting.

Another significant development of this period was use of religion for mass mobilization. Tilak started the Shivaji and Ganpati festivals in Maharashtra mainly to draw out the masses. In Bengal, people marched the streets singing *Bande Mataram*. The literature of the period had religious overtones, Bankim Chandra Chatterjee's *Anand Math* being one such example. Added to this was the British policy of divide and rule.

Consequently, while these public events united the Hindu middle classes, they alienated Muslims, who abstained from the Swadeshi Movement. In fact, even during the Home Rule Movement (1916–1918) and the Non-cooperation Movement (1917), the Muslim middle class maintained its distance. Their involvement began later, after World War I, in the form of the Khilafat Movement. Thus, one finds nationalism taking on different forms for different sections of society.

The period between 1920 and 1947 was one of great turbulence in the political and social history of India. The demand, which began with swaraj during the Khilafat and Non-cooperation Movements in 1919, had, by 1942, turned into a call for 'Quit India'. From reconciliatory to extremism to militancy to 'Gandhism', the struggle for independence incorporated all the ideologies of all the different social groups aiming for a single goal—freedom. The highlights of this period were two distinct approaches to the national movement: revolutionary and Gandhian, and it is these two approaches that impacted the politically active middle class the most and caused a split in its ranks. While the older generation looked up to Gandhi as its natural leader, the younger generation, which was influenced by world politics as well, found his method of non-violence inadequate to bring in the desired revolution. Motivated by the Russia's Bolshevik Revolution of 1917 and Irish Rebellion of 1916, it opted for armed resistance. This, here, is also an indicator of generational conflict within the middle class.

On the social front, India was grappling with its diversities of colour, race, and creed, and trying to evolve as a nation. The formation of the Muslim League in 1906 and the Hindu Mahasabha in 1915 had already created a schism in society which had brought communal tensions between Hindus and Muslims to the fore. Rise of caste movements, such as the Nair movement in Kerala or the Satyashodhak movement started by Jyotirao Phule in Maharashatra against Brahminic dominion, were another chink in the social armour of the country. Then there were class interests that exerted pressure on an already weakened social structure. The elites, the working class, and the educated urban middle class joined the movement with abandon; however, the 'aspirational' middle class remained loyal to the British.

Journalist Madhukar Upadhyay, who has done in-depth research on Gandhi and even recreated the Dandi March for the BBC India, believes that it was the aspirational middle class that did not support Gandhi. 'They (the middle middle-class) thought money was a guarantee to be accepted by society, because when you fight for your identity, money is the easiest way to be recognized.' This section of the middle class did not associate with Gandhi until the very end. In fact, he upholds that they firmly believed that Gandhi's presence on the Indian scene was highly detrimental to the nation. Their sentiment remained the same till the end. 'Even today, it exists...because they are still thinking in terms of money, in terms of acceptance in society.'[3]

The only positive aspect of colonial rule was that it did succeed in unifying the country under a centralized system of administration, replacing the heterogeneity of kingdoms, which provided a common platform that could be, and was, used in promoting nationalism.

Gandhi entered Indian politics against this background in 1917. His initial years were spent in understanding India and its people as he toured the country as advised by his political guru Gopal Krishna Gokhale. 'Gokhale told Gandhi that his idea of Indian classes was not perfect,' says Upadhyay. 'He asked Gandhi to take a tour of the country for a year and abstain from making any political comment. Basically, Gokhale was introducing Gandhi to the lower-middle and lower classes that were later assimilated into the Congress by Gandhi, making it a mass organization. Gandhi was looking to the future whereas the others were looking to the past because they didn't have the vision to look into the future.'

Hence, Gandhi became the bridge between the upper class and the masses. This was crucial, as there was a disconnect between the elite and the upper-middle class—which was urbanized and mainly drawn from the upper caste groups—and the rural lower-middle class as well as the poor. As a result, for the first time in the history of the Congress, there were speeches made in Hindi (earlier they would be delivered in English) at the Lucknow convention in 1916. It was Gandhi who brought the lower-middle and lower classes to these conventions. His biggest victory was that he could mobilize the masses at every level—upper, middle, and lower—and across different sections of society, which were hitherto untouched by national fervour. This can be seen in his decision to support the Khilafat Movement, which was widely criticized by the Rashtriya Swayamsevak Sangh (RSS) and opposed by some senior Congress leaders. Yet he managed to bring the Muslim middle class, which was hitherto anti-Congress or supporting the British, into national politics as the Khilafat leaders joined hands with the Congress.

Non-cooperation could not achieve its goal of swaraj as promised by Gandhi (he promised to deliver it in one year); it did, however, achieve moderate success in terms of people's participation as thousands of students left government-run schools and colleges; teachers resigned from their posts; lawyers gave up legal practice; foreign clothes were burned and shops selling them were picketed;

and legislative council elections were boycotted. Once again the focus shifted to swadeshi as khadi and locally made goods were promoted. According to an official estimate, 6,306 out of 23,887 college students (26.4 per cent) and 45,006 out of 196,548 high-school students (22.9 per cent) left the British education system during the Non-cooperation movement, while the number of students in the national schools increased from 13,468 to 15,000.[4]

Also, the movement had a pan-Indian appeal. S. Sathyamurthy in Chennai roped in theatre artists to promote the movement. Similarly, Ayyadevara Kaleswara Rao and Justice Muhammad Ghulam Mohiuddin of Andhra Pradesh were the first to resign from their government posts in response to Gandhi's call for non-cooperation. In Bihar's Tirhut division, people refused to pay taxes and boycotted foreign goods. Similarly, in Kerala, the United Provinces, Bengal, and Assam, too, the movement had huge mass appeal. In Gujarat, the Municipal Corporation of Ahmedabad supported the movement by protesting against the government's control over children's education and started national education in the town. After the Nagpur Congress session, Sardar Vallabhbhai Patel, who was the municipal councillor at the time, proposed this idea which was approved by the board. The government records state that 'the School Committee also accepted this proposal, which drew resentment from the British, especially the deputy education inspector, who was denied the authority to conduct examinations by the municipal board. Despite facing strong opposition, the municipality persisted with its decision and moved forward with the Non-cooperation Movement. The government responded by implementing severe measures, such as the opening of new schools outside the municipality's control to obstruct their efforts, but it was unsuccessful. On February 9th, 1922, the council was suspended.'[5]

In Punjab, though, the movement was only partially successful. Records suggest that women participated in the movement in huge numbers as satyagrahis in Jalandhar. They also engaged in more constructive activities such as teaching and spinning yarn on the charkha. In fact, a charkha club for women was founded in 1921 in Jalandhar with twenty-five girls and women as its members. 'The members of the club met every Sunday and spun for around four to five hours. The thread then prepared was sent to the Swaraj Ashram in Lahore for the use of the freedom fighters. The club succeeded in bringing women from the seclusion of home to mainstream political activity. During the Non-cooperation Movement, Punjab became one of the states with large-scale female participation.'[6]

Nevertheless, a contrary view states that the Non-cooperation Movement did not garner the support of the people of Punjab who remained indifferent to it. A government report dated 6 October 1920 states:

> In the Punjab, no children have been withdrawn from schools and no lawyers have given up their practice. On the contrary, over 500 graduates applied for admission into the law college and only 300 were admitted. This year's admission constitute a record which is Punjab's most emphatic answer to Mr. Gandhi and his non-cooperation scheme. The Arts colleges and high schools in the Punjab are usually full and the managers would feel thankful if these institutions were a little less overcrowded than is the case at present.[7]

Still, the movement became a game changer in Indian politics because: a) it had a pan-Indian appeal; and b) it was a movement led by the educated, urban middle classes.

The highlight of the movement was the boycott of the Prince of Wales's visit to India in 1921. The *Bombay Chronicle* brought out a series of reports on how the city prepared for the arrival of the prince. Apart from advertisements calling for the boycott of the visit, the Congress leaders held meetings urging people not to be a part of the welcome group. The 14 November edition of the *Bombay Chronicle* reported that the students of Bombay held a public meeting at the Marwadi Vidyalaya Hall to protest against the university's decision to welcome the Prince of Wales and give him an address. The meeting was presided over by Sarojini Naidu. Covering the prince's arrival in the city, the report states:

> While the officials and their men marched towards the Fort, with a number of sight-seers, to greet the Prince on his landing and to witness the pomp, a large number of people were marching in the opposite direction, towards the Elphinstone Mills, where a huge bonfire had been arranged and Mahatma Gandhi was to make a speech. In spite of the distance, in spite of the odd hour, and in spite of the blazing sun and absence of any useless show, nearly sixty thousand persons had gathered there to hear the message which Mahatma Gandhi was going to deliver to them. A huge bonfire (of foreign clothes) was arranged for the occasion and it was set on fire by Mahatma Gandhi.
>
> Within the city there was the silence of an English Sunday. Not a gharry plied. Not a shop was kept open except the eating houses which now by general consent are expected not to observe Hartal. The only mode of communication in the City was the tramway. But a crowd which observes that every other means of transit has been closed in obedience to the national sentiment, does not relish any exception. [8]

Though the *Times of India* reported that Bombay had 'lived up to its great traditions', the Prince's visit was greeted by hartals, strikes, and 'total boycott'.

> On the day of his arrival, hartals paralyzed dozens of towns across India. Similar strikes followed the royal tour to Lucknow, Benares, and Allahabad. When the Hindu University conferred an honorary degree on the Prince, 'practically all the students refused to be present,' Edward wrote to his father, King George V. 'It was quite humorous the way the university authorities tried to 'kid' me by filling up the empty students' seats with high school boys, boy scouts & Europeans'. In Allahabad, the streets were so empty

> even the government's lavish spending could not hide the disinterest of the locals from the foreign press. Along the 'festooned and garlanded' parade route, they reported, barely 1,000 people came out to cheer the prince.[9]

However, Gandhi's goal of a peaceful and civil disobedience remained unfulfilled as reports of violence breaking out in the city trickled in. His belief that the country was not ready for mass civil disobedience was reinforced by the Chauri Chaura violence on 4 February 1922 in Uttar Pradesh, prompting him to stop the Non-cooperation Movement while it was reaching its peak. 'Every time mass civil disobedience has been imminent some popular violent outburst has taken place indicating that the atmosphere in the country is not non-violent enough for mass civil disobedience.'[10]

It was not that violence had not reared its head all this time, it had always been there in spurts. In fact, in a way, the genesis of the national movement lay in violence, the greatest example being the revolt of 1857. Though it did not have a pan-Indian appeal, the revolt did make the middle class become aware of its own failings. It created in it a need for political representation to safeguard its own interests and established the fact that the British were not invincible.

When Gandhian philosophy became the guiding principle of the movement, violence took a backseat, though sporadic incidents of violence continued in which government buildings were burned down and railway tracks and telegraph lines were damaged. But the sudden withdrawal of the movement after the Chauri Chaura violence left the youth disappointed with the Congress leadership and the principles on which the movement was being carried on. And, in the frenzy of their heightened nationalist emotions, these young, educated revolutionaries, coming from economically well-to-do families, once again started gravitating towards militancy, especially in Punjab, where the Ghadar Movement had taken root, and in Bengal.

The Bolshevik Revolution of 1917 and the armed Irish insurrection of 1916 gave strength to these revolutionary sentiments. Though the Ghadar Movement could not sway the masses in India, especially Punjab, to the extent it wished, it did succeed in sowing the seeds of armed revolution in the minds of the youth. It also promoted ideas of brotherhood and secularism through its ideology, which 'considered concern for religion as unworthy of revolutionaries'.[11]

Thus, we find a highly disappointed and dissatisfied Ram Prasad Bismil forming the Hindustan Republican Association (HRA) in 1923. It was later renamed Hindustan Socialist Republican Association (HSRA), and included prominent members like Sachindra Nath Sanyal, Jogesh Chandra Chatterjee, Bhagat Singh, Rajguru, Sukhdev, Ashfaqullah Khan, and Chandra Shekhar Azad—all ex-satyagrahis in their twenties and thirties belonging to the middle class.

As these middle-class youths were perpetually low on funds and weapons; their tactics included pillaging and thievery. Funds were organized through looting of government treasury, as happened in Kakori where a train on Lucknow–Saharanpur section, carrying a government chest, was robbed by the HSRA activists. Similarly, a daring plan of a daytime heist was concocted and was executed on 26 August 1914. This was the famous Rodda arms heist conducted by the young revolutionaries of Atmonnati Samiti and Dhaka Mukti Sangha. The revolutionaries wanted a pan-India armed revolution to drive the British out which required a large supply of arms and ammunition and a British consignment of foreign-made arms was just the right target.

The most fascinating aspect of the Rodda arms heist was that it was pulled off without firing a single bullet and the theft was discovered by the British only after three days. The cache of fifty stolen Mauser C96 semi-automatic pistols and around 50,000 7.63×25mm Mauser cartridges was then distributed among the revolutionaries throughout India.[12]

The arms thus acquired were distributed across India and used in some of the most iconic revolutionary events that took place around then. Some of the arms were passed on to the HSRA, which used them in the Kakori Train Robbery of 1925. The famous Chittagong Arms Robbery of the 1930s was also executed using these weapons. Rash Behari Basu, the key organizer of the Ghadar Movement, carried one of these pistols with him. Even Bhagat Singh and Chandrasekhar Azad owned at least one Mauser pistol each.

The educated middle-class youth were growing tired and dejected of a struggle that seemed endless, and at times pointless, especially since most of the star revolutionaries were either killed or serving life sentences. Also, they did not have the support of the masses, which made it difficult for them to arrange for funds and arms, or even get new recruits. Evading arrests was also difficult most of the times. Getting youngsters to opt for a life full of danger, which in most cases ended up in them being shot dead, was not an easy task. In a message from his death cell, Bismil urged the youth to give up arms and 'not work in revolutionary conspiracies'. Bhagat Singh, for his part, had lost faith even before his arrest and had become a Marxist. In a letter to his comrades, written on 2 February 1931, he says:

> Let me announce with all the strength at my command, that I am not a terrorist and I never was, (except) perhaps in the beginning of my revolutionary career. And I am convinced that we cannot gain anything through those methods. One can easily judge it from the history of the Hindustan Socialist Republican Association. All our activities were directed towards an aim, i.e., identifying ourselves with the great movement as its military wing. If anybody has misunderstood me, let him amend his ideas. I do not mean that bombs and pistols are useless, rather the contrary. But I mean to say that mere bomb-throwing is not only useless but sometimes harmful. The military department of the party should always keep ready all the war-material it can command for any emergency. It should back the political work of the party. It cannot and should not work independently.[13]

Meanwhile, the Congress continued with its swadeshi drive. The coming of the Simon Commission to India, to assess the constitutional reforms of 1919, once again roused anti-British sentiment among the masses. The commission did not include a single Indian. The educated Indian middle class viewed this as an insult as they believed that India's fate should be decided by Indians themselves. 'Simon Go Back' became sort of a war cry with students. Protests were organized in different parts of the country. Anti-Simon demonstrations and hartals greeted the commission wherever it went. One such protest was led by Lala Lajpat Rai in Lahore. Though the protests were non-violent, the police lathi-charged the protestors, hitting the Punjab Kesari on the head. He later succumbed to his injuries.

By the end of 1928, anti-British sentiment had become palpable among the Indian masses. India seemed ready for the next phase of the national movement. This time, the demand was for purna swaraj. The Civil Disobedience Movement needed a strong subject that could give it the much needed drive by invoking nationalist feelings among the urban as well as rural masses. Gandhi chose the subject that touched the life of every Indian—he decided to break the salt law, which had been severely criticized in the past too.

The twenty-four-day Dandi Yatra started from Sabarmati and was concluded at Dandi in Gujarat, on the Arabian Sea coast. The Civil Disobedience Movement (1930) had begun. This was the first movement at the national level where rural India also participated in large numbers. And this was the first one where women, from rural areas as well as urban lower-middle and middle classes, came out in huge numbers.

The government's response to the Salt Satyagraha was brutal. The lone foreign correspondent, Webb Miller, who witnessed the protest at Dharasana, wrote in his report published in about a thousand newspapers worldwide:

> The scene at Dharasana during the raid was astonishing and baffling to the western mind accustomed to see violence met with violence, to expect a blow to be returned and a fight result... My reaction was of revulsion akin to the emotion one

> feels when seen a dumb animal beaten: partly anger, partly humiliation. In eighteen years of reporting in twenty-two countries, during which I have witnessed innumerable civil disturbances, riots, and rebellions, I have never witnessed such harrowing scenes as at Darsana... Sometimes the scenes were so painful, I had to turn away momentarily.[14]

The report changed the world view on the British rule of India. All senior Congress leaders and Gandhi had been arrested, yet the movement continued. Jawaharlal Nehru got a six-month jail term under the Salt Act. His arrest gave a fresh impetus to the movement as it intensified, resulting in an even harsher repression. People hit back by 'intensive picketing' of foreign cloth and liquor shops. In Bombay, two hundred volunteers 'secured six donkeys, decked them in foreign clothes—hats and all—and dividing themselves in three batches', took them around popular streets and urged the masses to light all foreign clothes on fire. From 17 April, women volunteers from Sabarmati Ashram, who were led by Kasturba Gandhi, 'launched on the picketing of liquor shops'.[15]

By 1942, the demand for Quit India had been raised. In the decade since the Dandi March, new twists and turns had appeared on the Indian political scene: the Indian National Congress had expanded its presence in the country; the Muslim League and Hindu Mahasabha had gained prominence; the two-nation theory had started becoming a reality as the Muslim League passed the Pakistan resolution in its 1940 Lahore session; and Subhash Chandra Bose resigned from the Congress and formed the Indian National Army, or the Azad Hind Fauj.

Unfortunately, Gandhi's 'Do or Die' call at the start of the movement fell flat as he, along with all prominent Congress leaders, was imprisoned even before the movement was launched. In the absence of a strong leadership, the movement became directionless. People resorted to hartals, took out processions, and held mass meetings. In the past, major participation came from the urban educated middle classes, with the petty bourgeoisie and the lower middle class joining in only later, by 1920–21. By 1942, the base of the movement had expanded to include peasantry, including landless peasants, and the depressed classes; and this had made the nature of the movement volatile. The uncoordinated efforts proved to be highly detrimental. The repression was severe as the movement was crushed with brutal force and Indian National Congress was declared an unlawful association.

One of the major reasons for the failure of the Quit India Movement was that it did not get the support of all communities. 'I would say large sections are there,' says historian Mahajan, 'however, we have to see the varied picture all the time. Just to give a small example, the Communist Party of India did not support the Congress in 1942 because the Soviet Union was an ally of Britain and the United States.' They believed that if the Soviet Union was in alliance with the allies, then it 'could not be an imperialist war'. This distanced them from the Congress, which held the thought that it was an imperialist war and they had to fight it. Now, owing to the hold of the communists over labour, 'in Bombay, for example, which was very big, the working class did not take part in the 1942 movement'.

As World War II drew to a close, the question of India's freedom once again took centre stage in the British Parliament, where the Labour Party was in power. Finally, under the Indian Independence Act of 1947, British India was divided into two new dominions: India and Pakistan.

The social outcome of these events proved to be far greater than the political one. As the national movement entered its last leg, rifts in the Indian society started becoming wider. Hindu vs Muslim, Brahmin vs non-Brahmin, urban vs rural, educated vs uneducated, traditional vs modern, and men vs women—these divisive forces were counter-balanced by a single emotion, nationalism. Different ideologies impacted the masses differently. Hindus were being influenced by the Arya Samajis on the one hand and the Hindu Mahasabha and the RSS on the other. Muslims were being mobilized by the Muslim League using the Khilafat and Khaksar Movements as tools.

The seeds of religious discord were sown after the 1857 revolt. While the growing animosity between the Hindus and Muslims has largely been attributed to the divide and rule policy of the British, after careful study of the social changes that took place in the first half of the nineteenth century, one cannot ignore the fact that the rising aspirations of an emerging middle class were, in fact, at the very helm of this animosity.

The social reforms brought in by Raja Ram Mohan Roy, along with the introduction of Western education, gave Hindus a head start in the socio-political and economic spheres, whereas Muslims were still nursing the loss of their political and social privileges. Under the Mughals, Muslims had enjoyed political and social hegemony. Most of the top positions were occupied by them. Linguistically, too, they had an edge over the others as the court language was Persian. Following the British conquest of India, Muslim jagirdars and zamindars lost their political and social clout, especially after the 1857 revolt. The ensuing insecurity prompted the Muslim community to turn to religion and shun all that the new rulers introduced, including the newly-implemented education policy and the new thought that was defining the contemporary world. By the time Muslim reformer Sir Syed Ahmed Khan's efforts produced results, Hindus had already progressed significantly. It was a functional necessity for the British to keep all the top and key posts to themselves, leaving the mundane clerical jobs for the natives. This restricted the job market, resulting in rising discontent among the expanding middle class, and it was this discontentment that the imperialists used to further their policy of divide and rule, as was seen during the Swadeshi Movement.

Interestingly, the middle class adopted a dual character during the freedom movement. On the one hand, it participated and even led from the front, while on the other hand, it aligned itself with the British and was more interested in being a part of the British power system.

As Misra points out, the nature of the middle class was nationalistic in orientation, while its character was mainly sectarian. 'I am not saying that they only started sectarian movements, but I would say that the middle class was responsible for caste consciousness in a big way, because it could argue for identity.' This new middle class was educated and upwardly mobile. It was aware of its roots and its history of relationships with other castes and could easily articulate caste consciousness. Thus, we find that by the late 1930s, the role of the middle class had not remained limited to nationalism, it included caste consciousness, region consciousness, and language consciousness too.[16]

The complexity of the middle class character can be gauged from the fact that while it led the national movement, it also led the reform movement that was not rooted only in the upper caste but permeated the lower sections of society. For instance, Savitribai Phule, wife of Satyashodhak Samaj founder Jyotiba Phule, and her associate Fatima Begum started the first girls' school in India in Pune. They created awareness among the lower castes. 'The middle class could play such a role too.'[17]

For the new middle class, boycott of everything British was paradoxical, to say the least, as it owed its existence to them. This explains its blow-hot-blow-cold attitude towards the national movement. The upper class had the resources to sustain themselves and the lower classes had nothing to lose. It was only the middle class that needed to protect its interests. Adopting an anti-British stance was, hence, a difficult call for them, and the reason why many chose to stay away.

6

The Feminist Movement in Pre-Independent India

The question of gender equality is universal in scope. When one speaks of subjugated and exploited women, it is not the queens and begums one is talking about, but women from humble backgrounds. Save for a few societies like Egyptian and Byzantine, women in the ancient world had fewer rights than men. In ancient Greece, for example, women could not vote, own, or inherit land. Their role was limited to keeping house and rearing children. The same was true of Roman women, who could not attend, speak, or vote in political assemblies, let alone hold any position of political responsibility. In China, apart from being in a subordinate position in society, women were subjected to physical exigencies such as foot-binding, widows could not remarry, and baby girls were often abandoned. By mediaeval times, the situation of women had marginally improved, especially in the High Middle Ages in Europe.* They could get educated and enjoy almost equal economic rights. However, socially, they were still battling great inequality as they didn't have voting rights and couldn't exercise their right to choose a partner of their own liking.

In India, the status of women has been an extremely complex issue. At the outset, it needs to be clarified that the information regarding their status in society is extremely limited. Also, the references available are conflicting. Thus, one can only gain a perspective from the available texts (the Vedas, Upanishads, the

*Scholars divide the middle ages into three periods: Early Middle Ages (476–1000); High Middle Ages (1000–1300); Late Middle Ages (1300–1500). See Joshua J. Mark, 'Women in the Middle Ages', Worldhistory.org, 18 March 2019.

Ramayana, and the *Manusmriti*) regarding the status of women in ancient India. The very fact that all three major components of life, namely, wealth, knowledge, and power, are associated with women—popularly Lakshmi, Saraswati, and Shakti in Hinduism—speaks volumes about the power an ordinary woman held in pre-Vedic and Vedic times. But, as records show, by the Middle Ages she had lost her position of prominence in society.

The status of ordinary women in society changes drastically as it progresses from ancient to mediaeval times. The Vedas recognize women as Shakti. Some of the hymns in the Rig Veda are said to have been composed by women rishis (scholars) and philosophers like Vishvavara and Apala.[1] The eighth Brahmana of the Brihadaranyaka Upanishad has references to Gargi participating in a philosophical debate, organized by King Janaka of Videha, with Brahma Gyani Sage Yajnavalkya.

By the end of the Gupta period, the status of women had declined to a great extent. While sati was not yet a general practise, it had started getting wider social acceptance. As religion became institutionalized, many of the rights that women enjoyed earlier were curtailed. The age of marriage was lowered, which meant girls could not get educated, nor did they have any say in marriage. Widow remarriage, though not banned, was looked down upon.

Describing women as worthless, Manu writes: 'For women no sacramental rite is performed with sacred texts, thus the law is settled. Women are destitute of strength and destitute of the knowledge of Vedic texts and are as impure as falsehood itself. That is a fixed rule.'[2]

In the mediaeval period, the position of women differed from region to region. Some parts of India, in northeast and south, had matrilineal societies, where women dominated. In matters of property, a large number of documents like bainama (sale deeds), hibanama (gift deeds), nikahnama (marriage contract) prove that women, both Hindu as well as Muslim, enjoyed the right to inheritance of parental property. 'There are also references of a daughter inheriting the whole property in case there was no male inheritor. In 1730, there is reference of a Brahman father bestowing a house on his younger daughter by way of sila (gift) and tabarru (voluntary) donation. The women were free to sell or mortgage the property without any difficulty'.[3]

Records suggest that women could exercise their financial rights, however, their social oppression had intensified as several restrictions were imposed upon them. They were generally confined to their homes. Polygamy, child marriage, female infanticide, and purdah system had become firmly entrenched in society. The practice of sati or jauhar among Brahmins and Kshatriyas had taken a religious form (it being the dharma of the widow to follow her husband into the afterlife). Though some Mughal emperors, like Akbar, tried to ban the practice, they were unsuccessful in doing so. As for Muslim women, though Islam allowed widows to remarry, they, too, had to maintain strict purdah and bear with polygamy and child marriage.

Women from royal backgrounds were educated—the *Humayun Nama* was written by Humayun's half-sister Gulbadan Begum and Shah Jahan's daughter Jahanara Begum was a Sufi scholar and wrote biographies of Sufi saints Moinuddin Chishti and Mullah Shah. There is a strong possibility that the upper- and middle-class women also had access to education. The majority, however, remained illiterate. A study of Mughal miniature paintings bring to light that 'painting was not an exclusive male profession'. There were three women painters Nadira Bano, Sahifa Bano, and Ruqaiya Bano from the time of Akbar and Jahangir. In *Gulshan Album*, in Tehran's Imperial Library, is a signed painting of Nadira Bano. 'According to the inscription on the surviving miniature, Nadira Bano was the daughter of Mir Taqi a calligrapher at Jahangir's court, and a pupil of Aga Riza, the well-known painter in the service of prince Salim during Akbar's reign'.[4]

By the eighteenth century, the decline of Muslim rule had become quite evident. As Delhi's power waned and it became clear that the ruler had become too weak to keep the Islamic identity of the community intact, religious reformists took the onus of protecting this identity on themselves. This led to a further marginalization of Muslim women as Islamic reformists started addressing women and their conduct according to the standards of the Quran. And this was done through fatwas. Not only did these so-called reforms curtail women's rights significantly, they drove them out of public spaces as well.[5]

An important source of information on the condition of Muslim women in the eighteenth century was recently discovered in Germany. The book titled *Tuhfa-tul-Zaujain* (A Gift to Husband and Wife) written by Shaikh Mohammed Qutb-ud-Din in 1851 (or 1891, there is ambiguity regarding the date), was presumably lost until it was found in the Sprenger Collection of the Berlin Staatsbibliothek. The book details the duties of a woman and man as per the diktats of the Quran. In the chapter on divorce, the author mentions that 'trivial excuses are sufficient for them (people) to blurt out talaaq.'[6]

There were instances of resistance against patriarchy, though. In the 1700s, Maharani Ahilyabai Holkar (1725–1795), the Holkar Queen of the Maratha Malwa kingdom, ascended the throne and ruled for thirty years after the death of her son. She did not perform sati after the death of her husband Khande Rao Holkar.[7]

The author of the article that shed light on women painters, Dr Angbin Yasmin, categorizes female performers as middle class. They have been depicted in miniature paintings and find mention in the written records of the time. 'We find different classes of dancing girls started emerging in the accounts—domnis, paturs, kumachnis, parishans and laulis. Where the paturs were the celebrated class of Hindu performers, the laulis on the other hand, were Muslims. Their association with the court distinguished them from others who performed in markets and streets.' These women belonged to the middle class but were considered socially inferior. By the time the British came, women in the Indian subcontinent had been completely relegated to the background, both politically as well as socially. Their presence in public spaces was negligible.

Ironically, it was men who realized the pitiable state the women were in and pushed for reforms for their upliftment. 'If you look into the history of women's rights, most of the time (in the colonial era), you will find that men fought for the cause of women,' remarks Mohapatra.[8]

The biggest example being that of Raja Ram Mohan Roy and Swami Dayanand Saraswati, who started a social reform movement aimed at uplifting the status of women. The foundation of the Brahmo-Hindu School (1822), where boys and girls studied together, was the first major step in this direction, which had a cascading effect on society.

Tracing the history of women's movement in India in her book *The History of Doing*, author Radha Kumar notes that in the 'early years of movements for women's rights, it was more or less taken for granted that the difference between the sexes was such that their roles, functions, aims and desires were different. And hence not only had they to be differently reared but differently treated in general. Over time this difference was itself adduced as a major reason for reforming women's conditions.'[9]

Nevertheless, the most peculiar aspect about middle class women in pre-Independent India has been that, despite the social restrictions, they came to play a decisive role in the freedom movement as facilitators, participants, reformers, and even executors. During the Revolt of 1857, scores of women warriors such as Jhalkari Bai, Uda Devi, Asha Devi, Umda, Habeeba, Shobha Devi, etc. fought against the British. These women came from the lower-middle and middle classes. Though the movement was crushed, the valour of these women continued to inspire others.

As the national movement gained momentum, the participation of women increased. Sarojini Naidu, Kamala Nehru, Aruna Asaf Ali, Annie Besant, Madam Bhikaji Cama, and Kasturba Gandhi were known names. They belonged to the upper caste and upper-middle classes, were educated, independent, and had strong connections within the Congress. Those who contributed to the movement—

either directly as satyagrahis or indirectly by boycotting foreign goods and spinning the wheel—belonged to the lot of ordinary women, coming from middle and lower-middle classes, most of them illiterate and steeped in traditions and had, probably, never been in public spaces before. The most dynamic role, however, was played by the unsung women revolutionaries who took to arms against British oppression.

Pritilata Waddedar of Bengal was one such fighter. Coming from a middle class background, this teacher joined the revolutionary group of Surya Sen and Nirmal Sen. Under Surya Sen, Waddedar, along with Kalpana Datta, trained in martial arts, lathikhela, and gun fighting. By the age of twenty-one, she was on Bengal's most wanted list. She led the attack on the Pahartali European Club and in the ensuing fight sustained bullet injuries. However, to avoid getting arrested, she swallowed a cyanide pill.

At fourteen, Suniti Choudhury was the youngest revolutionary when she, along with her accomplice, Shanti Ghosh (15), assassinated a British magistrate.

A report in the 17 December 1931 issue of *The Adelaide Chronicle* edition reads: 'Bengal experienced a terrible revival of terrorist activity this morning, when Charles Geoffrey Buckland Stevens, district magistrate and collector of Comilla, East Bengal, was shot dead by two Indian women anarchists. This is the first occasion in the history of the terrorist movement that an outrage against officials has been perpetrated by women.'

The women were hoping to be sent to the gallows. However, their dreams of being martyrs were dashed when, owing to their minor status, they were awarded life imprisonment. The disappointed duo commented, 'It is better to die than live in a horse's stable.'

In a 2019 interview with the *Times of India*, recounting the life of her revolutionary mother Suniti Choudhury, Bharati Sen says:

> These women never thought about their contribution. It was a job that needed to be done. They didn't think it was a

huge thing. Much later, when the head of the department of political science had asked my mother a similar question about her contribution, she had said: I am grateful that I have had the opportunity to serve my country.

On the social front, too, women were ready to break the glass ceiling. Rukhmabai's iconic legal battle against her husband's demand for conjugal rights led to the drafting and passage of the Age of Consent Act way back in 1891, at a time when it was considered a woman's duty to submit to her husband's demands. The Bombay High Court ruled in favour of her husband, Dadaji Bhikaji. The ruling stated that in case she did not comply with the court order she would go to jail. Rukhmabai opted for the latter. The matter was finally settled in 1888 outside the courts after a monetary compensation was paid to Dadaji in lieu of the dissolution of marriage.

After her divorce, Rukhmabai completed her studies and went on to become a practicing doctor, joining the league of Anandibai Joshi and Kadambini Ganguly. One of the first two women graduates (the other being Chandramukhi Basu) in the entire British Raj, Kadambini's journey was also fraught with struggles. She had to face severe backlash from the bhadralok for her decision to study medicine. The Calcutta Medical College refused her admission on the grounds that there was no history of women studying there. However, ultimately, she prevailed.

Besides the history attached to them, what makes the contributions of these women invaluable is the direction they gave to their frustrations and rage. Their fight was not just against the British but against the patriarchal Indian society too. All these women came from middle class backgrounds. All of them struggled to fulfil their dreams and at every step, they had to prove themselves. Take, for instance, the case of Pritilata. Even though she was inducted into the revolutionary camp of the Jugantar group, she, and many other revolutionary women like her, had to prove their worth as actual revolutionaries who could plan and lead attacks. These women were ready to break taboos in pursuit of their passions, be it fighting the oppressors or the oppressive social norms.

Ramabai Ranade, Aruna Asaf Ali, Fatima Sheikh, Dr Usha Mehta, Captain Lakshmi Sahgal, Madam Cama, these women represented the aspirations of scores of educated upper and middle class women who wanted to break free from the shackles of societal bonds. Their bravery, at times at a personal cost, inspired women to come out and participate in the freedom struggle in large numbers. One such inspiring story is of Madam Cama. On 21 August 1907, at an International Socialist Conference being held in Stuttgart in Germany, Madam Cama unfurled the first version of the tricolour and declared: 'This is the flag of Independent India. I appeal to all gentlemen to stand and salute the flag.'[10] Her participation in the movement led to her exile from her beloved country, which resulted in her estrangement with her husband who remained pro-British.

With such a rich history, one wonders why, then, Indian women have lagged behind in social and political spaces. The answer, according to Madhukar Upadhyay, lies in economics. 'In early India, women were liberated. Women could choose their partners. The whole concept of swayamwar is based on the fact that it's the woman who has the decision-making power. Until social distinction was based on mental capabilities, women matched men. They were on equal footing. But when money started becoming the basis of distinction, women started being viewed as weaker sex, less productive.... And this started in the mediaeval period.'[11]

Upadhyay maintains that until the early decades of the twentieth century, there was a deliberate attempt to suppress women. While upper-class women enjoyed certain privileges, the position of middle- and lower-middle-class women further deteriorated as social norms became more rigid. One major consequence of that was the absence of women from public spaces. 'There were no women leaders in the Congress, till Gandhi brought in Sarojini Naidu. And when Gandhi went to Champaran in 1917, twenty-four women filed statements against the British in front of Gandhi. He gave them strength just by being there.'

One other crucial factor highlighted by Radha Kumar is how the shift in the movement happened from defining the suffering of women and the need for reform to emphasizing women's right to be treated as 'useful members of society' to the right of self-determination.

Unlike early nineteenth-century reformers, who stressed that gender difference was no reason to dominate over women, later reformers contested that as this difference highlighted the social usefulness of women, it had become a social necessity to provide them with proper care. Early feminists concurred with this view. Says Radha Kumar, 'When it came to the sphere of rights, for example, feminist demands for parity with men (in property rights, to suffrage and education), cut across the affirmation of gender-based difference, for these said that in these spheres at any rate men and women were equal, or the same. To this extent, pre-Independence feminists clung with one hand to gender-based definitions of themselves while reaching with the other for an existence based on equality and sameness rather than complementarity and difference.[12]

Even Gandhi, for that matter, though he proclaimed that he was 'uncompromising in the matter of woman's rights...I should treat daughters and sons on an equal footing of perfect equality', initially, tried to keep women's participation limited to providing logistical support to the satyagrahis: boycott of foreign goods, and spinning of the wheel, which had become a national symbol of freedom struggle. When he listed out people who would accompany him in the Dandi March, the group did not include a single woman satyagrahi. His contention being that he didn't want them to 'face police brutality'. It was only after Kamaladevi Chattopadhyay argued with him that he relented and changed his strategy and asked Sarojini Naidu to lead the Dharasana Satyagraha.

Gandhi was considered the father of the women's movement in India as he had feminized Indian politics. But his view was restricted to the spirit of endurance and suffering embodied in the mother. The fallout of such a thinking was that, while it talked about women's respect and honour, it did not question the fact that women were typecast as caretakers.

Since pre-Independence, women have had to constantly struggle to prove their relevance both socially as well as politically. It, undoubtedly, creates self-doubt which has a negative impact on one's productivity. Anand Kumar raises some pertinent questions: Why were the backward people, SCs, Dalits, tribals, and women (from both Hindu as well as Muslim communities) missing from the mainstream freedom movement? Was it a structural problem or open male-centric strategy?

The answer lies in the way the movement progressed. One needs to keep in mind that this was a time when parallel movements, at different levels, were taking place in the Indian subcontinent. Backward castes were pushing for their rights under the leadership of Dr B. R. Ambedkar. The clash between Marx-influenced revolutionaries and pro-Gandhians had become more pronounced. The formation of the Muslim League and talk of two-nation theory had created a rift in society. And, in the midst of it all, there was the question of gender inequality, even among revolutionaries.

For the middle class, it proved to be a highly challenging phase, as it had to deal with societal and regional pressures while at the same time thinking and acting on a national level. As the movement gathered momentum, all other issues, but for the two-nation theory, took a backseat, and there was a concerted effort at gaining Independence. Thus, the issue of gender equality in the true sense did come to the forefront during the freedom struggle.

7

Gandhi, Nehru, and the Middle Class

The two-nation theory, which had been gaining ground as an idea, was going to be a reality soon, and this had complicated the process of attaining independence. Problems were aplenty: What would be the guiding principles of the new state? How would normalcy be restored in Partition-affected areas? How would the refugee question be solved? What kind of state would India be? What were to be the economic goals for a nation deep in debt? But perhaps the biggest of them all was: what kind of relationship would the two neighbouring nations have, given their long history of co-existence? In the midst of it all, the question concerning the role of the middle class in the rebuilding of the nation was, in a sense, lost.

The middle class was expanding. With the increase in the number of schools, colleges, and universities, a whole generation of English-educated middle class professionals including doctors, teachers, engineers, bureaucrats, journalists, and corporate houses had come up. It was the middle class that took the lead in the Non-cooperation Movement yet, Gandhi seemed to ignore it in his addresses initially. By the late 1930s, Gandhi's attitude towards the middle class had started undergoing a change. The reason, according to historian Tara Chand, was that Gandhi needed educated and responsible leaders (he associated the middle class with urban India) to guide the masses. He wanted to organize the masses, the rural poor, the peasantry, and the working class, in his fight against imperialism. 'Therefore, in spite of his scepticism about the educated, he tried to maintain his hold upon the middle class Indian National Congress. The Congress also realized that without the support of

Gandhiji and his cohorts from the villages, the British Government could not be made to yield to the people's will.'[1]

But what is more interesting to note is the shift in the middle class, whose involvement till now was minimal, towards the freedom movement after Gandhi appeared on the Indian political scene.

Madhukar Upadhyay contributes it to the competitiveness of the middle class, to their constant struggle to be a notch above the rest. It is the same logic that works here. 'You got the acceptance in society because of language and financial status and because of your access to the powers that be. Now that you have attained that, and you are a part of the middle class, what next? Your growth is not just money, there are other things that you have achieved.' And it was this novelty factor, he argues, that drew them to Gandhi. He was propounding different ideas. Ideas that were exclusive. Most of the people who had gone abroad for studies were middle class and upper caste, and almost all of them joined the government to represent Indian interests. For these people money was not an issue (most had landed property), they wanted to do something different, and that opportunity was provided by Gandhi.[2]

Also, Gandhi had delivered. With his unique methods, he had been able to secure a win against British might in South Africa. For the middle class this was a remarkable feat: being rooted in one's traditions and yet being able to stand up to the oppressors in a foreign land, and force them to mend ways. 'Besides,' says Upadhyay, 'the upper middle class was looking to associate with Gandhi to elevate itself.'

Gandhi's growing influence in Indian politics can be measured by the fact that from being denied membership in the Servants of India Society despite Gokhale's urging, in 1916, in a span of eight years, by 1924, he became the Congress president and wrote its constitution, making it a mass organization. In 1934, he resigned from the Congress, citing differences with his co-workers, and retreated from active politics. Gandhi's focus was entirely on rural areas. The middle class did not fit into his scheme of things. His views on economy clashed with those of the other Congress leaders, most of whom belonged to the upper-middle class.

Gandhi had strong views regarding industrialization. He did not agree that it was the answer to India's problems. Instead, he stressed on developing the village economy as 'real India lived in its villages'. Gandhi's idealism talked of simple living and high thinking, which were inconsistent with a speedier and complicated material life.

> Whether such plain living is possible for an isolated nation, however large geographically and numerically, in the face of a world armed to the teeth and in the midst of pomp and circumstance is a question open to the doubt of a sceptic. The answer is straight and simple. If plain life is worth living, then the attempt is worth making, even though only an individual or group makes the effort.[3]

It is this philosophy that led to differences between him and the other leaders of the time, including Nehru, Bose, and Patel. Unlike them, Gandhi's goal was much larger than freedom. During one of his meetings with Lord Reading, the viceroy, Gandhi said that his movement was religious, 'designed to purge Indian political life of corruption, deceit, terrorism and the incubus of white supremacy'.[4]

'To him it was evident,' says Tara Chand, 'that the fight for freedom was not between the Government and its armed forces on the one side and the educated middle class Indians on the other. In fact, he disliked "the hardness of heart of the educated". He thought they were too much enamoured of parliamentarianism and offices to put their heart into the struggle which demanded extreme and prolonged sacrifice. His approach to the problems of India was, thus, fundamentally different from that of the educated class. Naturally, his preference was for the masses whom he wanted to train as soldiers for the impending war against the imperial system.'[5]

According to Kumar, it was the outcome of the collaborative phase of the middle class that saw Gandhi's exit from the political platform and his entry onto the social platform.

What is peculiar about Gandhi is that, though he was against industrialization and capitalism, he did not oppose them. In fact, he implored the capitalists to support the fight for democracy. Nehru tries to explain this contradiction in Gandhian philosophy in his autobiography:

> ...why with all his passion for non-violence he is in favour of a political and social structure which is wholly based on violence and coercion? Perhaps it is not correct to say that he is in favour of such a system; he is more or less of a philosophical anarchist. But as the ideal anarchist state is too far off still and cannot easily be conceived, he accepts the present order... If the means are right, the end is bound to be right. That, I think, is the main background of his thought. He suspects also socialism, and more particularly Marxism, because of their association with violence. The very words 'class war' breathe conflict and violence and are thus repugnant to him.[6]

On his part, Nehru's bourgeois mindset (owing to his background) underwent a transformation after his involvement with the peasant movement. He acknowledges the fact that the politics at the time was of the middle classes and for the middle classes. While the Moderates represented the upper-middle class and prospered under British rule, and wanted it to continue, the Extremists represented both the upper as well as the lower-middle classes. In essence, they were cut off from the larger section of society, the rural poor. In 1920, he admits that he was 'totally ignorant' of the situation of labour in factories and fields, and that his 'political outlook was entirely bourgeois'. He understood that there was 'terrible poverty and misery', and the politically free India should first handle poverty. He says, 'But political freedom, with the inevitable dominance of the middle class, seemed to me the obvious next step. Just then a new interest developed in my life which was to play an important part in later years. I was thrown, almost without any will of my own, into contact with the peasantry.'[7]

Though Nehru adopted a more socialistic stance, he did not undermine the importance of the middle class in independent India. In fact, the difference of opinion between Gandhi and Nehru on the nature of the state resulted in an argument via letter between the two on the eve of Independence.

The India of Gandhi's dream, which he envisaged in *Hind Swaraj*, was drastically different from that of Nehru's. In Gandhi's words, his 'ideal village will contain intelligent human beings. They will not live in dirt and darkness as animals. Men and women will be free and able to hold their own against anyone in the world. There will be neither plague nor cholera nor smallpox; no one will be idle, no one will wallow in luxury. Everyone will have to contribute his quota of manual labour. I do not want to draw a large scale picture in detail. It is possible to envisage railways, post and telegraph offices etc. For, me it is material to obtain the real article and the rest will fit into the picture afterwards. If I let go the real thing, all else goes'.[8]

Nehru, on the other hand, was an advocate of industrialization, which he thought was the only way to build a peaceful society. He believed that technical advancement was imperative for India to attain independence. 'I am not thinking for the moment in terms of just armies but rather of scientific growth. In the present context of the world we cannot even advance culturally without a strong background of scientific research in every department.'[9]

'Nehru's attitude was to underline the role of the state, underline the planning, industrialization, economic development and bring social change through that. Nehru wanted people to go beyond their narrow ideology. For Gandhi, the transformation of society was much more to do with transformation of the self,' remarks Mohapatra.

Nehru was quite perceptive of the class conflict based on economic interests that had started emerging in Indian society, and believed that it needed to be addressed effectively. He did not agree with the Marxist theory of realizing change with the revolutionary overthrow of any particular class; instead, he wanted to bring about a peaceful transition from backwardness to progress and development in all aspects of human life. These were the beliefs that shaped his policies after Independence.

8

Middle Class Shift to the Right

Unchecked religiosity often leads to destruction. In India, the destruction came in the form of the Partition with the country being divided along religious lines. Partition, was as much a middle-class creation as Independence was, and though the real issue on which it was sought was political, the tools acquired to achieve it were socio-religious, and the decision to use these tools was taken by leaders such as Muhammad Ali Jinnah and V. D. Savarkar, who first propagated the two-nation theory in his presidential address to the Hindu Mahasabha in 1937. These leaders had massive sway over the middle classes. This brings us to the question: Was Partition an expression of middle-class intolerance towards religious and ethnic diversity?

A study of the history of the Indian subcontinent reveals that though religion had become intertwined with politics centuries ago, it never really led to the communalization of society as is visible today.

Religion has been an inextricable part of the socio-political milieu of India, right from ancient times. And religious violence was not only a mediaeval Indian phenomenon, it existed in ancient India too. Unfortunately, most historians and scholars have not paid much attention to the extent of religious violence that marred ancient societies. In his book *Against the Grain*, historian D. N. Jha lists a number of instances that portray the extent to which religious violence could escalate. Describing one such incident, Jha writes, 'Around 185 BCE, Pushyamitra Shunga overthrew the Buddhist Mauryan dynasty, destroyed the Ashokan pillared hall and the Kukutarama monastery in Pataliputra. He is also said to have vandalised the famous Sanchi Stupa, burnt down the Ghositaram monastery in Kaushambi, and killed Buddhist monks wantonly. As a consequence, the Buddhist Sanskrit work, *Divyavadana*, describes him as the "great persecutor" of Buddhists.'[1]

Religious conflicts were quite common in the mediaeval period, too. There have been instances of temples and mosques being desecrated and fights over street processions during festivals like Muharram and Holi, but they did not result in the ghettoization of society, as the demolition of the Babri Masjid in 1992 or the subsequent 1993 Mumbai bombings, or the 2002 Gujarat riots did. Maybe because there was no concept of 'India' as such then, or maybe because news travelled at a much slower pace. Or, as historian Prathama Banerjee states, the reason why there was no ghettoization of society was because 'neither all Muslims nor all Hindus were involved in them (conflicts) as well defined or clearly bounded totalities'.

Also, the nature of these clashes had more to do with economy rather than religion. For instance, the Satnami revolt against Aurangzeb was not just a clash between an orthodox Muslim ruler and a Hindu sect but an uprising of marginalized people (peasants, artisans, tribals, and untouchables) against systemic oppression by the upper castes (feudal lords) and the state taxation policy. According to historians, Satnamis were a monotheistic sect who believed in leading a life based on good conduct rather than rituals and any particular philosophy.[2]

Thus, communalization of the Indian middle class started under the British Raj. The British occupation of India began after their victory in the battles of Plassey and Buxar as we've seen. Being of a different race with a different language, culture, and belief system, it was not easy for the British EIC to rule over a mass of people as diverse as in the subcontinent. This became clear from the Revolt of 1857. By the end of the nineteenth century, the British had become aware of the rising threat of public agitation against them, a result, they deduced, of the new education policy which introduced

Indians to Western ideas. How seriously the British took the matter can be gauged from a letter written by the secretary of state for India, George Francis Hamilton, to Lord Curzon, the viceroy, in 1899, stating that the '...real danger to our rule in India, not now but say 50 years hence, is the gradual adoption and extension of Western ideas of agitation and organisation, and, if we could break the educated Hindu party into two sections holding widely different views, we should, by such a division, strengthen our position against the subtle and continuous attack which the spread of education must make upon our present system of Government'.[3]

It was probably the same fear that prompted Lord Curzon to partition Bengal in 1905, though the reason provided was that it was too big a province to be administered by a single provincial government. He appointed Sir Bampfylde Fuller, an Irishman, to cope with the complexities and estrangement arising out of it. Historian Manmath Nath Das states that it was Fuller who, through keen observation and study, came up with the idea of using these differences to their advantage. 'Fuller worked on a different hypothesis. The Hindus and Moslems, though they spoke a common language and formed a common society, had several differences. These differences, if elaborated, might create a new Moslem attitude towards the movement (Bande Mataram Movement) itself. This policy was sure to prove beneficial to the British by breaking Bengali solidarity.'[4]

Minto endorsed the view that the future of the British empire was in grave danger of a 'political upheaval' of an alarming nature brought on by educated youth. In a letter to Major J. B. Leslie-Rogers, 15 March 1909, he states, 'It is in my opinion sheer madness to disregard rising ambition, the creation of which an administrator is so largely responsible for—the strong hand will become stronger still in recognizing them—it will lose strength and pile up unnecessary evils for the future if it does not.'[5]

In fact, according to Das, presupposing that the Muslims favoured the partition, Fuller tried to build up a 'Moslem opinion' in his favour by giving them minor posts in the government against the rising anti-partition Hindu agitation. The growing tide of nationalism was characterized by Hindu-Muslim unity, which was becoming a threat to British dominance by fuelling the nationalistic sentiment. 'Anti-British agitation was slowly reaching the educated Moslems. At no other time, therefore, was the necessity so keenly felt for understanding political developments in the two communities, and never before had the administration attempted to establish a permanent pattern in Hindu-Moslim relations vis-à-vis their relationship with the British government as during 1905–10. The story naturally began with the partition of Bengal, and it finally ended in the partition of India, forty-two years later.'[6]

The partition of Bengal in 1905 not only stemmed the rising tide of the national movement but also succeeded in driving a wedge between Hindus and Muslims. Aside from religious differences, the two communities were also divided in terms of class. In Bengal, the majority of the landlords were Hindus whereas Muslims formed the bulk of peasantry and landless labourers. Added to the religious discrimination were the atrocities of the upper caste feudal lords against the lower caste, lower-middle class, and poor peasants, which resulted in their indifference towards the national movement in the first place. The use of Hindu festivals, religious symbols, and bhakti songs in the Swadeshi Movement, a popular way of mobilizing the masses, widened the rift between the two communities. In fact, many scholars have questioned Gandhi's use of religion in the freedom movement. The Muslim middle class saw it as an assertion of the Hindu faith and did not support the Swadeshi Movement.

The insecurity and fear that Hindus, constituting the majority, would prevail over them pushed the Muslim leaders, backed by the state, to create an alternative to Congress, which would safeguard Muslim interests. This resulted in the formation of the Muslim League in 1906.

In 1909, the British introduced constitutional reforms in India. According to Chandra, the reforms were aimed at curtailing the growing unity between the two communities and 'divide the nationalist rank'. And to achieve that, they brought the Morley-Minto Reforms, which introduced the 'system of separate electorates under which Muslims could only vote for Muslim candidates in constituencies specially reserved for them. This was done to encourage the notion that the political, economic and cultural interests of Hindus and Muslims were separate and not common. The institution of separate electorates was one of the poisonous trees which was to yield a bitter harvest in later years'.[7]

However, this was also the issue that saw Hindu–Muslim cooperation reach its peak as the Lucknow Pact of 1916 led to the Congress and the Muslim League uniting in favour of separate representation for Muslims. It had become clear to the leaders of the Congress and the League that a united front was a must to achieve their goal of purna swaraj. The move was opposed by rightist leaders like Madan Mohan Malviya, B. S. Moonje, and Tej Bahadur Sapru. They accused Tilak of surrendering to the Muslims.

Addressing the Lucknow session, a revitalized Tilak answered:

> There is a feeling among the Hindus that too much has been given to the Muslims. As a Hindu I have no objection to making this concession. When a case is difficult, a client goes to a lawyer and promises to pay him one-half of the property if he wins the case. The same is the case here. We cannot rise from our present intolerable condition without the aid of the Muslims. So in order to gain the desired end there is no objection to giving a percentage, a greater percentage, to the Muslims. Their responsibility becomes greater, the greater the percentage of representation you give to them. They will be doubly bound to work for you and with you, with a zeal and enthusiasm greater than ever. The fight is at present a triangular one.[8]

This had a major impact on the Hindu as well as Muslim middle classes, who added strength to the movement.

Perhaps the biggest factor that eventually led to the political shift of the middle class to the right was the formation of right-wing organizations like the Hindu Mahasabha and the RSS.

Madhukar Upadhyay begs to differ. He believes that the shift to the right happened much before. A look at the literature of that period (the later part of the nineteenth century) will reveal that the talk of Hindu revivalism had started much before the RSS came into existence. 'It was only after Gandhi came into the picture that Premchand and others started writing about assimilation.'[9]

Another interesting theory espoused by Upadhyay is that the Partition interrupted the move towards the right. As Partition became a reality, survival took precedence over everything else, stalling the movement towards the right. The first few decades after Independence went into rebuilding the nation and re-establishing refugees. Once that was done, the shift towards the right restarted. 'It was temporarily halted by two things: Independence, led by Gandhi, and Partition, which led to violence.'[10]

The middle-class shift to the political right was thus a gradual process that started sometime in the 1880s. It gained momentum during the Swadeshi Movement and at the time of the Partition, but the social distancing between communities happened only in the last decade of the twentieth century with the demolition of the Babri Masjid.

9

The Middle Classes of the World

Between the mid-eighteenth century and World War II, Europe underwent a series of changes, both social and political, that had a huge impact worldwide. The most noteworthy, however, was the emergence of a new middle class and the monumental transformation it went through during this period. It is not that middle-income groups did not exist in mediaeval Europe. Even then, society was divided on the basis of wealth, status, and power. In fact, by the eleventh century, Europe witnessed the establishment of burgs (fortified towns) inhabited by a group of people, apart from peasants and nobility, distinctly professional in character and engaged in various commercial activities.[1]

Towards the end of the mediaeval period, Europe was in the thrall of what is known as the Commercial Revolution that gave stimulus to commercial activities as new lands were discovered and explored by voyages patronized by England, Spain, Portugal, and other nations in Africa, Asia, and the New World. The surge in foreign trade was paralleled by an expanding middle class, with divergent regional, ethnic, and cultural characteristics, leading to the creation of distinct national identities. Thus, one sees a gradual rise of nation states in the second half of the nineteenth century in Europe.

Rise of the Middle Classes in the West

Eighteenth-century Europe witnessed two major developments that not only transformed their society and politics but had a significant impact on the world too. These were the Industrial Revolution and the French Revolution. The former led to the rise of capitalism driven by market economy; the latter, to ideas of equality and freedom of the individual. The former promoted imperialism which resulted in the colonization of half the world, whereas the latter gave the impetus for resistance against imperialism. The colonization of India was a result of the Industrial Revolution, the impulse to fight it came from the French Revolution.

The transition of European society from a strictly feudal set-up to a modern society with a prominent middle class happened gradually, over half-a-century, and the development differed from country to country. In modern towns that had come up by the latter half of the eighteenth century, a prototype of the middle class in the form of burghers existed and it was here that the bourgeois culture first developed.

By 1750, the feudal structure of European society had given way to the putting-out system, where goods were being manufactured by hand as there were no machines or factories. Nevertheless, heightened commercial activity, a result of voyages of exploration, saw a surge in overseas trade and creation of chartered companies, money economy, and increased economic specialization. This necessitated the establishment of institutions of economic activities like banks and stock exchanges. By the mid-eighteenth century, the stage was set for the Industrial Revolution.

Though feudalism had been in decline, its social aspects were still in order, especially in the countryside where peasants were expected to be loyal to their lord and master. The Industrial Revolution, however, resulted in a shift in power to urban areas, thereby undermining the influence of the landed gentry.

The first to experience this technological marvel was England. Between 1760 and 1840, several technical innovations resulted in machines replacing men. Goods that were being created by hand started getting mass-produced in factories leading to increased productivity. Rapid industrialization transformed the rural agrarian society of Britain into an industrialized urban setup, creating a need for schools, healthcare centres, banks, etc.

The social implication of the revolution was immense as it strengthened the position of the middle 'sorts' in British society and helped them emerge as a class, one that owned factories, coal mines, railways, among others. As this class gained more economic power, it started developing political aspirations as well.

Flourishing trade and commerce and growing managerial bureaucracies created a demand for clerical staff like secretaries and bank tellers as well. These white-collar workers comprised the lowest rung of the middle class and their jobs required them to be educated. Though their working conditions were only slightly different from the working class, most white-collar workers did not like to be associated with the blue collars. The employers encouraged this segregation by setting up separate payment systems and benefit programs, fearing a union of interests might lead to labour unrest.

The Industrial Revolution soon spread to the other European nations and the United States. The first to be industrialized on the European continent were Belgium, France, the German states, and then North America. In 1815, these European states were still largely agrarian. And though they did experience population growth and improvement in agriculture and foreign trade, the pace of the economic growth was extremely slow as compared to Britain.

If the Industrial Revolution paved the way for a more modern world as far as science and technology went, the French Revolution (1789) promulgated the ideals of liberté, égalité, fraternité that questioned traditional feudal authority. This was a time when Europe was both united and divided. The Age of Reason (Enlightenment), preceding the Industrial Revolution, had resulted in the development of a modern world across Europe. Centuries-old customs and traditions were replaced by individualism and scientific thought. This thought was reflected in the cultures of the continent and mirrored in their literature. The social changes that followed the Industrial Revolution were also more or less the same across European countries. However, rising nationalism deeply divided the nations.

The French Revolution was a result of the socio-economic changes sweeping across Europe at the time. The feudal system was disintegrating and increased commercial activity had resulted in the rise of wealthy commoners called the bourgeoisie, who had started harbouring political ambitions. Even peasants, who were better educated now, became aware of their rights and wanted to do away with the feudal system altogether. Also, higher standards of living had reduced the mortality rate, which led to the rise in population and, eventually, greater demand for food and consumer goods. As the economic crises deepened, voices of social reform began reverberating through France and a revolution was deemed necessary based on the ideas of Baron de Montesquieu, Voltaire, and Jean-Jacques.[2] Powerful works by French intellectuals, writers and thinkers, often satirical in nature, reintroduced the masses to the ideas of Voltaire and Rousseau that talked of religious tolerance, rational thought, criticism, and human progress. These philosophers challenged conventional beliefs and questioned established facts and opinions.

The French Revolution had a decisive impact on the world, perhaps even more than the Industrial Revolution. For it led to the establishment of the first democratic state in the world.

The lasting impacts of the French Revolution were the 'principles of democracy, liberty, merit, equality and sovereignty'. The revolution in 1789 gave way to a century of 'revolutionary upheavals which culminated in the Russian Revolution and the establishment of Soviet Russia'. The French Revolution 'fundamentally' moulded the Western notions of rights, citizenship, secularism, free expression, merit, legal governance, sovereignty, and democracy—ideas which continue to steer global events even today.[3]

The British reaction to the French Revolution was two-fold though. Those championing the cause of social reform greeted the news with much enthusiasm. These included 'dissenters excluded from political office by the Test and Corporation and Subscription Acts, members of the middling orders denied the vote by antiquated constituency boundaries and a restricted suffrage, and Parliamentary Whigs whose ambitions for office were blocked by Pitt's firm hold on power'.[4] But then, there were conservatives like Edmund Burke who were critical of the reforms, which they thought would destroy the French state, and feared the 'bloody' revolution might spread to England.

Nevertheless, English-American writer Thomas Paine's *Rights of Man* (1791), which became the basis of the French Revolution, advocated human rights. It denounced hereditary government and asserted that a nation was free to choose its government and the role of that government was to protect its people and their rights as individuals. *Rights of Man* sparked a controversy among British intellectuals. But it had the desired effect on the masses as it revitalized reform societies like the Society for Constitutional Information (SCI) and gave impetus to the rise of some new associations organized by commoners who challenged the control exercised by the privileged. One such organization was political reformer Thomas Hardy's London Corresponding Society (LCS) which was formed early in 1792, and pushed for the democratic reform of the British Parliament. The party drew its strength from tradesmen, shopkeepers, and workers, who had been living in tough conditions with long working hours and meagre salaries.

Though the early reformers failed in their attempt to bring reforms to the British Parliament, as the LCS was ultimately suppressed, they did succeed in creating class consciousness among the working class, prompting William Ewart Gladstone, a liberal parliamentarian who later became prime minister, to comment, 'Every man who is not presumably incapacitated by some consideration of personal unfitness or of political danger is morally entitled to come within the pale of the Constitution.' Thus, the growing clamour for democracy finally pushed the British Parliament to pass the Reform Act of 1832 that paved the way for the middle class to enter the political system. And gradually, the right to vote was extended to the working class as well.

The biggest social change that the Industrial Revolution had brought about in England was that men were no longer defined by their family background. Instead, their identity came to be based on the kind of work they did. Land ceased to be the only source of income. New professions requiring skills and higher degrees of education sprang up across England, including the countryside, as manufacturing increased and new factories were set up.

In 1840, graphic artist George Cruikshank came up with a caricature called 'The British Beehive'. It showed English society, with the royal family at the top, divided by class and profession, a 'broad middle section including booksellers, mechanics, weavers, jewellers, glaziers, tea dealers and inventors; and at the bottom the cabmen, shoeblacks, coalheavers, sweeps and dustmen'.[5]

But wealth alone was no guarantee to social security. As the middle class ranks swelled, class distinctions became important to distinguish between old middle class (lawyers, doctors, etc.) and new middle-class (businessmen, traders). To be a distinguished middle class gentleman, one had to behave like one, and this was increasingly becoming a source of anxiety for the men who came from humble beginnings. To help them cope with the exigencies of the new lifestyle, a variety of manuals, like 'How to Behave' and 'Hints From a Gentleman', were available, teaching men how to behave like a gentleman and be presentable at dinner parties, how to converse and bring the conversation politely to a close, how to shake hands, how to stand or sit gracefully, how to carry themselves at soirees, among others.

It was not just men, but middle-class women, too, who had to follow certain social rules and regulations to maintain their status in society. Middle class women were discouraged from doing any sort of work, including house work, which was left to a battalion of specialized servants. Even lower-middle-class women were expected to keep at least a maid to do the manual job. 'The real function of a middle-class wife,' says historian Kathryn Hughes, 'was to display her husband's financial success by stocking her home with material possessions—what's been called the "paraphernalia of gentility". Carpets, pianos and paintings, the fancier the better, were all advertised in the new women's magazines such as Sam Beeton's "Englishwoman's Domestic Magazine" and sent a message not only about their owners' wealth but also their patriotism. Being a consumer had become a civic duty.'

The European middle classes displayed similarity in challenging the authority of the 'nobility, absolutism and religious orthodoxy'. However, historians debate the impact of the French Revolution on the socio-political framework of France, with many maintaining that the Revolution did 'little to change the balance of power among the political and social forces in the country'.[6]

What makes this period most intriguing and significant is the changing role of the middle class in defining the socio-political environment of the continent. Surprisingly though, 'in a state which became the leading industrial power in continental Europe in 1914, with a wealthy entrepreneurial and a traditional and influential bureaucratic and professional middle class, it will be interesting to ask why aristocratic values, and indeed the aristocracy itself, continued to dominate, and actually became even more entrenched as the ruling elite.'[7]

According to German social historian Jurgen Kocka, the unifying and defining characteristics of the European middle class can be explained by two theories: relational and cultural.

Despite differing with each other in many respects, the various stakeholders constituting the middle class had a unifying factor; they were critical of the aristocracy and opposed the privileges enjoyed by them. This new class was secular, educated, believed in self-reliance and achievement, and it created an identity for itself away from the nobility, though it did acquire some cultural aspects of them.

> Civil servants were agents of the state, but they were simultaneously part of the emerging middle class. Still, the various subgroups of the emerging middle class were to some degree united by their common opponents: the nobility,

> unrestricted absolutism, and religious orthodoxy. They developed common interests and experiences and a certain degree of shared self-understanding and common ideologies. In this way, the middle class constituted itself as a social formation that encompassed various occupational groups, sectors, and class positions.[8]

Another social demarcation that had become prominent by the latter half of the nineteenth century was between the middle and the working classes. The middle class sought to distance itself from the working class. And to give itself a distinct identity from both the nobility as well as the labour class, it developed a culture of its own, with emphasis on education, independence, and rationality. It derived prestige and influence from individual achievement.

As Kocka says, 'For bourgeois culture a specific ideal of family life was essential: the family as a purpose in itself, a community held together by emotional ties and fundamental loyalties.'[9] However, as the family system was patrilineal, it created an inequality between the sexes as women eventually came to be confined to homes. This middle-class culture flourished only in towns and cities as it required a certain economic status and security to be classified as middle class.

By the twentieth century, the middle class in Europe had grown in 'wealth, cultural influence and political power'. In the mid-nineteenth century, political instability and threat from below had forced the middle class, which always looked for stability and security, to compromise on its liberal ideas and enter into an alliance with the elite. Added to that was growing nationalism that had acquired imperialistic, racist, and ethnic connotations. It was no surprise, then, to find the middle class shifting to the right.

The culmination of this could be seen in the rise of Nazism in Germany and Fascism in Italy. The end of World War I saw the emergence of radical groups all over Europe, but it was only in Italy and Germany that they could come to power.

According to Misra, 'In Germany, the old middle class was studied and it was found that the middle class had formed an alliance with the working class and this alliance gave boost to an ideology which is known by different names: Fascism in Italy, Nazism in Germany. And an important section of this middle class belonged to the old middle class.'[10]

Fascism was the first post-war mass movement of the middle class that grew in response to 'a shattered political order, a highly politicized and fragmented body politic, a revolutionary threat, and a profound loss of faith in the market mechanisms',[11] and led to the formation of totalitarian regimes in both the European countries. As social and economic changes after World War I seemed to 'threaten the very basis' of Western civilization, the 'remedy for it had to be equally drastic or total. Using techniques of mass mobilization pioneered by the Left, tactics of combat forged in the trenches of World War I, and modern means of mass communications, Fascism and Nazism promised a new and unified national or racial community.'[12]

The rise of Fascism is a prime example of the ambiguity of the middle class, especially in times of crisis. It highlights some important characteristics that are unique to this particular class. Foremost among them is that whenever its security is threatened, the middle class seeks collaboration with the powerful. But Fascism was not an overnight development. The conditions for its rise were in the making for some time. The expansion of the middle class, development of mass communications, mass mobilization, and a fragmented middle-class political party structure, all contributed to the development of Fascism.

Usually, it takes many years and includes 'continuous measures and legislative changes' that 'kill' the existence of political and civil rights. In Italy, it took six years 'to legally move from a liberal democracy to a dictatorship. Hitler, admittedly, did it much faster, just two years after his election victory in 1933'.[13]

PART II

Independence to Economic Liberalization

(1947–1991)

∽

10

1947: Independence and Social Movements

The struggle for independence, which culminated in the creation of two separate entities—India and Pakistan—was the most significant event of the twentieth century in the subcontinent and had far-reaching impacts on its political and social constitution, repercussions of which are felt to this day. That being common knowledge, what is significant about the Partition is how the social classes, especially the middle classes, of both India and Pakistan, reacted to this development and how it shaped the two countries over time.

The years following Independence were characterized by nation-building in both countries. The story of Pakistan began with a twin tragedy, the first was the shared pain of the Partition and second was the death of its founder, Qaid-e-Azam Muhammad Ali Jinnah, a year later. Jinnah's demise proved to be the undoing of Pakistan, as he passed away without leaving a documented vision of what form this new state was to acquire, a glimpse of which can be seen in his speeches made at various times between 1940 and 1946. The final shape that Pakistan took was a far cry from the one envisaged by the Qaid-e-Azam. In his historic speech on 11 August 1947, he told the Constituent Assembly: 'You are free to go to your temples, you are free to go to your mosques or any other place of worship in this state of Pakistan. You may belong to any religion or caste or creed—that has nothing to do with the business of the state.' He did not wish Pakistan to become the theocratic state it is today.

India, on the other hand, after gaining dominion status, went down the path of social democracy. The founding fathers spent three years, from 1947–50, crafting a Constitution that declared it to be a sovereign socialist secular democratic republic, operating on the guiding principles of social, economic, and political justice; 'liberty of thought, expression, belief, faith and worship; equality of status and opportunity'; and sought to promote 'fraternity assuring the dignity of the individual and the unity and integrity of the nation'.[1]

It is in the light of these fundamental rights enshrined in the Constitution that one needs to see the development of India and its people over the years.

A major factor influencing Indian society and politics, perhaps more than freedom itself, was the Partition. Freedom was a natural outcome of almost a century of struggle against colonialism. Partition, on the other hand, was the result of a more recent phenomenon, which started with a demand for a separate state for Muslims in 1940. Independence was a result of rising nationalism brought about by imperialism. This, says historian S. Irfan Habib, was an 'inclusive nationalism', which reflected the diversity of India. But, during the national movement, one saw the rise of two distinct strands of nationalism based on religious identities: Hindu and Muslim. 'Such nationalisms were not essentially anti-colonial and were more interested in using history to legitimize their political ideology of religion-based nationalism to endorse the political mobilization that they sought.'[2]

The British had always projected the two communities as monolithic entities, with different ideologies, interests, and goals. Thus, Muslim nationalism resulted in the creation of Pakistan. Hindu nationalism, though on the fringe, cried for a Hindu rashtra, and right-wing organizations such as the Hindu Mahasabha and RSS, which became the tools to achieve this goal, just as the Muslim League was in the case of Pakistan.

Post-Independence, the social framework of the country, specifically the north and northeastern parts of India, underwent a significant change as scores of Punjabi and Sindhi refugees from West Pakistan and Bengali refugees from East Pakistan poured into India.

These were the most trying times for the country. Emotions were running high. And, according to French historian Lucien Febvre, 'emotions are contagious'.

Febvre asserted emotions brought together individuals, at times acting as initiators and at times being followers, to create a 'system of inter-individual stimuli' that could take various forms in response to a situation and create a variety of reactions or 'modes of sensitivity'. In essence, 'emotions, contrary to what is thought when they are confused with mere automatic responses to the external world, have a particular character which no man concerned with the social life of other men can any longer disregard'.[3]

The middle class needs to be studied keeping its 'emotional factor' in mind. This also explains the inconsistencies in the behaviour of the various groups within the class in a diverse country like India. Misra is right in saying that the 'middle class nature is of a nationalistic orientation, but its character is sectarian', as has been displayed at various occasions in the course of history, especially in post-Independent India.[4]

American historian Barbara Rosenwein makes a similar point in her theory of 'emotional communities', which states that 'people live in emotional communities', and that different emotional communities evaluate, endorse, and express these emotions differently. 'I (further) propose that people move (and moved) continually from one such community to another, adjusting their emotional displays and their judgements of weal and woe (with greater and lesser degrees of success) to these different environments.' Besides each group shaping and expressing emotions differently, according to her, 'within the same society contradictory values and models, not to mention deviant individuals, find their space.'[5]

It was this very characteristic that made the middle class in post-Independence India more diverse and pluralistic in nature. Heightened nationalistic fervour, enhanced religiosity, and growing caste consciousness shaped its socio-political outlook and left a deep impact on its character and behaviour.

'When Constitutional intervention took place post Independence,' explains Misra, 'then the nature of recruitment of the middle class changed.' This also changed its nature and also influenced the society differently. 'When the high caste people, feudal lords realized that their role in the current scenario was questionable, they developed a nationalistic orientation. It was natural.'[6]

Thus, the post-Independence era, till economic liberalization in 1991, marks the evolution of the Indian middle class from a thin layer of mostly high-caste educated Hindus to a growing confederate of social groups. They had diverse goals and aspirations, and that influenced their nature and social character, consequently resulting in various social movements characterizing this phase.

Social Movements by the Middle Class

When Nehru spoke from the ramparts of the Red Fort declaring that India was now a free country, his 'Tryst with Destiny' speech, brimming with hope for the future, carried an undertone of pain inflicted by a divided India.

The biggest challenge before the newly-appointed government was to bring peace to the strife-torn country. The period between 1900 and 1947 saw several social uprisings highlighting caste, gender, and class-based issues. However, these voices were either assimilated into the freedom movement, for instance, the peasant movements of the Bardoli agitation in the Surat district of erstwhile Bombay Presidency became a part of the 1928 Non-cooperation Movement and took on a nationalistic character, or were temporarily drowned out in the heat of the mo(ve)ment, as one sees in the case of the social movement demanding equal rights for Dalits.

After the country attained freedom, these issues resurfaced. So, the political, economic, and social challenges were compounded by the issues of caste, class, and gender.

Post-Independence, as new educational institutes opened up and urbanization increased with the establishment of industries, the middle class grew with lower income groups and people from rural areas, lower castes, and Adivasis and other minority communities entering the segment. This transformed the nature of the middle class and its 'changed social character and roots led to a number of tribal movements, ethnic movements, state and language movements'.[7]

The impact of this change can be gauged from the number of social movements marking this period. Each movement, whether it was related to language or the women's liberation or the Dalits, left a deep impact on the middle-class behaviour. In fact, many of these movements were led by the middle class itself.

The Refugee Crisis

Post 1947, about a million refugees migrated into India following the Partition. Partition was not a tragic by-product of the national movement, instead it should be seen as a tragedy in the making for the past three-quarters of a century. This is not because it divided the subcontinent territorially, but that even today, more than seven decades later, the Hindu-Muslim divide runs deep in Indian society.

There are several social and political factors responsible. Many of those suffered during the Partition have found it difficult to move on. Politicians have, time and again, revisited the tragedy for personal gains. They have kept the pain alive, rather than providing solace to the wounded.

Nevertheless, another factor that warrants close attention is that there has been no attempt to understand how deep the scars inflicted by the Partition run or gauge the extent of psychological damage that has been caused to people, both Hindus and Muslims.

It is a historical fact that a number of Muslims were not in favour of the Partition. Hence, when the inevitable happened, they opted to stay on this side of the border. According to the 1951 Census of India, the Muslim population in divided India declined from 42,400,000 in 1941 to 35,400,000. In effect, based on the census, a mere 7,226,000 Muslims went to Pakistan (both East and West). Moreover, along with Hindus and Sikhs, many Muslim families migrated from the newly formed state of Pakistan to India. One such migrant family is that of legendary actor Yusuf Khan, better known by his screen name, Dilip Kumar.

In The *Psychological Impact of the Partition of India*, authors Alok Sarin and Sanjeev Jain stress the need to discuss the psychological impact of the Partition on people. 'As psychiatrists, we have been intrigued by the lack of discussion, historically, in Indian mental health discourse, on the psychological scars and damages caused by the Partition.'[8]

The study of the psychological impact of a tragedy of such a magnitude, according to them, was essential as was done in Europe in the aftermath of the World War II and the Holocaust. There the 'psychological impact was deliberated upon in great detail, and a consensus was achieved that it would "never again" be allowed to happen'.[9]

The idea behind such debates was to understand and explore the impact of 'prejudice, trauma and displacement' on the mental health of the victims. The authors state that these issues were underlined by psychiatrists and doctors, and it 'led to the development of humanistic schools of psychotherapy, greater acceptance of diversity, as well as ensuring that medical services develop certain global and universal principles of practice and ethics (e.g. the Nuremberg Code) that were clearly enunciated, and shared'.[10]

Partition has been the biggest disaster of human displacement to impact South Asia, the effects of which are felt to this day. However, as the authors point out, no attempt has ever been made to evaluate the trauma that has been caused by the violence following the creation of new states in the region and its impact on the mental health of those who lived through the chaos. Consequently, people did not get the required medical attention and, as it happened, most refugees internalized their feelings of anger and fear. Also, Muslims were not the only community the people turned against, limited resources pitted different groups among the Hindu migrants against each other, too.

Thus, the emotional dimensions of the Partition remained unexplored, a critical overlook considering the trans-generational effect it carried. The book quotes R. B. Davis, a psychiatrist and one of the founding members of the Indian Psychiatric Society, recounting a case at the Allahabad symposium in 1949:

> The symptoms...ran the whole gamut of political belief, over a few years, from being an admirer of Subash Chandra Bose, then the Communist party, then with welfare of the untouchables, and finally a sense of guilt and a suicide attempt following the assassination of Mahatma Gandhi. The experience of psychiatric disease, in all its forms, is thus influenced by identity, socio-cultural ideas and stigma, and also the politics of the day.

This illustrates the importance of the psychological evaluation of victims of displacement coupled with violence.

The refugees belonged to different classes, and this difference determined the kinds of experiences they would undergo during their displacement. One interesting theory states that the duration of the journey was indicative of the class of the migrants as it was dependent on the mode of transport employed by them. For instance, a majority of people coming from rural areas in West Pakistan walked hundreds of miles over weeks to cross into India. They were essentially farmers and landless labourers, belonging to the lower-middle and poor classes. They moved in caravans carrying their farm equipment and livestock with them. Those belonging to the middle classes travelled by train in highly cramped conditions. The shortest duration, and by far the safest, was by air travel, which was availed of by the upper-middle and rich classes. In fact, most of them had shifted their wealth across the border months in advance before the Partition took effect and the resulting mayhem began.

The most noteworthy aspect of displacement was the emotional response the refugees faced from the locals on both sides of the border. These responses determined the formation of 'emotional communities'. While Punjabi Muslims migrating to Pakistan were assimilated into the Punjabi community across the border, Muslims migrating from Bihar, Uttar Pradesh, Bengal, and other states of India, were termed muhajirs in Pakistan. The muhajirs settled mainly in the Sindh province, forming an ethnic minority there. Pakistan's politics has been greatly influenced by the muhajir issue.

In India, the refugees settled mainly in Punjab, Delhi, Haryana, Gujarat, and Maharashtra, contributing to the demographic changes in these areas. By the fifties, Delhi, which had lost almost one-third of its population as resident Muslims migrated to Pakistan, was once again teeming with people from diverse backgrounds, including displaced Muslims. The biggest change that the refugees initiated was urbanization as the city expanded to accommodate the refugees. According to a 2018 *Hindustan Times* report, in response to 329,000 of 900,000 people leaving for Pakistan, around '495,000 Hindus and Sikhs from Western Punjab, Sindh and Northwest Frontier poured in almost simultaneously... From 198 sq km in 1951, Delhi's urban area grew to 323 sq km in 1961'.

Loss of property, lives, and the atrocities faced by women during the Partition, on both sides of the border, are well known. What is perhaps not discussed in as much detail is the treatment meted out to these immigrants who had crossed over, or made to do so, to live in their 'own country'. Most of the refugees were middle class* And this challenge was compounded by the response of the locals who saw them as troublemakers. Historian Deepra Dandekar talks

*One of the greatest mass migrations in history was today nearing completion as a 75-mile convoy of uprooted non-Muslim population continued to pour over the Pakistan border into India from the most fertile areas of West Punjab. The convoy included shopkeepers, artisans, doctors, lawyers, and once-rich landlords. The old and sick died on the way, but the convoy moved on, blood from torn feet of the weary immigrants staining the dusty road. See 'A report on refugee movements after partition', The National Archives, Source 4, Catalogue Reference: DO 142/416, 6 October 1947.

about five types of emotional responses that the refugees had to face. Not only were they termed as 'violent' and accused of 'spreading partition violence within peaceful Indian society, especially places that had not undergone partition or witnessed rioting' but their 'claimed entitlement to prosperity' was also questioned. The pity shown by the locals added to their humiliation.[11]

A majority of these refugees were from urban areas and belonged to the middle class. These traders and businessmen, teachers, restaurant owners, etc., who settled on the outskirts of Old Delhi brought along with them their own language, culture, and cuisine. It was this class that added to the middle segment of the city significantly. Most of these refugees were educated, upwardly mobile, and entrepreneurial. Raunaq Singh's Bharat Steel and Apollo Tyres, H. P. Nanda's Escorts Group, Bhai Mohan Singh's Ranbaxy and Dharampal Gulati's Mahashiyan Di Hatti (MDH) are some of the companies that were born out of the refugee settlements of Delhi.

Talking about his book *Delhi: A Novel*, Khushwant Singh, veteran journalist, writer, and historian, reflects on how the culture of the city underwent a transformation after the Partition. 'Punjabi replaced Urdu as the language of the people, and their emphasis was on eating...So many dhabas and eateries came up. They did well for themselves. They worked very hard and they loved showing off. They built bungalows, bought cars, entertained, their marriages were vulgar displays of ostentation with brass bands, lights and bhangra dancing. The element of the rat race had come in. The competitive spirit…anything you can do I can do better was very much there.'[12] This one-upmanship has since been a distinct feature of the middle class in Delhi.

While Delhi's quiet and courteous middle class tehzeeb made way for the lively commotion of the refugees, Bombay started a quiet journey to becoming the financial capital of India. It proved to be the preferred choice of Sindhis. The community did not face much physical violence as compared to the others,* nevertheless, its loss was colossal. Along with their material possessions, the Sindhis also lost their homeland, culture and, to a certain extent, their language. Undaunted, they strove for success and placed a huge emphasis on empowering men as well as women.

The Sindhis (Hindu) were a flourishing community in their home in Pakistan. They were mostly urban and constituted the upper-middle and rich classes of the Sindh province, and were one of the most economically advanced groups in the country.[13] After their exile, the Hindu Sindhis, most of whom came empty-handed, set about achieving the same status in a new land, amid new people and with limited resources.

Professor Chanda Kathuria is a second-generation Sindhi whose parents migrated from Pakistan after the Partition. 'They worked so hard for the first 20-30 years that they just took a jump from nothing to directly into the middle income group and from there to the rich section. Because they were on a fast track, they couldn't bear losing everything. My parents left everything in Pakistan. As my mother would recall, they came with only a few clothes and were living on railway platforms. They forgot about their rituals, customs, traditions, language, religion...they forgot about everything. You will see that there are more inter-caste marriages among Sindhis and Punjabis. Sindhis are very dynamic and resourceful, and huge risk takers.'[14]

Her statements point to two distinct characteristics that make the Sindhi middle class unique: first, they are not caste conscious or ritualistic; and second, their adaptability to situations is remarkable. For instance, before the Partition, though middle-class Sindhi women were educated, they did not work. But after the displacement the community faced, women took to working as telephone operators,

*Sindh experienced fewer cases of physical violence, and more frequently, reports of looting, destruction, and distress sale of property. This was because the province was not divided and went to Pakistan. Moreover, Sindhis did not migrate en masse to India during Partition—their evacuation continued for three years. See 'The Partition', Partitionmuseum.org, < https://www.partitionmuseum.org/partition-of-india>.

secretaries, etc. to support their families. Those who could not leave their homes would make papad or pickle, or stitch clothes or babysit for neighbours. They never declined an opportunity to supplement their income. Another characteristic of the Sindhi middle class is its tendency to economize. Instead of fretting about trying to earn more, the emphasis was on economizing by limiting their needs and doing most of the work themselves. However, education was never compromised. Today, the community hardly has any poor sections. Most Sindhis belong to the upper-middle and affluent classes. According to 2019 data, Sindhis, who comprise 0.30% of the population, add 20 per cent to the GDP of the country, and their contribution towards the total income tax is 24 per cent.[15]

The 1951 Census of India shows that refugees constituted 2 per cent of India's population at the time. Barring the four southern states of Tamil Nadu, Karnataka, Andhra Pradesh, and Kerala, refugees were resettled in all the other states of India from Jammu and Kashmir in the north to Maharashtra in south, and Rajasthan in the west to Assam and Tripura in the east. It will not be incorrect to say, then, that the combined experience of the Partition and displacement has shaped the character of the emerging middle class in the northern part of independent India. As the competition intensified, the struggle for opportunities and resources drove a wedge between the Hindu and Sikh refugees. Muslims were the worst off. Their neighbourhood was called 'Mini Pakistan' and was often attacked by refugees seeking revenge. India has since been on a religious pot-boiler.

The middle class internalized emotions of hate, fear, insecurity, suspicion, and distrust. The extent to which these emotions impacted the psyche of this class can be judged from the following observation made by a middle-class media professional who spent a better part of his childhood in Janakpuri, one of the biggest refugee colonies in Delhi. 'I am a 1983 pass-out from Kendriya Vidyalaya Janakpuri. All through my schooling years (from grade 2–12), I did not have a single student from the minority community in my class. In fact, there was not a single Muslim family in my neighbourhood. We were not exposed to their culture at all. For us, they simply did not exist. We knew about them only through Hindi movies. So, when the BJP government came to power, my school's WhatsApp group was full of Hindu nationalistic messages. By this time, I was working and had made quite a few Muslim friends. Also, I had shifted from Janakpuri to Ghaziabad. Most of my classmates, however, still lived in Janakpuri. When agitations against the Citizenship Amendment Bill, brought by the BJP, were going on, I was shocked at the deep hatred shown by some of my classmates against Muslims.'

The generations that came after Partition carried the seeds of religious disharmony. For the likes of Hindu nationalist organizations, such as the RSS and Hindu Mahasabha, these proved to be fertile grounds to operate in, the outcome of which could be seen in the demolition of the Babri Masjid in Ayodhya in 1992.

This does not mean that Gandhian ideals had been completely discarded. If the mayhem stopped, it was because of those ideals. The assassination of the Mahatma put an abrupt end to the violence. His death revived the Gandhian philosophy of *ahimsa parmo dharma* and stalled the growing influence of the RSS on society, though for a short period of time. Gandhi stood for compassion towards the poor. The middle class, who had alleviated him to the status of a saint, followed his example with utmost conviction, but steered clear from his stern opposition to any vulgar display of wealth. Nehru's vision of a modern India based on development of science and technology, too, deeply resonated with this urban-centric and upwardly mobile class, which was brought up on Western concepts of reasoning and free thinking.

Despite Gandhian values, the duality of the Indian middle class remained very much intact. The caste system was considered evil, something to be discarded, as long as it remained on the periphery of upper-caste homes. So, while the middle and upper-middle class vehemently opposed the caste system in public, within the confines of their homes, the bias remained strong as ever.

Writer Ved Mehta narrates a rather interesting anecdote. While conducting interviews for his book *Mahatma Gandhi and his Apostles*, he spoke to Jankidevi, wife of businessman Jamnalal Bajaj, who was one of the patrons of the Mahatma. After Gandhi died, she became a disciple of Vinoba Bhave, who was considered the spiritual successor of Gandhi, and participated in the Bhoodan movement. The interview, excerpted below, is an example of the superficiality of upper-caste middle class and elites when it comes to lower castes as well as minorities.

> 'I walked with Vinobaji for years,' Mrs. Bajaj says. 'Ten or 15 miles a day, begging land for the poor. It was very hard changing camp every day because I never eat anything I haven't prepared with my own hands. Everyone knows that Muslims and Harijans have dirty habits.'
>
> 'How did you manage in Gandhi's ashrams, where you had to eat food communally prepared by Muslims, Harijans, and all sorts of other people, whatever their caste of religion?' I ask.
>
> 'In the ashrams, everyone was very clean,' she replies, 'We all ate out of each other's hands. But everyone knew that Muslims and Harijans outside the ashram had dirty habits, Hare Ram, Hare Ram.'[16]

Jankidevi lived with the ideals of Gandhi, with simplicity. She replaced her gold and fine silks with khadi and stepped out of purdah at the behest of her guru. But the roots of caste proved to be too deeply entrenched.

Another incident underlining this fact, happened when Gandhi opened the Satyagraha Ashram at Kochrab near Ahmedabad. Gandhi wanted to start his fight against untouchability from there. However, he had to face strong protests and even boycott from the neighbouring community when he admitted Dudabhai, an 'untouchable', and his family into the ashram.[17]

Such contradictions have always been an integral part of the Indian middle class ethos. Likewise, the concept of 'unity in diversity' was, and has been, just an attractive promotional package for international tourists concealing a highly complex and volatile mixture of different religions, regions, languages, and castes.

Little wonder then that the post-Nehruvian era was marked by a multitude of social movements fighting against religious, regional, caste, and gender biases. Ironically though, these movements were initiated by the middle class, against the middle class, indicating the increasing role of this growing segment in matters concerning society, politics, and the environment.

Two major reasons can be attributed to this development. First, the middle class had become aware of its strength. The struggle for independence was still very fresh in the minds of the people. However, these nationalistic sentiments differed from community to community, and came to the fore once the common goal had been achieved. And second, the growing influence of education.

Education was one of the sectors that got priority after Independence. Nehru's dream India needed educated, young, and rational minds. Keeping that goal in mind, scores of new schools and colleges were opened. As a result, lower- and middle-income groups started moving into the middle class. Over time, increasing state intervention in educational institutions saw people from rural areas, lower castes, and ethnic groups become a part of this class, making it highly pluralistic in nature.

Social movements were, thus, a natural outcome of the clash of interests of the people of this eclectic class. Misra views it as a middle class feat. 'By the seventies, the middle class had started expressing itself in different ways. Now the question is why did the middle class start with these identity related movements? The answer is simple: I believe that middle class is the most articulate class among old classes. It has something to do with knowledge. So, it is very natural that it would be able to articulate its case. The middle class has the capacity to argue, to change.'[18]

Language Protests

The best example of this middle-class articulation, which had a far-reaching impact on the subcontinent, is, perhaps, the language revolution of East Pakistan which resulted in the creation of Bangladesh. What started as a cultural movement on 21 February 1952, when students in large numbers came out in protest against the imposition of Urdu as official language, became a political reality in 1971. State action against the agitating students, in which some students died and many were injured, fuelled the protests with many people including politicians, teachers, writers, poets, and journalists joining it. Jinnah had, in his 1948 speech in Dhaka, amid thunderous applause, proudly proclaimed that the state language of 'Pakistan is going to be Urdu and no other language'. However, by 1956, the Pakistan government had been forced to recognize Bangla as the official language of East Pakistan. [19]

In neighbouring India, too, a demand for formation of states based on languages was gaining ground. It started in the 1950s with Indian freedom fighter and revolutionary Potti Sriramulu floating the idea of a separate state for Telugu speaking people. His demand was rejected by both Prime Minister Nehru and Chief Minister of Madras State C. Rajgopalachari, and Sriramulu went on a hunger strike, forcing the central government to concede to his demand. What followed was the linguistic reorganization of India—carving out states on the basis of the language being spoken in the region.

The middle classes are highly protective of their regional identities, which not only highlight their ethnicity (which is a major source of social cohesion as well as conflict) but gives them a unified voice too in this diverse nation.

This is the reason the Sindhi middle class fought for inclusion of the Sindhi language as a non-regional language in the Eighth Schedule of the Indian Constitution. Sindhis, after Partition, were a community without a region. They were a cultural, electoral, and linguistic minority, which had to compromise on their traditions and culture and adapt to the local customs in order to survive. Their culture was an amalgamation of Sufi Islam and Hinduism that the locals could not really comprehend. They were meat-eaters; this made it difficult for them to get a house in a Gujarati neighbourhood. Territorial loss was a severe setback to their culture. Now, the only thread tying them together as a community was their language.

Their efforts bore fruits when in 1967 Sindhi became the first language to be added to the Eighth Schedule of the Indian Constitution. This ensured Sindhi Hindus' linguistic identity and gave them political recognition. This had a great significance for other linguistic minorities who referenced the Sindhi campaign for their own recognition.[20] Over the years, any attempt at imposition of a language deemed 'foreign' to a region or culture is vehemently opposed by the people. In 1937, politician and social activist E. V. Ramasamy, better known as Periyar, launched the first agitation against Hindi-imposition in the erstwhile Madras Presidency. The agitation was against the compulsory learning of Hindi in schools and garnered much support among the middle classes. An attempt was made again post-Independence when, in his address at Thiruvananthapuram on 21 May 1950, Sardar Patel stressed on the need for the people of South India to learn Hindi lest they 'lag behind both in central organisations and central government'.[21] Finally, a compromise was reached when Nehru gave a personal assurance in Parliament that there will be no imposition of Hindi on non-Hindi members. Then, in 1964, violent protests swamped Tamil Nadu when the state government introduced the three-language formula (English, Hindi, and Tamil) in the Madras Legislative Assembly after Nehru's death.

The issue of language once again came to the forefront in 2022 when Home Minister Amit Shah declared that the official language of running the government would be Hindi. 'Now the time has come to make the official language an important part of the unity of the country. When citizens of states who speak other languages communicate with each other, it should be in the language of India.'[22] And once again, voices of dissent are being raised, even within the BJP.

On 12 April 2022, while addressing a press conference, state BJP president, K. Annamalai, categorically said that the Tamil Nadu BJP would never accept imposition of the Hindi language over the state.[23] After the backlash the home minister's comments faced, there has been no update on the issue. BJP's 2024 election manifesto also did not mention its 'One nation, One language' drive. Nevertheless, the central government has been accused of promoting the same. In March 2023, the Food Safety and Standards Authority of India (FSSAI) issued a directive to the Tamil Nadu federation of milk producers, asking them to use the word 'dahi' on the curd packets instead of 'curd' in English and 'thayir' in Tamil. The same was to be done on other dairy products such as butter and cheese. This led to a major controversy in Tamil Nadu and other southern states including Karnataka. The FSSAI had to withdraw the directive.[24] One aspect of these language movements, as pointed out by Misra, was that from a nationalist orientation the middle class was shifting towards a sectarian orientation. The middle class's fears were not totally unfounded. History is replete with instances where cultures were lost when the associated languages lost their status or were imposed upon by another language. One such example is Prakrit, which was used in early Ashokan edicts but got replaced by Sanskrit by the end of the third century CE.

'When a language dies, its speakers decide to migrate,' says G. N. Devy, renowned for his research on language. 'First, they migrate to another language and then they physically start migrating to another region. The second thing that happens is that their traditional livelihood [is lost]. They may have some special skills and that disappears. Thirdly, a unique way of looking at the world disappears. Every language is a unique worldview.'[25]

This makes language an essential aspect of culture. It carries the cultural ethos of a region, its history, in the form of folklores and oral narratives. It defines the people of the land and gives them a regional identity, which is why the question of language is so dear to social classes.

Middle Class and the Environment

Often, the middle class is accused of being opportunistic and self-centred. However, if one examines it sociologically, one would find that every class prioritizes its own interests. Misra argues that the middle class, by its very existence, is placed in a tight spot and is always 'pressurised' by both the other classes. So, that's why, says he, 'perhaps, the nature of the middle class becomes like this (self-centred).... Because it becomes an existential problem for the middle class.'[26]

The working class looks up to the middle class to champion its cause. The pressure to stand with them and fight for their rights is contradictory to its own ambitions and aspirations. The middle class acts as a balancing factor in society; however, it has to work within the confines of the rules and regulations set by the elite. And it is expected to toe the line. The same rules don't apply to the rich. A few years ago, the apex court issued a statement saying, 'India cannot have two parallel legal systems, one for the rich and resourceful and those who wield political power and the other for small men without resources without capabilities to gain justice.'[27] So there is a pressure of performance from the top as well. Also, while on the one hand, it feels threatened by the lower class, as it strives to enter the middle-class bracket (which would heighten the competition for resources); on the other hand, the elites, identifying themselves as 'middle class' avail of subsidies marked for the middle class and the poor. As Sambuddha Mitra Mustafi says, 'Like the rich in the United States who use the "job creator" tag to lobby for tax breaks, India's elite has devised the middle-class narrative to capture more public resources like fuel, food and education subsidies, often at the cost of the country's poor millions.'[28] The elites use their economic might and connections in the corridors of power to influence policy formulation. For instance, according to the 2020–21 income tax data, the rich, who constitute around 1 per cent of the Indian population (as per the *Economic Times* report of 20 Mar 2024) with an income of above 1 crore, declared 38.6 per cent of their total taxable income, making them 0.016 per cent of the 6.6 per cent population who filed a tax return.[29]

This middle-class insecurity is also heightened by the Marxist theory which states that the middle class is no class and will wither away as a class in times of crisis. It will ultimately split, with one section joining the bourgeoisie and the other becoming a part of the proletariat. This constant threat is taken as an existential problem. So, for the middle class, its own interests become more important.

Nevertheless, there have been times when the middle class has risen to the occasion to fight for what it considered morally and ethically right. The Chipko Movement, Narmada Bachao Abhiyan, and Silent Valley Movement were three such milestone movements of the seventies and eighties. These movements were initiated to protect the environment as well as safeguard the rights of the poor and the marginalized living in those areas.

The Chipko Movement was iconic because of its multifaceted identity. It was at once a fight between rural values and urban concepts, between powerful men and simple, illiterate women, and between lower class need and upper-class greed. It signified much more than protecting the environment, it signified the empowerment of women too. Above all, it was a movement initiated by the lower- and middle-middle class, involving students, social activists (CPI activists), and environmentalists (Sarvodaya workers). They mobilized the locals against the exploitation and degradation of the forests.

Chipko was not the first environment-based activism to have taken place in the hills of Kumaon and Garhwal. Back in 1930, villagers in Tiladi were gunned down by the prime minister of the maharaja of Tehri while protesting the encroachment of their rights to the forest in a manner similar to the Jallianwala Bagh massacre.

Territorially, agriculture was not really feasible at this altitude, nor were there other sources of employment, leaving the villagers no choice but to depend on the forests for their survival. However, a growing frequency of natural disturbances, like landslides and drying up of water sources, had made it clear that this was a limited resource which needed to be used judiciously and protected at all costs, especially from the commercial activity of the triad of contractors, bureaucracy, and politicians. In 1970, flash floods in the Alaknanda submerged areas far downstream, highlighting the need to restore the ecological balance in the area. Protests broke out in Purola, Uttarkashi, and Gopeshwar against 'indiscriminate logging by outside contractors'. Another flashpoint between the disgruntled inhabitants and the government officials was the limitations put on the villagers' traditional rights to the forest. The villagers wanted the ash tree to be included in their haque-haquooks (traditional rights to the forest), which the divisional forest officer declined saying the ash tree was a 'foreign currency earning species' and the villagers were not allowed to use it to make farmyard tools. Yet, at the same time, an Allahabad-based sports company, Symond's & Co. was granted permission to fell ash trees for commercial use.[30] This blatant patronage of larger economic interests while ignoring the locals' needs, sparked off the Van Bachao movement under the leadership of environmentalist Chandi Prasad Bhatt in Chamoli district in 1973.

It was a movement led by a Gandhian and fought on the Gandhian principle of ahimsa. Bhatt proposed that the villagers hug the trees. So, when the contractor and his men came, armed with their axes, the villagers simply stood in front of their beloved trees, hugging them, giving the protest its name, Chipko Movement. The contractor had to return empty-handed. But that was not the end of the story.

The story of Chipko took a turn in 1974 when, in response to the government auction of more than 680 hectares of forest land near Reni village in Joshimath to a contractor from Rishikesh, the women of Reni made a collaborative effort to drive the men out of the area. They encircled the trees, forcing the labourers to abandon their plans and return. The news of the women's bravery spread like wildfire, and so did the movement. Chipko had now metamorphosed into an eco-feminist movement. It resulted in the imposition of a ten-year ban on 'commercial forestry in Reni and in nearly 1,200 square kilometres of the upper catchment of the Alaknanda' in 1976 by the government, which was extended by another ten years in 1985.[31]

As a movement, Chipko succeeded at many levels. It empowered women and made them aware of their rights. It underlined the importance of letting people exercise their right to manage their environment. It was imperative as these poor and lower-middle class people depended on the forests for their livelihood, and any policy related to the forests had to be made keeping them in mind. This was the message the activists wanted to communicate.

'A distinction is necessary between what happened locally and the national and international movement that grew out of it. Chipko put forests on the political agenda in the country. The Forest Conservation Act of 1980 and the very creation of the environment ministry are due to the consciousness created by Chipko.'[32] Chipko did create a positive impact on environment for some time, but it ultimately fizzled out and unplanned logging and construction continued in this eco-sensitive area, the latest being the Char Dham project which, despite protests by the locals and environmentalists, aims to improve connectivity between four Hindu pilgrimage sites: Kedarnath, Badrinath, Gangotri, and Yamunotri.

Nevertheless, what Chipko could not achieve the Silent Valley Movement did. In this people-versus-state fight, which drew masses from across all sections of society, it was the people who emerged victorious.

In 1970, the Kerala State Electricity Board (KSEB) proposed that a hydroelectric dam be built across the Kunthipuzha River running through Silent Valley. Under the proposed project, four units of 60 megawatt (MW) each were to be installed in the state. The project, argued the state, would fulfil the state's electricity requirements and irrigate an additional 100 square kilometres of land in the Mallapuram and Palakkad districts, besides boosting the economy by providing employment to thousands during the construction phase.

However, the project presented a grave threat to the evergreen forests and the flora and fauna of the region covering an area of over 237.52 square kilometres in the Palakkad district. The dam would have submerged around 8–9 square kilometres of forest area, destroying its biodiversity.

In 1971–72, Steven Green, an American zoologist conducting research on the rare lion-tailed macaques, and Romulus Whitaker, a herpetologist, raised concerns about the threat to the valley. Whitaker wrote to the Bombay Natural History Society about the need to conserve the valley. This brought public attention to the issue. A task force set up by the National Committee on Environment Planning and Coordination (NCEPC) to analyse the environmental impact of the project made a futile attempt to convince the state government to scrap the project. The project received the go-ahead from the Planning Commission in 1973, but could not take off due to insufficient funds.

By the end of the seventies, a number of conservationists and environmentalists had joined the anti-dam movement started by the NGO Kerala Sasthra Sahithya Parishad (KSSP) way back in 1966.

This movement was initiated by eminent people including scientists such as V. S. Vijayan, a wildlife biologist, ornithologist, and environmentalist; conservationists like Salim Ali; and several environmental groups like Friends of Trees, Parisara, and Society for Promotion of Environmental Conservation. Unlike other movements that started from grassroots and moved to the top, this one was top-down, with scientists, bureaucrats, litterateurs, and the educated upper-middle and middle classes forming the base. They took the movement to the masses through Sasthra Kala Jathas, street plays, songs, and dances.

The other interesting aspect of the movement was that instead of being a rhetorical protest, the movement was backed by scientific argument and that made it a much discussed topic nationally as well as internationally. Also, prominent members of the movement conducted environment awareness sessions throughout the state. In an interview dated 1 February 2018, renowned ecologist Madhav Gadgil, who later went on to chair the Western Ghats Ecology Expert Panel (WGEEP), told *Mongabay India* that the KSSP was a popular science movement in the seventies and eighties in Kerala, and they had a 'scientifically well-informed argument' that they were able to communicate to the public successfully.[33] In 1983, the hydroelectric project was called off and Silent Valley was declared a protected area. The story of Silent Valley has been one of the most successful middle class environmental initiatives in the history of modern India.

The third and, perhaps, one of the longest running movements in India (over thirty-eight years), is the Naramada Bachao Abhiyan.

In 1985, a protest began in Madhya Pradesh and parts of Gujarat and Maharashtra against the government resettlement and rehabilitation policy of more than 2.5 million people who were set to be displaced by the construction of dams along the Narmada River. According to the plan, 30 large dams, 135 medium dams and 3,000 small dams were to be built along 1,312 kilometres of the Narmada from Madhya Pradesh to Gujarat. Out of these, only the Sardar Sarovar dam was in Gujarat while the rest were in Madhya Pradesh. The height of the dam was to be 138.68 metres and it would have submerged 38,000 hectares of land, and displaced 244 villages, with a total population of approximately 250,000 people.

Social activist Medha Patkar, a politician and a social activist, petitioned the Supreme Court against the project in 1985 citing the poor resettlement and rehabilitation policy of the government and got a stay order on the construction work. That marked the beginning of the Narmada Bachao Andolan, a mass movement which was a coalition of Adivasis, farmers, and social activists like Baba Amte, who came from a middle-class background.

In 1998, the court 'stayed work but vacated it on condition that permission would be granted after a review of the affected areas. In 2000, the court allowed construction on condition of supervised R&R (resettlement and rehabilitation). By 2004 it stood at 110.64 metres and by 2006 it had permission to rise to 121.92 metres'.[34] In 2014, when the BJP came to power at the centre, permission was granted to construct the dam to its full height and install sluice gates at the top while around 21,000 families were still awaiting resettlement and rehabilitation.

Narmada has been a highly controversial issue with people supporting and opposing it with the same fervour. Political partics have encashed it to their own advantage. The Narmada project was envisaged by the first prime minister Jawaharlal Nehru and deputy prime minster Sardar Vallabhbhai Patel. The project spanned four decades and three parties at the centre (Congress, Janata Dal, BJP), and was finally completed in 2017.

While social activists had been agitating against the building of the dam, citing problems in the rehabilitation of displaced tribals and farmers of Madhya Pradesh, the people of Gujarat supported it wholeheartedly as it meant continued water supply to the arid lands of Saurashtra and Kachch. Also, the Gujarati middle class viewed the dam as part of Gujarati asmita and culture.

The stories of middle-class participation in environment protection movements raise a very pertinent question: Is the middle class genuinely concerned with environment protection?

There is no straight answer to this question, for the simple reason that the middle class differs from region to region. The rural middle class is closer to nature. All its activities are governed by the environment surrounding it. For instance, a study conducted in the Kadalundi-Vallikkunnu Community Reserve in Kerala observed:

> We documented a positive association between traditional fish trap deployment and waterbird counts and diversity. This suggests that the traditional fishing practices in KVCR, if promoted and managed adequately, could enhance waterbird abundance and diversity. Low impact fishing practices such as the bamboo fish traps that enhance waterbird abundance could serve as a model for sustainable utilization of fish resources, provided proper monitoring and evaluation instruments are in place.[35]

The urban middle class, on the other hand, shows contradictions in behaviour when it comes to environmental protection. The use of plastic continues unabated; however, tree-planting activities have increased significantly. There is a conscious effort by a section of the middle class, to the point of aggression, to make vegetarianism and veganism a way of life. Yet, power consumption has gone through the roof and the number of cars on roads keeps increasing. But there is a section of people who are genuinely concerned with the cause, who work towards bridging the gap between urban-dwellers and nature through camps and nature trips. Dr Salim Ali was one. And there are numerous who followed him. They are inculcating a love for nature in young minds, and it is their indomitable spirit that keeps the hope alive.

The Neo-Buddhist Movement: The Caste Factor

The Neo-Buddhist movement started by Ambedkar created a space for the depressed classes both in politics as well as economy. Ambedkar was from Maharashtra and belonged to the Mahar caste, which formed the lowest strata of Indian society, the 'untouchables'. They were considered outside the chaturvarna system.

Many scholars believe caste to be the creation of British. When we talk of caste, inevitably the reference is made to the untouchables. Among the lower castes, the 'untouchables', or Dalits as they are referred to now, form the lowest rung of social hierarchy. Incidentally, the Rig Veda, the earliest literature, makes no mention of untouchability. In fact, as per G. S. Ghurye, the Rig Veda frequently mentions only three classes of society—Brahma, Kshatra, and Vis—'it is only in one of the later hymns, the celebrated *Purushsukta*, that a reference has been made to four orders of society as emanating from the sacrifice of the Primeval Being'.[36] Now, such being the case, it becomes imperative to understand the origins of Dalits as a group, as they have come to play a big role in Indian politics. Indian political theorist and Dalit activist Kancha Illaiah Shepherd maintains Dalits were historically Shudras. He believes them to be the original inhabitants of the Harappan civilization. In a 2021 article in *The Wire*, he claims that the 'Dalits were separated from Shudras and made an untouchable section of the Shudra varna'.

His contention, that the Dalits originally belonged to the Shudra varna, is based on the fact that the social status of the Shudras, as described by the religious texts, was that of slaves and that there could not have been any strata lower than that. He puts forth an interesting argument regarding the formation of the Dalit community and the reason they were kept out of the chaturvarna system.

'It may be that once Brahminism declared leather and leather-related instruments untouchable, the section of Shudras who specialised in leather were declared untouchable too. During the Vedic period, though the economy was called pastoral, we can assume that leather goods were part of economic life; evidence for this comes from our present Adivasi society, which is very similar to the Vedic pastoral society. Even in our own time, the Adivasi community's deep forest village economies have developed work specialisations. A section of their society has the specialised role of transforming animal skin into leather and to turn that leather into bags, ropes and other leather instruments and essential commodities.'[37] The Dalits came to be a force the day Ambedkar, along with close to 400,000 followers, converted to Buddhism. That, according to the visionary that Ambedkar was, was the only recourse to getting equality in society. His belief was that Hinduism was founded on the basis of inequality, whereas Buddha fought inequality all his life. Hence, the first step towards organizing the Dalits was conversion to a religion that treated all equally.

The Dalit Panthers was one of the outcomes of this. The organization was founded on 29 May 1972, by educated Dalit youth from the middle class. Despite a very specific name, the Dalit Panthers was not a closed organization. To the Panthers, the Dalits included anyone who was politically exploited and was a victim of caste or religious bias. They represented women, Scheduled Castes and Tribes, and other minorities as well.

The organization lasted only five years after which it disintegrated due to infighting among its founding members: Namdeo Dhasal, Raja Dhale, J. V. Pawar, and Arun Kamble. Even in that short a time, it left a deep impact on the people. This was the first time a segment of society considered meek and voiceless had asserted itself so violently, as against Ambedkar's movement which was rather humane. Ambedkar had approached the social problems academically and sought to find solutions legally and through policies. In contrast, the Dalit Panthers were a resistance group modelled on the revolutionary Black Panthers of the US, a social organization that fought against police brutality. They used literature to rouse anti-feudal sentiments among the masses. The founders of the Dalit Panthers, too, were literary figures in their own rights. In that sense, one can call it a literary movement.

Ambedkarite Today traces the beginning of the Dalit movement to the sixties. It was a time when media was dominated by the upper castes. Dalit intelligentsia understood the might of the pen and sought to express itself and reach out to the masses through poetry and prose. Thus, it was the despondency and frustration felt by the educated Dalit youth that gave birth to the Dalit Literary Movement. 'This young generation or the new Dalit intelligentsia wanted to articulate themselves in their own words and in their own style, without a sense of borrowedness.

In other words, this was an attempt by the Dalit Panthers to un-caste the literary world.'[38]

In their poetry, street plays and theatre, Dalit litterateurs told stories of oppression, of how Dalit women were raped, how the men were murdered at the slightest pretext, and how even basic human rights were denied to them. They talked of revolution, of taking forcefully what was due to them rather than waiting for it to happen. And it was this militant outlook of theirs that attracted the Dalit middle class towards them, expanding their base.

Unfortunately, the movement fizzled out too soon. Yet, it did manage two highly significant achievements: first, it consolidated Dalit groups, which had become directionless after the death of Ambedkar, into a single political unit, especially since the Republican Party of India had lost its way and was pandering to the needs of the rich and powerful; and second, it motivated the Dalit urban middle class to fight aggressively for their rights.

This phase in the post-Independence history of India has played a crucial role in defining the present middle class. It was during this phase that conflicts that had been simmering for a long time between different communities took centre stage as political leadership increasingly became power-hungry, reducing politics to a game of numbers.

11

Caste in Education: Mandal Commission

One of the highlights of the interim period between the year of Independence and the year of liberalization was the introduction of the Mandal Commission Report. The commission was set up under the Morarji Desai government, but it was the V. P. Singh government that implemented it, leading to much social and political chaos. It was the middle class that was affected the most, and so the voices of dissent were the loudest among them. But talk of caste and reservation were not new, their roots were strongly embedded in the past. The Mandal report made caste the central issue of Indian politics; it also created a deep divide in society between pro- and anti-reservationists, especially among the student community, and created a new identity among the middle classes.

Generally, a political or economic revolution is preceded by a social or religious revolution. Take, for instance, the French Revolution. The genesis of the French Revolution lay in the existing inequality among the masses. The revolution itself was an outcome of the new ideas of equality and democracy propagated by enlightened philosophers such as Voltaire and Rousseau, who not only influenced French society but also served as an inspiration for the world to follow. India, too, responded with great fervour. But the Indian story differed from the rest of the world. Here, the social and political revolutions commenced almost simultaneously. The Indian National Congress was formed in 1885, and two years later, in 1887, its social reform cell, the Indian (National) Social Conference, was founded.

Now, herein lies the contradiction. While the Congress was aiming for political unity to fight for representation in the government, the Conference was seeking to bring social issues like caste, polygamy, and child marriage to the national level. And this presented a dilemma for the leaders of the time as to which of the two should take precedence. Of course, the political wing of the Congress favoured political reform over social reform. Dr B. R. Ambedkar raised the issue of social reform in a speech he wrote for the annual conference of the Jat-Pat-Mandal of Lahore in 1936.

> The gentlemen who presided over the sessions of the Social Conference lamented that the majority of the educated Hindus were for political advancement and indifferent to social reform, and that while the number of those who attended the Congress was very large and the number who did not attend but who sympathised with it even larger, the number of those who attended the Social Conference was very much smaller. This indifference, this thinning of its ranks, was soon followed by active hostility from the politicians.'[1]

The speech, however, remained undelivered as the conference, which he was to preside over, was cancelled. The reason given by the organizers was that the views expressed by him would not find favour with the conference in general.

By the 1930s, the Social Conference was but a spent force, though it did manage to highlight the issues of child marriage, polygamy, and untouchability at the national level. Hence, the struggle for independence took precedence over social reform.

Ambedkar's contention that to achieve its political goal India had to first achieve its social goal did not receive much attention. There were two reasons for it. First, the Indian middle class wanted representation in the government, and so politics was a priority; second, most of the social reformers were high-caste Hindus, and while they did promote inter-caste marriage and fight against untouchability, the annihilation of caste as proposed by Ambedkar, which would have resulted in the total breakdown of the existing social order, was not something they wanted.

On his part, Ambedkar was convinced that without tackling the issue of caste, India was not 'fit for political power'. He found the argument that caste was a division of labour to be in defence of the discrimination.

In contrast, social reformers like Ram Mohan Roy, Ramakrishna Paramhansa, and his disciple, Swami Vivekananda, while denouncing caste-based discrimination, did not turn against the Hindu religion. In fact, in a speech given at Kumbakonam in 1897, Vivekananda said:

> There is a law laid on each one of you in this land by your ancestors, whether you are Aryans or non-Aryans, Rishis or Brahmins, or the very lowest outcasts. The command is the same to you all: that you must make progress without stopping, and that from the highest man to the lowest Pariah, everyone in this country has to try and become the ideal Brahmin. This Vedantic idea is applicable not only here but over the whole world. Such is our ideal of caste as meant for raising all humanity slowly and gently towards the realisation of that great ideal of the spiritual man who is non-resisting, calm, steady, worshipful, pure, and meditative.

Caste remains a highly debated subject as historians and scholars hold distinctly different views on its origins. While many scholars believe that it was the British who compartmentalized Indian society into castes, historians say otherwise. Eminent historian Romila Thapar traces the origin of lower castes back to the mid-first millennium CE. She maintains that by then 'the exclusion of the Chandala and others that formed the lowest jatis was well established. Buddhist texts state that other communities generally listed as excluded tended to be Adivasis—such as Nishadas, Pukkasas, or in low occupations such as Venas and Rathakaras. Little is said about why they are low jatis. Forcing communities to live outside the settlement immediately marks them out as excluded. Had this not have been required, they may over time have merged into the general population of not-so-low jatis'.[2]

As complex as the caste system was, it was not surprising that, post-Independence, Indian society and politics came to be influenced by it. As the middle class expanded, the cracks in society became wider, and it got divided into diverse groups with different orientations, constituting different vote banks. Nehru had warned about this in his *Discovery of India* that the Indian social structure 'carried within it seeds of destruction'.

Which is why, recognizing the implications such a system would have on the creation of a democracy, certain legal and institutional provisions were made in the Constitution, albeit temporarily, to create a system that would enable the depressed classes to participate in democratic politics on an equal footing.[3] This inevitably led to the emergence of the educated Dalit middle class. Over the years, caste came to play a major role in electoral politics, influencing the selection of candidates, voting patterns, and even political alliances.

After Independence, the focus shifted to rebuilding the country. Hence, middle-class orientation, form, and patterns kept changing from time to time. 'Here, one should be mindful of the fact that the middle class is not always holding a pan-Indian ideology,' says Mohapatra. 'The Scheduled Caste middle class will be talking about caste justice, the tribal middle class will be talking about development displacement, and middle class women will be talking about gender rights. So, different middle classes will be articulating their interests in different ways.'[4] Thus, a middle class varied in form and ideology emerged in post-Independent India. And, more often than not, these ideologies created clashes of interests among the stakeholders involved. The biggest example of this is the Mandal Commission Report, which created a divide in society along caste lines. Mandal became a burning issue on which elections were fought, won, and lost.

In a country where caste dictated all aspects of life and more than half the population belonged to depressed classes, creating a nation based on the ideals of liberty, equality, and fraternity was next to impossible. This was why there was a need to bring reservations in education, employment, and legislatures. The idea was to provide them with an equal base so that they could participate with full vigour in the development of the nation. The proposal was made in 1882 by William Hunter and Jyotiba Phule. However, British Prime Minister Ramsay Macdonald introduced it in 1933 in the form of Communal Award. After Independence was achieved, while framing the Constitution of India, the Constituent Assembly made a provision for reservations for the socially backward classes, so that the goal of social equality was achieved.

According to Article 15(4) of the Constitution: Nothing shall prevent the State from making any special provision for the advancement of any socially and educationally backward classes of citizens or for the Scheduled Castes and the Scheduled Tribes.

Articles 341 and 342 of the Constitution specified the castes and tribes that came under the purview of Scheduled Castes (SC) and Scheduled Tribes (ST), resulting in 'compensatory discrimination via reserved positions' at the national and state levels in education and public service. And though references to other socially and educationally depressed groups were made, their identities were not specified. Hence, they were deprived of the privileges extended to the SCs and STs.

To address this anomaly, the central government, under the leadership of Morarji Desai, constituted the Mandal Commission in 1978. The Commission, headed by B. P. Mandal, who was also the chief architect of the report, was tasked with determining 'the criteria for defining the socially and educationally backward classes' and 'to recommend steps to be taken for the advancement of the socially and educationally backward classes of citizens so identified'.[5] The report takes note of the fact that the upper castes, especially Brahmins, who had established themselves as custodians of higher knowledge, had acquired a flair for intellectual pursuits, whereas the Shudras, who had been deprived of social, economic, cultural, and educational privileges, had remained unlettered.

Just how crucial this task was for the development of the country can be gauged by the following observations made by renowned political theorist Rajni Kothari in his book *Caste in Indian Politics*: 'As

Brahmins entered the institutions of higher learning, the professions and the services, everywhere they formed cliques from which the non-Brahmins were excluded. Between 1892 and 1904, out of 16 successful candidates for the ICS 15 were Brahmins; in 1914, 93 out of 128 permanent district munsifs were Brahmins; in 1944, 452 out of 650 registered graduates of the university were Brahmins.'[6] After a delay of about eleven years, the report was finally implemented on 7 August 1990, under the prime ministership of V. P. Singh. In fact, Singh had fought the election based on the issue. Writing for *The Wire* in 2020, Singh's grandson, Indra Shekhar Singh, shares why his *bubba* implemented the controversial report.

> The day I was sworn in, it was clear that the BJP would not allow the government to function beyond two years, as they wanted to run the government themselves. So I already knew that we would have to work very hard to implement the promise in our manifesto to implement the Mandal Commission. It was the sole mission of my prime ministership to free millions of Indians and their children from the clutches of an oppressive system and give them social justice. I had a duty to break (the) status quo and free these people in India's villages.

The announcement met with fierce resistance as Delhi resonated with anti-quota stirs. Protests and counter-protests rocked the capital as students took to the streets. The most vivid picture of the anti-quota movement is of Rajeev Goswami trying to immolate himself. Rajeev was studying at Deshbandhu College, Delhi University, when the reservation policy was announced. In a 2015 interview with *Indian Express*, Rajeev's father, Madan Lal Goswami, disclosed that his was not an impulsive act. Rajeev and two of his friends had threatened to take the drastic measure unless the government backtracked on the issue. On the fateful day, Rajeev's friends backed out, but he stood his ground. Rajeev survived with 50 per cent burns and became the face of the movement. For a while, Rajeev joined politics when he became the president of the Delhi University Students' Union (DUSU). But soon, he called it quits to start his own business. Rajeev passed away in 2004 due to jaundice. He was thirty-three. Madan Lal said he was 'proud' of his son. 'I was repeatedly overlooked for promotion, unlike my colleagues belonging to reserved categories. Reservation has to end,' he was quoted as saying.[7]

Rajeev's act inspired many to follow his lead, some not as lucky as him. Nearly 200 students attempted self-immolation, out of which around sixty-three succumbed to burns. An *India Today* report dated 30 October 1990, states that 'of the six people in Chandigarh that *India Today* spoke to, four had attempted suicide only after having heard on television about another person having taken recourse to it. Saroj Saini, 15, for instance, swallowed naphthalene balls after hearing on TV that Rajeev Goswami had burned himself. "I wanted to be the first girl to do it," she told her relatives. Similarly, Shama Gupta of Chandigarh, who died of burns in the last week of September (the first such case in Chandigarh), torched herself after hearing on TV that a Chandigarh girl had consumed poison.'[8] The anti-reservation movement was largely an urban middle-class phenomenon, mobilizing large sections of middle-class students, professionals, lawyers, and even members of the press. Despite being a volatile subject, the Mandal agitation did not have a pan-India appeal. In South India, aside from a few protests in Andhra Pradesh, it remained a non-issue. Gujarat gave a tepid response to the call of anti-reservation. In Punjab, barring Chandigarh and a few areas surrounding it, the reaction remained weak. And in Bihar, a violent anti-reservation agitation was countered by the pro-reservationists in equal measure.

However, the movement was an uncoordinated, unorganized spontaneous reaction of an upper-caste middle class to a purely political decision that led to more chaos than any significant impact on the government. It drew its strength largely from tragic acts performed by the students. The only achievement of the movement, if one could call that, was the entry of apolitical students into politics. Despite the prime minister's assurance that the commission's recommendations would not be applied to educational institutes, promotions in government jobs and recruitments in the defence and police forces, the students refused to back down, and the agitation took a serious turn as the entire Hindi belt was rocked by a spate of self-immolations.

The incidents of self-immolations following the example of Rajeev compels one to delve into the psyche of the middle class to understand why they resorted to such an extreme measure and what came of it. According to an *India Today* report, the department of psychiatry in Chandigarh's PGI decided to study '20 suicide cases to go into the psychological profiles of the suicide victims and the reactions of their parents'.[9] A survey conducted revealed that the parents were 'glorifying the incendiary acts of their children'.[10] The sentiment that the students were fighting for a greater cause was high among the protesting students as well as their families. Setting oneself on fire is, perhaps, the most dramatic and emotionally stimulating statement one can make. It sends a strong message.

Psychologists have, however, cited reasons other than reservation issue for such a drastic step. The age of adolescence is marred by conflicting emotions, raging hormones, and teenage angst. A youngster is going through different stages of development mentally, physically and emotionally, which makes him or her highly reactionary. In such a state, any negative feeling often results in volatile behaviour.

Take, for instance, the case of thirteen-year-old Chetan Gautam of Delhi. He still had many more years before the Mandal effect would have impacted him. Yet he set himself on fire. On the face of it, his act was a harsh warning to the government to roll back the policy. He even said, as quoted by the magazine, that there was no point as he would not get a job even if '[he happened] to get 70% marks. Somebody with just 30% will get what is [his] due'.[11]

Chetan was too young to fully understand the implications of the reservation policy. He was probably carried away by the sentiment of self-sacrifice prevailing in society at the time. Many attempted the act solely because of peer pressure. Atul Aggarwal was one such twelve-year-old. Atul had shifted to Delhi only a year before and felt quite out of place. Speaking to *Indian Express* in 2015, he narrated how he 'got carried away' by the anti-Mandal sentiment and his life post the incident. 'Everywhere, people were only talking about the Mandal report. Rallies were being held, roads were blocked, youngsters were killing themselves. As a child, I felt I should be part of this movement though I did not understand what it stood for.'[12] Atul sustained 55 per cent burns.

The students saw it as a noble cause, a fight for their rights, a fight for equality. They unleashed their pent-up frustrations with vengeance. And the fact that they were seen as heroes and the act was being legitimized by their parents—they 'did it for the country', they would say—made them even more determined.[13]

A third aspect of the movement, as the report points out, was media publicity that came with these so-called acts of bravery. The report quotes the head of the psychology department at the All India Institute of Medical Sciences (AIIMS) as saying: 'The otherwise lost souls started finding mention in newspapers. In an epidemic, the degree of exposure you get overtakes pain, the thought of death or even rational thinking.'[14]

He was not exaggerating, as the first question that Monica Chadha, a nineteen-year-old who tried to immolate herself, asked her mother, a day after her suicide attempt, was whether her photo had appeared in the newspaper.

In 1997, the Department of Psychiatry, Postgraduate Institute of Medical Education and Research, Chandigarh, published a paper on the Psychological Study of 'Self-immolation' in India. Over all, twenty-two young students in the age group of 13–36 were studied. This is what they had to say when asked about what they thought of the reservation:

> 61% of them said that all forms of reservation were wrong. Nearly 39 of the subjects reported that their families had suffered because of reservations. In total, 67% of the cases felt that engaging in an act of deliberate self-harm was justified. About 64% of the subjects reported that they had attempted self-immolation in order to pressurise the government to withdraw its controversial policy. Assessment of personality characteristics revealed that 17 subjects had high aspirations and were ambitious, 16 subjects were impulsive, and only 5 subjects rated themselves as altruistic.[15]

Apart from Delhi, the other states that witnessed large-scale protests were Haryana, Uttar Pradesh, Orissa, Himanchal Pradesh, Punjab, and Bihar, where they turned violent, claiming several lives. South India, on the other hand, remained relatively calm. The reason was that states like Tamil Nadu and Maharashtra had already made reservations for the socially and economically backward.

Political parties politicized the issue as per their convenience. Initially, there was just constitutional intervention in the matter, but now political intervention also began. Pseudo- and semi-religious political groups started interfering in the matter. Mandal heightened caste-based distinctions and, as a result, caste organizations flourished. 'These existed earlier too,' says Misra, 'but they were in the form of caste panchayats. Now, they were proper organizations.'[16] And according to him, the intervention of these politico-religious groups led to the rise of the communitarian nature of the contemporary middle class. Added to this was the competition in the politico-economic sphere. Insecurities pertaining to jobs and one's future initiated a demand for reservation, be it the upper class or the lower class, backed by political parties.

Misra is categorical when he says that the middle class is not very conscious of equality as its class goal or class interest. 'Equality may be a value for society at large, or it may be an ideal, not a value, for a class too, but it is logically not appropriate for the middle class because it is not a homogeneous class either economically, culturally, socially, or even politically.'[17]

According to him, it is a heterogeneous class, and this is also the case with inequalities. 'I doubt that the middle class has ever been an advocate of equality.' Judging from the history of the middle class, not just in India but across the world, one can say that equality can be used as a 'camouflage' to achieve certain objectives under its garb. 'But when the question of providing equality comes as some kind of distribution of rewards of any kind to the whole society, then the middle class doesn't support that argument.'[18]

If one were to view the entire issue objectively, it becomes clear that the anti-Mandal stir was a manifestation of middle class fears and insecurities heightened by the belief that reservation would give undue advantage to a section of people while increasing competition for the rest. The issue of reservation drove a wedge between students.

India Today did a cover story on the reservation issue. The story, published on 15 October 1990, quoted a political science researcher from Delhi University as saying: 'We used to have Hindu College vs St. Stephens or Miranda House vs Lady Sriram College rivalries. Now they are forcing us to think on caste lines.' Another student from King George Medical College, Lucknow, was quoted saying that 'ever since the Mandal Commission report was announced and our agitation started, our Yadav and Gujjar friends have stopped talking to us.'[19]

While the issue of Mandal did raise the debate of inequality persisting in Indian society and provided an opportunity to the depressed sections of society to participate in the political and economic development of the country, it also led to increased caste consciousness among people in general and raised questions on the issue of meritocracy for selection in government-run educational institutes and public workspaces.

Perhaps the only positive outcome of Mandal at the time was that it educated students about politics and politicians, especially how politicians exploit such situations for furthering their personal agenda. Which is why when senior BJP leaders such as L. K. Advani, who was the president of the party, and M. P. Madan Lal Khurana went to the hospital where Rajeev was undergoing treatment to meet his parents, they were booed away by the students. They were clear: 'Only those publicly against the Mandal Commission can join us.' Advani couldn't say that as the implementation of the Mandal Commission Report was part of the BJP election manifesto. Even the Congress (I) did not oppose the report. However, Congress leaders in Delhi, S. S. Ahluwalia and Subhash Chopra, gave open support to the agitating Delhi University students. And in Bihar, Congress (I) MLA Aditya Narain Singh led a violent rally against the Yadavs.[20]

The worst outcome of Mandal politics, however, was the rise of 'Kamandal politics' by the BJP. Mandal gave political legitimacy to caste-based identity politics. The introduction of Mandal recommendations changed the political set-up of Bihar as the backward classes started identifying with their caste more than their Hindu identity. This spelled doom for the BJP in the state. And to regain lost ground, the BJP started the 'Mandal' versus 'Kamandal' discourse. With religion joining the fray with class and caste, Indian politics was transformed forever.

12

Middle Class Women and the Feminist Movement

In the struggle for independence, women, across class and caste, came out of their homes in large numbers to participate in rallies and gatherings. Many courted arrest. Strong, fearless, determined, they took the movement forward wherever and whenever the need arose. If not directly, they supported the movement indirectly. Nehru's declaration of independence was received with much jubilation by all sections of society. The dream of a new India was within reach. Hindu-Muslim, lower caste-upper caste, rich-poor, men-women, these distinctions would be mitigated, and India would set an example of unity in diversity before the world.

'At the stroke of the midnight hour, when the world sleeps, India will awake to life and freedom. A moment comes, which comes but rarely in history, when we step out from the old to the new, when an age ends, and when the soul of a nation, long suppressed, finds utterance,' said Nehru in his famous *Tryst with Destiny* speech.

Gaining freedom was one thing but sustaining it and ensuring that all stakeholders were given their due was a different matter altogether. Despite sustained efforts at social reforms, divisions along caste and religion remained intact. And the growing middle class kept reinventing its identity based on them.

For women, the change that was witnessed during the freedom movement turned out to be transient. Once freedom was attained, a majority went back to being caretakers of the family. Though the Constitution granted equal rights to women in civil liberties and education, and empowered states to adopt measures of positive discrimination in their favour, the ground reality did not change for them much.

The 'why' can be answered thus: a) Though the representation of women as shakti has been accommodated in the Indian patriarchal society through religion, their status in society is defined by the laws of Manu. As devis, they are the epitome of power, beauty, and benevolence, revered by men, but as women they are considered second class citizens, economically and socially dependent on men; and b) Social reformists, especially in the thirties and forties, talked mostly about educating women and removing social evils such as polygamy, child marriage, and sati, whereas the need to make women financially empowered was not stressed upon.

As a matter of fact, even during the freedom movement, women's roles were fashioned according to the patriarchal notion of gender. In fact, even Gandhi, while giving a clarion call to women to join the movement asked them to 'sacrifice like Sita'. The constant reinforcement of their 'traditional' image and a misplaced belief that any other role would undermine their role as custodians of Indian culture and tradition prevented them from progressing.

Journalist Madhukar Upadhyay believes that except for Gandhi and Nehru, the others did not provide the kind of leadership that was expected of them. Women never got the support. 'Had there been, after Gandhi, two to three more tall leaders for another two generations fighting for women's rights, things would have been different.'[1] An article by Dwijendra Nath Thakur highlights an important point that in the West the 'notion of "self" rests in competitive individualism where people are described as "born free yet everywhere in chains", by contrast in India the individual is usually considered to be just one part of the larger social collective, dependent for its survival upon cooperation and self-denial for the greater good'.[2] Thus, women's participation in the freedom movement, according to Ivan John, was 'for the purpose of that common agenda of freedom for the country and Gandhiji's call, of course. And because they idolized Gandhiji and his values and what he was fighting for, they came out and participated and fought along with everybody else. But as soon as that goal was achieved, they went back into the kitchen.'[3]

John's statement speaks volumes when seen in context of women's issues. During the British Raj, it was easy for women to identify the outsider as the enemy and fight him. It was Indians vs British. But post-Independence, as women had never thought in terms of gender inequality, there were no visible enemies.

Consequently, one finds that in the initial decades after Independence, the involvement of middle class, educated women in nation-building was almost negligible. The concept of 'feminism' as understood by the West was missing in India. Here, a woman was considered to be the anchor of the family, one who kept the family together, produced heirs, and inculcated traditional and cultural values in them.

Another critical point made by Thakur is that India being a heterogenic society has multiple patriarchies, and hence multiple feminisms. This means feminism in India has a different orientation. 'It has changed over time in relation to historical and cultural realities, levels of consciousness, perceptions and actions of individual women and women as a group,' says Thakur. This is why perhaps Indian feminists have resorted to carving out a separate identity for feminism in the country.

Since the reform movements of the nineteenth century, one encounters different phases of feminism in India. The #MeToo movement brought to the surface the inherent divisions among feminists in India, as they failed to raise a unified voice against the sexual exploitation of women. Indian feminism is layered: There are moderate feminists, radical feminists, Marxist feminists, cultural feminists, and Caste (Dalit) feminists; and they all fight for different things.

Writing on the different waves of feminism India witnessed, Srila Ray raises some pertinent questions: What is feminism; and, more importantly, who gets to define it? 'The Indian case is evocative of a more general and global predicament that contemporary feminism seems to find itself in,' she writes. 'Across the north and the south, there is a new visibility, potency, and legitimacy to feminist knowledges, affects, and struggles, but there is also an intensification of internal contestation, charge, and conflict. If feminists are unable to respond in a unified voice to sexual violence, then they are also faced with an increased backlash from patriarchal forces, not to mention the threat of "co-option" from external agents, such as the state, the market, neo-liberal capitalism, and right-wing nationalisms (Farris and Rottenberg 2017).'[4]

Feminism as a concept, therefore, does not have a single definition. It incorporates different beliefs and varies from person to person, based on the belief they follow. For example, for a liberal feminist, progress is measured by the number of women occupying positions of power earlier dominated by men. The emphasis is on social equality. A liberal feminist would rather change existing laws and create opportunities for women than bring about a change in society. In contrast, socialist feminists work towards reforming the society. They associate women's oppression to the Marxist ideology of exploitation, and equate domestic work, marriage, and childcare to the exploitation of women by a patriarchal system.

Marx viewed women's oppression as a product of economic, social, and political structures of capitalism. Marxist sociologists maintained that the development of class society resulted in exploitation of the proletariat by the bourgeoisie, which in turn led to the oppression of women. Marx believed that once liberation from class oppression was achieved, gender oppression would also come to an end. However, not all socialist feminists subscribe to this view.

A third category is of radical feminists who, similar to socialist feminists, strive to bring about equality in society by bringing in significant social change.[5]

After the initial phase of feminism, where social reforms were introduced and women started talking about political participation and their role in independent India, the decades following Independence saw a lull in women's development. Despite more women enrolling in schools and colleges, their status in society remained unchanged. They were still economically dependent and socially deprived.

The first feminist movement in post-Independence India that created national headlines was the 1972 Anti-Price Rise Movement in Bombay. War and drought had crippled the Indian economy, leading to escalating prices for essential commodities. This was the time when black marketeers ruled, and hoarding had become a menace. By 1972, the economic situation of the country had worsened to the extent that women were forced to come out on the streets to protest. These were educated middle-class women who were joined by those from the working class. In September, representatives from seventy women's organizations collaborated and formed the Mehengai Pratikar Smyukta Samiti (Anti-Price Rise Women's United Front) to fight rising costs under the joint leadership of Mrinal Gore of the Socialist Party, and Ahilya Ranganekar of the CPI-M (Communist Party of India-Marxist). Women from all walks of life, and different political groups, were invited to join the movement. From deputations to ministers to meetings and conferences, gheraos and dharnas, all possible avenues were tried but to no avail. The demonstrations continued for three years.

The Anti-Price Rise Movement gathered new momentum in 1973 when prices of milk increased, prompting women to enter the government-owned Aarey Milk Colony and stop the trucks from leaving. 'They accused the government of progressively reducing the fat content in the milk' to charge a higher price and sell low fat milk. Thirty women gheraoed the agricultural minister on 17 January 1973 for more than four hours, and demanded a price reduction. Further, they asked for his resignation, 'who according to them, was in league with the affluent sectors of society'.[6]

The unique ways in which the protests were carried out demonstrated women's prowess as revolutionaries in their own right. In February 1974, women gathered at around 1,000 places in the city of Mumbai and expressed their agitation by, simultaneously, beating thalis with rolling pins, sounding a warning to the government and a wake-up call to other women to rise against injustice.

It was a movement by the women for the women, and it had continued for three years. Though it could not accomplish much, the movement did succeed in drawing the middle-class women out of their comfort zones to demand and fight for what was rightfully theirs. Also, it busted the myth that women had neither interest nor any voice in political matters as men did.

However, what it failed to do was highlight the issue of female oppression. As Radha Kumar observes, 'Neither of them (Anti-Price Rise and Nav Nirman movements) seem to have asked, for example, why an increase in domestic expenditure should be the concern primarily of women rather than men, and to this extent they seem to have accepted that the family was women's sphere. Nor do they seem to have challenged women's role as consumers rather than producers, or to have asked why the family should be tended as a unit of consumption rather than production.'[7]

The fact that women offered bangles to officials to signify their unworthiness for public office seemed to reiterate rather than challenge patriarchal typecasting of women. With the declaration of Emergency, the movement came to an end, but it did manage to initiate a change in society.

While a beginning had been made, there were larger issues that remained unaddressed—violence against women being one of them. It existed then and it exists now. Earlier, there was no legal protection given to women against physical abuse, but now there are laws that can be availed. That women are unaware or don't approach the law, fearing disgrace, is another matter.

It was the Mathura rape case of 1978 that pointed out the urgency of addressing this issue. Mathura, a fourteen-year-old Adivasi girl, was brought to a local police station for questioning regarding a family dispute. She was in a relationship with a boy and was planning to elope with him. While in custody, she was raped by the two officers in charge of the investigation.

Despite being uneducated and poor, Mathura filed a case against her perpetrators. The Sessions Judge found no satisfactory evidence that proved that Mathura was a minor when the incident took place. The court found Mathura's testimony 'riddled with falsehood and improbabilities' and came to the conclusion that though she had had sexual intercourse in the police station, rape could not be proved. Further, the court noted that she was 'habituated to sexual intercourse' and in all probability would have surrendered herself to the constable, but fearing that her aunt and lover would get angry with her, she pretended to sound virtuous before them. Based on this judgement, the District Judge acquitted the appellants. The High Court, however, reversed the Sessions Court's order on the grounds that, as both the accused were strangers, it was highly unlikely that Mathura would make any overtures to them. Thus, the High Court termed the intercourse rape.

The matter reached the Supreme Court (September 1979) that reversed the High Court judgement on the basis of reasonable doubt. The Supreme Court judgement was based on three factors: firstly, Mathura did not resist or call out for help while she was being violated; secondly, there were no visible signs of physical assault on her body; and thirdly, the two-finger test revealed that she was 'habituated to sexual intercourse'. The court also found the girl to be untruthful as she reportedly changed her statement filed in the FIR against one of the accused during the trial. Hence, it pronounced the accused not guilty.

The verdict created uproar in the country. Feminist groups organized a nationwide anti-rape campaign through demonstrations, poster marches, street plays, and public meetings, and sent petitions to Members of Legislative Assembly and the prime minister. It was one of the most defining feminist movements of the time. Their biggest objection was regarding the 'two-finger test', which, for a long time, was the only way to prove that a woman had been raped. During the test, a doctor would insert two fingers inside the vagina of the victim to check whether the hymen had been ruptured. Going by the number of fingers admitted and the elasticity of the hymen, the doctor would then say whether the woman was 'habituated to sex' or not.

The verdict overlooked two major issues. First, to assume hymen could only get ruptured through sexual intercourse was medically incorrect, unscientific, and illegal. And second, it was presumed by the sitting judge that a woman could have sex only after marriage. The bench totally disregarded consensual pre-marital sex.

Appalled by the callousness with which the case was handled by the courts, women came out in large numbers to protest the verdict. These were educated middle class women who, seeing the indignity suffered by the victim, questioned both the method as well as the verdict, which seemed to question the morality of the victim, resulting in victim shaming.

Recounting the incident and how it brought about changes on rape laws, writer Nishtha Shanti states that the 'courts went so far as to say that since Mathura was "habituated" to sexual intercourse, she perhaps initiated sexual intercourse, seduced the police officers, and then came out and cried rape in an effort to seem "virtuous" in front of her brother and partner'.[8]

Widespread opposition eventually forced the central government to amend rape laws. In 1983, a new category was added to the criminal law dealing with rape with the following directives:

1. Courts would presume that a woman saying she did not consent to sexual intercourse was telling the truth.
2. In-camera rape trials were to be conducted as closed proceedings and identity of the victims would not be revealed.
3. Custodial rape was clearly defined, and the burden of proof was shifted from the accuser to the accused.
4. It was made clear that henceforth women could not be called to the police station before sunrise and after the sunset.

As both incidents cited above portray, feminism was gaining ground in India and was addressing issues related to patriarchy as well. Yet, it failed to emerge as an organized movement that represented women from all sections of society. Not only were the feminists divided on ideology, but their emotional needs and desires also varied considerably.

The feminist movement of the seventies and eighties was inherently middle-class in character. The women participating in the movement were educated and essentially from urban areas. They shifted the focus of the movement from women's practical gender needs, which centred around material inequality, as propagated by the Left, to more strategic gender interests like violence against them.

Nineties' liberalization had a significant impact on the feminist movement in India: it resulted in the rise of state feminism. Through legal reforms, women were provided the opportunity to participate in governance. However, the move led to rising concerns that it could further 'domesticate' gender. 'Concerns around the implications of state feminism were most evident in legal reforms to combat violence against women. Besides the fact that very little was achieved in the realm of law enforcement, feminists argued that such reforms inadvertently increased the power of the state, while reinforcing not just patriarchal, but also class–caste norms and normativities,' writes Ray. [9]

The issues related to caste and religion also created a problem for feminists as they were neither aware nor equipped to deal with them. The trials of Dalit women were not limited to gender, they stemmed from caste oppression too. And in the majority of cases, Dalit women faced persecution from upper caste women. Similarly, in the case of Muslim women, gender oppression was often cloaked in religious diktats and discrimination. The feminists of the seventies considered religion to be detrimental to women's rights, as was seen in the arguments regarding women wearing burqa or hijab. However, when it came to the Muslim Personal Law, they were reluctant to voice their opinion. After the Supreme Court judgement on the

Shah Bano case on 22 August 2017, though, women's organizations fought for Muslim women's rights.

One major drawback that hampered the growth of radical and socialist feminists was that they imposed their ideas on women, unmindful of their preferences. They visualized the modern woman as someone who challenged the traditional role ascribed to women, who were career-oriented and 'modern' in outlook. They assumed that the educated middle-class women would subscribe to their view.

John agrees. 'Ultimately, it boils down to what a woman wants.' He recalls his former principal Ananda telling him that 'if a woman wants to be a homemaker, because she desires so, then why do you want to label her as a traditionalist...You are casting judgement on another woman who wants to be a homemaker, who wants to look after her family.'[10]

The problem with radical feminists was that they wanted women to adhere to their definition of a 'modern' and 'liberated' woman.

There was a significant difference between the feminist movements of pre- and post-Independence India. While the former essentially focused on social reforms, the latter raised issues of gender equality, questioned gender-based division of labour, and fought against the stereotypical representation of women as envisaged by patriarchy. Though issues of domestic violence and abuse of women by other women in the family were raised by feminist groups, instances of female infanticide and dowry-related deaths continued unabated. And marital rape was not recognized as a crime (as of the writing of this book, there is still no law against marital rape in India).

Above all, most middle-class women were not aware of their rights as individuals. Many are unaware of them even today. Steeped in traditions and bound by family honour, middle class women, despite being educated, did not have the courage to break free and start anew, as Anandibai Joshi had done. What was required was a change in the mindset of people, especially women, which was hard to come by. It has still not.

13

Middle Class Politics from 1947–91

'Subjects follow their king: they are heathen if the king be irreligious; sinners if the king be a sinner and normal if their king be normal. As the king so the subjects…'

These lines from Chanakya's *Arthashastra* (267) aptly describe the current political mood of the country as it did more than three-quarters of a century ago, soon after India gained independence.

What makes the period between Independence and economic liberalization interesting is the way middle class thinking shifted from a socialistic outlook to revolutionary Marxist ideology to, finally, Hindu majoritarianism. It needs to be kept in mind that the middle class, during this period, was gradually expanding, and new categories were being formed that espoused different ideologies and represented different interests. State emphasis on education had led to lower castes and backward communities getting assimilated into the lower-middle class, leading to new socio-political formations, as was seen in the rise of Dalit political groups, that gained firm footing during this period.

As we saw earlier, senior journalist Madhukar Upadhyay feels that the shift to the right started much before Independence. 'If you look at the literature of that period…Much before the existence of the RSS, the literature was talking about the right-wing in terms of hatred towards Muslims. One such example is Bankim Chandra Chatterjee's *Anand Math*. It was only after Gandhi came into the picture that Premchand and others started writing about assimilation.'[1]

He theorizes that the Partition, in fact, stalled the move towards the right. 'The instinct of survival stopped the movement towards the right, which had started much before Independence, for a generation or two. When they (the middle class) got back on their feet, they reestablished themselves, and it came back. That's how I understand it and see it. It was temporarily halted by two things: Independence, led by Gandhi, and the Partition, which led to violence. In survival, the identity becomes secondary, money is more important.'[2]

However, there were other reasons that resulted in, if not stalling, then definitely slowing down the shift to the extreme right. Foremost among them was Gandhi's assassination. It stemmed the tide of religious fanaticism taking over the country post-Partition. Gandhi's death revived his principles in a middle class that was still influenced by the manner in which Independence was gained. The other reason was the ban imposed on the RSS on 4 February 1948, which lasted for eleven months. It was, however, the association with the assassination that cost the RSS dearly. It made the organization unpopular with the masses, who considered Gandhi a Mahatma.

Political leaders, though coming from different ideologies, presented a united front. In fact, Nehru's first cabinet included members from the Hindu, Muslim, Christian, Sikh, and Parsi communities. Apart from that, there were two members from the Dalit community and a woman cabinet minister too. Shyama Prasad Mukherjee, who served as the president of the Hindu Mahasabha from 1943–46, also found space in the Cabinet, though he later resigned and formed his own party, the Bharatiya Jana Sangh.

What political and economic greed could do to a people had become crystal clear under the 200-year British rule. Which is why, perhaps, despite having different ideologies, leaders of the time collaborated in their fight against imperialism. In essence, freedom was the result of a cumulative effort by multiple interests, which became part of Nehru's first Cabinet. It was, however, his vision that not only shaped the country's economy but impacted society as well. In a 1929 speech at the Lahore Congress after taking over the presidency of the Indian National Congress, Nehru shared his vision:

> I must frankly confess that I am a socialist and a republican and am no believer in kings and princes, or in the order which produces the modern kings of industry, who have greater power

over the lives and fortunes of men than even the kings of old, and whose methods are as predatory as those of the old feudal aristocracy. We must realise that the philosophy of socialism has gradually permeated the entire structure of society the world over and almost the only points in dispute are the pace and the methods of advance to its full realisation. India will have to go that way too if she seeks to end her poverty and inequality, though she may evolve her own methods...[3]

Nehru was inspired by the teachings of Marx and Lenin, however, he rejected the rigidity and violence attached to them, believing that the Marxist dogma was incompatible with the atomic age. This is why he opted for socialism.[4]

A report in the *Economic & Political Weekly*, published in 1964 analyzed the man behind the making of modern India—Jawaharlal Nehru. Nehru, said the report, abhorred ideas that ceased to grow with changing times. He believed that 'men as well as ideas should continuously grow with the changing environment which shapes them'.[5]

Why the Bolshevik Revolution appealed to the Indian middle class, according to S. Irfan Habib, was because it symbolized victory against oppression. He believes that in the current times, the ideology may not be 'very attractive'.[6] This was not the case in the struggle against colonialism, so 'Marxism came in very handy'. These ideologies, he believes, played a 'major role' in that phase to fight against oppression, poverty, and for rights, economic as well as social.[7]

Nehru belonged to the modern world; this was evident in his persona as well as his thinking. He knew that India would have to undergo industrialization if it had to grow, and do so at a fast pace, in a world becoming increasingly commercial. And this became a major point of contention between Gandhi and Nehru. Gandhi considered industrialization to be the root cause of the exploitation of the poor, whereas Nehru thought it to be the shortest and quickest way to alleviate poverty.

As the *EPW* report states, 'Nehru's mind was quite made up by the end of the thirties on industrialisation based on modern science and technology as the only radical cure for India's economic problems and since industrialisation had to subserve a social purpose, it had to be carried out in a socialist framework.'[8] It was Nehru's determination that resulted in socialism being accepted by the Congress party as well as the masses. And that became the political stance of the people, especially the middle class.

For the middle class, the formation of a welfare state was a welcome act. State intervention in the services sector and the nationalization projects it undertook created a need for skilled workers. This necessitated the growth of science and technology, administration and management, and education in general. The expansion of media, transport, and communication systems created opportunities for white collar workers. And as the functions of the state became more complex and secretariats expanded, new departments were created, making further additions to the white-collar, bureaucratic workforce.

Journalist Nagesh Prabhu states that 'during the 15-year period 1956–70, which was marked by the launch of the second Industrial Policy and Green Revolution, the public sector (central, state, local, and quasi-government bodies) provided employment to nearly 5.1 million people while the organized private sector absorbed 1.7 million people'.[9]

By the late 1960s, however, the disillusionment of the middle class with the state had started setting in. Nehru's missteps on the China and Kashmir issues, combined with the exigencies of the wars in 1962 and 1965 with China and Pakistan, led to a sort of disenchantment of the middle class with the Gandhi-Nehru philosophy. The bitter defeat in the 1962 Indo-China war had proved that idealism alone was not enough to fight for a place in the world. Also, the war shattered the myth of security and stability that the middle class thought had been achieved. Nehru's death not only marked the end of an era but left a void in ideology-based politics. The Left tried to fill in this void, as was seen in the growing influence it had over the masses, especially in Tripura, West Bengal, and Kerala. But by the turn of the century, it was a spent force.

The Indian middle class started participating actively in politics from the first half of the nineteenth century, with the rise of the bhadralok in Bengal. The reform movements initiated by them marked their presence on the socio-political platform of the country. The formation of the Congress made it official. Most of the leaders belonged to this class. Hence, the sway they held over the masses, especially students, was tremendous.

During the freedom movement, students played an important role in providing manpower for campaigns, street demonstrations, and carried out other movement-related activities. American author and researcher Philip G. Altbach chronicles the political lives of students pre- and post-Independence. He highlights two critical points: first, students who participated in the national movement largely came from urban middle and upper-middle classes and were upper caste, as lower caste and poor from rural areas did not have access to higher education; and second, perhaps more crucial, was the changing nature of the student movement, which started getting influenced by factors of caste, class, and religion. 'With a few isolated exceptions, the student movement in India has been unable to regain its sense of militant unity and ideological purpose,' observes the author. Students developed 'more active interest' in politics in the initial years of the twentieth century 'as the Congress grew more militant'. 'The articulate and militant nationalism of the Congress appealed to the students because it provided the opportunity for dramatic political action and promised speedy independence for India. The Congress leadership was based in the college-trained intelligentsia, but the influence of radical thought on the growing working class gave it added strength.'[10]

The first major agitation by students was during the 1920 Non-cooperation Movement. During the anti-Simon protests, Wilson College students, in erstwhile Bombay, played a significant role. They carried out a signature campaign against the Simon Commission and distributed pamphlets urging people to boycott it. Interestingly, the then principal, Rev. John Mackenzie, supported the students. And when the police came to arrest them, Mackenzie didn't let them enter the college premises. On 5 September 1930, the students unfurled the tricolour on the college building.

By 1936, an All India Students' Federation had been formed, and students from the middle class had become very active in politics. Post-Independence, however, student politics underwent a transformation. It lost its nationalistic outlook and was reduced to becoming a tool in the hands of political parties—the formation of the National Students' Union of India (NSUI), the student wing of the Congress party, and Akhil Bharatiya Vidyarthi Parishad (ABVP), the student wing of the BJP, being in point.

Altbach lists two main reasons for this transformation. First was the absence of any clear-cut ideology. Prior to 1947, there was a single goal in front of students: to oust the British from the Indian subcontinent. After India became independent, there was suddenly a vacuum as far as student revolutionaries were concerned. Even political leaders, who had encouraged them to participate in the freedom movement earlier, now reversed their position and asked them to 'stay out of politics' and concentrate on 'acquiring skills required for national development'.[11]

The second factor impacting the students' federation was its diversification. The expansion of education saw a number of new colleges and universities being opened post 1947. According to the statistics provided by Altbach, 'between 1950-60, the number of college students increased from 263000 to 645000. In 1966, more than 1094000 students were enrolled in about 2565 colleges'.[12] This increasing number led to the diversification of the student community as youngsters from lower caste, lower-middle, and working classes joined in, making it heterogeneous in nature. Not only were these entrants lacking in experience in activism, but their thought-process was also very different from that of the existing federation members. The new students did not want to jeopardize their careers for politics, so they stayed out of it.

Professor Sudhakar Solomon Raj, a retired Political Science professor from Wilson College, Mumbai University, currently heading its Mass Media department, presents a different view. The 1960s witnessed a rather crucial development in the form of the Naxalite movement, which captured the imagination and attention of the students who were seeking a cause to fight for. These idealistic youths found their answers in Marxism, and they joined the leftists in their fight for peasant rights. 'The students' body was very strong, and all of them (members) came from the middle class,' says Sudhakar, talking about the involvement of the middle class in politics and its leaning towards the Left. 'Even if you see the 1967 Naxalite movement started by Charu Majumdar, Kanu Sanyal, Jangal Santhal, etc., a lot of middle-class students studying in esteemed colleges and universities joined the movement. So, definitely, until the eighties there was a very active political space. That's one. Second, even if you look at the teachers' union, it began somewhere in the seventies. And it was completely manned by a middle class Left of the centre.'[13]

For the students brought up on stories of the freedom struggle, the Naxalite movement seemed to be their moment to effect a change in society. They were inspired to join the movement. Posters of Naxalbari adorning the walls of colleges in Calcutta and Delhi were a common site. A dated report in *Indian Express* states that Charu Mazumdar 'took a number of steps as well to entice students into joining the Naxal movement. He declared that the revolution was not just for the rural masses but rather a fight against everyone who was a "class enemy", which included university teachers, businessmen, police and, of course, the government. Naxalites took over Jadavpur University and Calcutta University. Presidency College in Calcutta and St. Stephens in Delhi became hotbeds for Naxalite activities'.[14]

Till Nehru was alive, his persona loomed large over the country. As a result, even though some of his policies were not well-received by the masses, they did not oppose them openly. But after his death, political atmosphere in the country changed, not only in the corridors of power but amongst the masses too. Famines and wars took their toll as the economy tanked. Shrinking resources and increasing population led to widespread discontentment among the middle classes. The diversification of the middle class also impacted its political outlook. Spread of education among the lower castes and Muslims started a process of upward mobility among them, too.

The 1969 split in Congress led to the rise of Indira Gandhi on the Indian political scene. It also marked the beginning of cult politics, which was seen during the Emergency. The war with Pakistan in 1971 and the creation of Bangladesh showed Indira's prowess as a politician. 'The problem with war is that it has a huge cost to the economy,' says Sudhakar. 'So from 1972 onwards, India suffered from stagflation. In 1973, there was this huge oil shock where, because of the 1973 war, oil prices went up four times. I remember the price of oil before October was 95 paise a litre, which went to ₹3.75. That almost four-fold increase was a huge shock for a lot of families.'[15] The 1970s were years of turmoil, for the Indian politics as well as society. The fallout of the 1971 war was rising discontentment among the masses, especially the middle class. By 1974, the country was in chaos. Food scarcity and rising prices led to demonstrations, looting, and arson, leaving almost a dozen people dead in Gujarat. There was already displeasure in the state over neglect by the central government, due to the absence of any big projects in the first Five-Year Plan, added to that was widespread perception that resources were being diverted to Maharashtra, this led to a Maha-Gujarat movement. The Navnirman Andolan, started by students, was a culmination of this rhetoric, and soon spread to the rest of the country. Once again, the middle class proved its political might as it answered the call given by veteran socialist leader Jayaprakash Narayan (JP) to fight against the Indira government over corruption, rising inflation, and recession. Bihar became the centre of action as the movement took the shape of Sampoorna Kranti, demanding the resignation of the prime minister.

The situation worsened with rising unrest among the workers of Indian Railways over pay rise and the regulation of working hours for drivers. The unrest soon took the form of protests, headed by the then union leader of the Railways, George Fernandes. He called for a nationwide rail strike. For almost three weeks, the lifeline of India remained shut as there were no drivers, station masters, guards, track clerks, etc. 'Better jail than rail' was Fernandes's cry. The Indira government complied. But she ensured that the unions agreed to running goods trains carrying essential supplies and at least one passenger train on trunk routes. As the situation deteriorated further, Indira Gandhi declared Emergency in the country. The year was 1975.

The middle class played a pivotal role in these agitations as it 'brought a managerial flair to mass agitations often marked by a high-level organisation, a clever use of communication technology and marketing gimmicks'.[16]

One of the uniting factors among the different middle classes was their resistance to the advancement of the deprived sections of society. Thus, mass agitations usually expressed the grievances of the upper and middle sections of society, and strived to expand economic opportunities for them.

As per an *Economic Times* report dated 10 April 1975, there was a growing disillusionment among the middle class against the movement led by JP even before the declaration of Emergency. 'The movement led by Mr Jayaprakash Narayan is not making much headway—and that is nowhere near achieving its goals of arresting corruption in public life and radically reforming the electoral, educational and administrative systems.'[17] JP's main strength came from the middle class. But it had started showing signs of discontentment. The movement was to be a 'total revolution' brought on by peaceful agitations. However, by the mid-sixties, as mentioned, the middle class had started becoming disillusioned with the Nehru-Gandhi philosophy. As we enter the seventies, we see a generational shift happening as well. Overall, the middle class was now more attracted to the philosophy of armed struggle as espoused by the likes of Chandrashekhar Azad, and the Gandhian values of non-cooperation and non-violence were limited to a certain section of people who had marched with the Mahatma in the fight for Independence.

In 1947, despite the blow of the Partition, there was euphoria among the people that now that the enemy was out, India would change for the better. However, the change proved to be elusive. To start with, the British had left behind an almost empty treasury. Added to that were the wars with Pakistan and China, and the twin droughts of 1965–66, followed by famines. Rising prices, high unemployment rate, black-marketeering, and a rapidly increasing population, all contributed to the frustrations of the people, especially farmers, who were in great distress. By the end of the seventies, peasant leaders were forming their own parties.[18]

To a disgruntled middle class of the sixties and seventies, the armed approach to achieve their goal was more appealing however, much to their chagrin, JP's movement was launched by peaceful agitations. Also, with the opposition divided, it did not see any alternative to the Congress.

The fact that the middle class acted purely keeping its own interests in mind was displayed when the government crushed the train strike brutally. In a biography of Indira Gandhi, journalist and author Inder Malhotra gives a detailed account of the way the agitators were dealt with.

> Over 20000 strikers were arrested; large numbers were mercilessly beaten up; and families of absentee workers were summarily thrown out of their railway quarters. The ruthlessness of the state machinery was widely known, but most of her middle class countrymen, including those who accused her of authoritarianism, applauded Indira for her 'firmness' in dealing with the railway strike. Their dichotomy

> was easily explainable. Many, if not most, of them were also sticklers for all the Westminster norms being observed in Delhi and were angry when Indira failed to do so. But they also wanted the trains to run regularly and did not want aggressive trade unionists to hold the country, or any business for that matter, to ransom.[19]

The Emergency has been an indelible black mark against the Congress. Surprisingly, once it was declared, the middle class accepted it without any resistance. It did come as a shock to politicians and the public alike, but as the situation returned to normalcy, it was, in a way, welcomed by the middle class, which was tired of agitations, protests, and strikes. Reminiscing about the day Emergency was declared, Malhotra, who was in Bombay at that time, says, 'When we drove (towards the *Times of India* office), I was surprised to see that there was no protest anywhere in the city. In the first days of the emergency, the same middle class that was protesting with JP against her was now in support of the Emergency! This was because, after three years of chaos, the public was seeing order. I was shocked.'[20]

It is not easy to evaluate the role of the middle class in either society or politics, but, for the most part, middle class loyalties lie with the state. It can be hypocritical, which is why one sees it providing leadership to the working-class movements yet at the same time supporting the bourgeoisie. Misra explains it thus: 'In the Indian situation, you see the middle class always supports the arguments of fascism. And it gives its support at every level, local level, family level, caste level, community level and the national level...but at the same time, the middle class also, as a civil society leader, lends support to democracy and the democratic argument.' This is why it does not develop any deep attachment to any political outfit.[21]

The middle class of the initial decades of independent India was identified as the 'Nehruvian civil service-oriented salariat, short on money but long on institutional perks'.[22] This explains why, despite heavy criticism of the government, most of the civil servants and government employees refused to resign. Public employment meant job security and a pensionable income, which were politically determined. Added to it was the charm of social prestige, a much-sought-after credential by the middle class.

This phase in Indian politics saw three major developments that influenced the middle class immensely: first, the creation of personality cults, which started with Indira Gandhi. Her bold decision to support East Pakistan in its struggle for independence at a time when the country was facing enormous problems of its own may have generated criticism, yet the victory over Pakistan brought her to the centre with a thumping majority. Then came the nuclear test at Pokhran. India had refused to sign the Nuclear Non-Proliferation Treaty in 1968. On 18 May 1974, India conducted its first nuclear test at Pokhran, sending shock waves around the world. The secrecy with which Project Smiling Buddha was completed (even the CIA was in the dark about it) added to Indira's persona as a fearless and determined leader, which made India a part of the exclusive Nuclear Club. That made a big impact on the minds of the middle class, which thrived on nationalism.

One key error on the part of Indira was to steer away from the traditional Congress strategy that took the middle path and represented all segments of society. She took on an approach that favoured the poor and called for 'Garibi Hatao', meaning 'remove poverty', along with the land reform programmes. These policies assured her an electoral victory but eroded the Congress's base among the lower-middle class. Also, increasing corruption in government ranks didn't help either, as the government failed to fulfil its promises, leading to general middle class apathy.

The second major development was the depoliticization of the middle class. The middle class favoured stability and security, as can be seen in their preference of public sector jobs and continued in one job for life. And this is precisely the reason they stopped raising their voices and agitating for social causes. 'If you look at the colleges, by the nineties social issues began to take a backseat.

Families were also telling the students to focus more on their studies. Maybe depoliticization starts around this time,' says Sudhakar.[23]

But that was not all. The behaviour of the middle class underwent a highly critical change during this phase. In that, it stopped questioning, even if the state was in the wrong. Sociologist Anand maintains that the deterioration of the politics of protest started during the Emergency. People started learning to 'live in silence'. For instance, even to ask for a salary revision, they could not take to the streets as they didn't feel safe. 'It is a very insecure middle class that can't resist market and state forces and lives a very hypocritical existence. Their own thinking is very radical, but when it comes to expressing it in public, they remain quiet.'[24]

The third, and perhaps the most crucial development was the growing influence of right-wing philosophy on the masses. Though the RSS had been banned as a political organization after Gandhi's assassination, it had continued working at the grassroots. The ban was lifted in 1952. The same year, the RSS laid the foundation of its first school in Gorakhpur, Uttar Pradesh.

But it was not just the RSS that was using religion to establish itself politically. Political leaders in general, as per Sudhakar, began to be overtly religious. 'Starting with Indira Gandhi. She would go to temples....' He maintains that one of the major contributors to the rise in religious fervour was the telecast of the TV series Ramayana and Mahabharata on Doordarshan.

'That created a very strong Hindu sensibility. That went on for more than a year. So your socialization is also focused a lot on the Hinduization. If you look at the Babri Masjid issue, the actual incident (a group of 50–60 people broke into the gated compound of the mosque and placed the idols of Lord Ram and Goddess Sita underneath the central dome) happened in 22 December 1949, but the BJP and the VHP revived it in 1988. And those days, Gujarat saw a lot of riots. If you look at the incidents of communal riots, they became much higher in the eighties and nineties, especially between 1988–93 when the number touched 3000 or something.

So, there were communities getting communalized. Ghettoization is mostly a phenomenon of the nineties. Once the ghettoization of spaces happened, the mindset followed.'[25]

By the time Rajiv Gandhi became the prime minister, the middle class had started showing a deep interest in politics. Still, it did not consider politics a career option. Rajiv's appeal was his clean image and progressive thinking. He introduced fresh faces in the Congress party, much to the delight of the middle classes, and brought in economic reforms to bolster the regressing economy. The focus was now on technological development rather than being a welfare state. However, he could not survive for long. The Bofors scandal cost him his seat.

By the late eighties, the BJP's rising rhetoric over Ramjanmabhoomi had started taking effect on the middle-class psyche, especially the urban upper-caste middle class that had been critical of the Congress policy of appeasement towards Muslims and the backward communities. They wanted an alternative to Congress that would represent their interests. The BJP's Hindutva agenda seemed to provide just that.

From a totally socialistic outlook in the initial decades of new independent India to an extreme right position, the Indian middle class saw a tremendous transformation between 1947 and 1992, which culminated with the Babri Masjid demolition. This was as much a result of the ideological bankruptcy of the political parties as it was of the growing diversity of the middle classes themselves. Growing competition and decreasing resources; rising corruption across all levels of government administration from clerks right to MLAs, MPs, and ministers; increasing differences between communities based on caste, religion, region and gender; and the government's failure to address the issues of a growing economic crisis all contributed to the rising frustrations of the middle class. How these frustrations manifested themselves in middle class nature became clear as India progressed towards the twenty-first century.

PART III

From Liberalization to the Present

(1991 Onwards)

∽

14

New Economic Policy: Crisis, Management, and Impact

The year 1991 marked the beginning of a new chapter in the socio-economic history of India. The shift from the traditional socialist approach of the Indian economy to a largely capitalist and market-based one has had a deep impact on the economic, political, and social outlook of the Indian middle classes. This effect is manifested in the choices they make as consumers, voters, and custodians of Indian social values and culture. These choices not only affect the market but policymaking as well, at the centre and state governments.

A BBC report on the Indian economy prior to the economic reforms states:

> Before the process of reform began in 1991, the government attempted to close the Indian economy to the outside world. The Indian currency, the rupee, was inconvertible and high tariffs and import licensing prevented foreign goods reaching the market. The labyrinthine bureaucracy often led to absurd restrictions—up to 80 agencies had to be satisfied before a firm could be granted a license to produce and the state would decide what was produced, how much, at what price and what sources of capital were used.[1]

At the time of Independence, the Indian treasury was nearly empty, and, seeing the conditions prevailing at the time, the popular thinking among Western countries was that India would not be able to sustain its independent status. The political leaders of the time had a mammoth task cut out for them: rebuilding a nation from ruins.

Post-Independence India's largely socialist approach to governance led to a closed economy, resulting in policies leaning towards protectionism. State intervention in all businesses at the micro level, especially in the labour and financial markets while protecting the interests of workers and consumers and keeping inequality in check, led to the growth of bureaucratic delays and a lack of incentives. In a bid to promote self-reliance, the emphasis was on import substitution, with the state monitoring industrialization. The public sector formed the bulk of the economy and an exhaustive system of licenses and regulations, plagued by red tape, became a deterrent to establishing new businesses.

The period between 1970 and 1980 witnessed great economic instability and crises around the world, impacting both developed and developing nations. While the world economy started recovering from recession in 1976, the situation deteriorated for developing countries due to rising debts and cutbacks in developmental aid by industrialized nations. In India, the effects of the 1971 war, droughts, and rapid population growth were heightened by the economic pressures of the decade. The big blow came in the nineties though. In 1990, Iraq attacked Kuwait, disturbing the delicate balance of power in the Middle East. The ensuing Gulf war led to an unprecedented increase in crude oil prices. According to an RBI report, the oil imports increased from an average of US$ 287 million per month in June–August 1990 to US$ 671 million per month. To make matters worse, the UN trade embargo on Iraq put a stop to exports to Iraq and Kuwait. The RBI pegs the estimated loss at about US$ 280 million.[2]

Furthermore, recession in industrialized countries and the breakdown of the USSR economy slowed world trade down considerably. Indian exports took a huge hit, while imports were steadily on the rise. A widening trade deficit, declining foreign exchange reserves, and an unmanageable balance of payment situation put India on the verge of defaulting on its external debts.

The enormity of the situation can be judged from a conversation between Deepak Nayyar, the then Chief Economic Advisor to the prime minister, and the Managing Director of IMF, Michel Camdessus. Nayyar had gone to the IMF asking for financial support and had told the director, in no uncertain terms, that 'if the Fund cannot extend a lifeline, we will bring the shutters down'.[3]

By the late 1980s, it had become apparent that the closed, state-controlled economy of India had run its course, and that stringent measures were required to save it from total collapse. It was, however, easier said than done. There was stiff opposition to the economic reforms from old socialist Congressmen as well as the opposition. The BJP had the backing of the traders who resisted foreign competition, the Left was ideologically and theoretically against capitalism and the National Front, which had come to be seen as the voice of the marginalized groups, saw it as the 'abdication of the state's responsibility and its role in upliftment or welfare work'.[4]

Politically, the P. V. Narasimha Rao government was on a slippery wicket. To start with, his was a minority government with a mandate of 244 seats, having the support of the National Front and the Left from the outside. A 'No Confidence' move could have sounded the death knell for the government, yet, Rao managed to survive one in Parliament on 15 July 1991, barely a month after assuming office.

Author Vinay Sitapati describes how Rao managed to pacify voices of dissent both within and outside the party. 'As before, he made use of the threat to the prestige of the nation,' he says, 'urging the Opposition to give up their maximalist ideologies in the face of calamity. He quoted a Sanskrit verse to make his point: "*Sarvanashe samutpanne ardham tyajati panditah* (Faced with total ruin, the wise settle for half)." That same day, on 15th July, 1991, Narasimha Rao asked for the note on industrial policy to be presented before the Cabinet—the final step before a policy is put into effect.'[5]

On the eve of the thirtieth anniversary of the reforms, talking about the necessity of such measures, Dr Manmohan Singh, who was the finance minister and the main architect of the reforms, remarked that they 'unleashed the spirit of free enterprise'. He said, 'The economic liberalization process in 1991 was triggered by an economic crisis that confronted our nation then, but it was not limited to crisis management. The edifice of India's economic reforms was built on the desire to prosper, the belief in our capabilities, and the confidence to relinquish control of the economy by the government.'[6]

The main objectives of the New Economic Policy were to reduce the fiscal deficit and introduce structural reforms in the economy. The drastic measures used to bring about the reforms opened the Indian market for private and foreign players. The new economic model created new opportunities, which resulted in the rise of a new 'liberalized' middle class showing a marked shift from the traditional, simplistic outlook towards consumerism, and promoting a new cultural standard in the process.

A report on the economic crisis of 1991 and its resolution by the RBI states:

> The objective of the reforms was to promote economic growth by reducing government intervention, enhancing domestic competition, and accelerating India's integration with the world economy. The government had already made significant policy changes in several key areas. Specific policy actions in a number of areas—notably industrial deregulation, trade policy, public enterprise reforms, and some aspects of financial sector reforms—were also the basis for a World Bank Structural Adjustment Loan (SAL), as well as sector loans. A number of measures were announced to strengthen competition between the private sector and public enterprises, where de facto monopoly power and soft budget constraints had been the root causes of inefficiency. Specifically, the number of industries reserved exclusively for the public sector was narrowed down to eight (relating to defence production, atomic energy, minerals and railways); the system of monitoring public enterprises was strengthened;

the budget constraints faced by the enterprises were hardened through a reduction in transfers and subsidies from the union budget; and the government announced its intention to sell up to 20.0 per cent of equity in selected public enterprises to mutual funds during 1991–92.[7]

The immediate impact of the reforms was seen in the economic growth of the country. The average annual growth rate increased in a decade from 6.3 per cent (1980–81) to 18 per cent (1991–92), and the GDP increased from 5.6 per cent in 1980–91 to 6.4 per cent in 1992–2001. The end of the 'License Raj',* brought on by liberalization, gave an impetus to local businesses by creating opportunities, besides encouraging competitiveness, in multiple sectors such as the automobile industry, telecommunications, research and development, and others. However, it was the services sector that witnessed unprecedented growth.

Impact on the Middle Classes

The most transforming effect of liberalization was seen on the middle class, which showed a remarkable shift from being a conservative spender to a consumerist. It changed the middle class's relationship with money. Traditionally, the Indian middle class had been an advocate of simplicity (the old middle class, especially in rural areas, still is). It would spend on essentials only, saving part of the income for the future. This was standard practice. Eating at restaurants, even in urban areas, in the 1970s and eighties, was not common practice. The middle class used public transport. Vacation

*The term License Raj was coined by freedom fighter and Swatantra Party founder C. Rajagopalachari to describe the system prevalent before the 1991 economic reforms wherein, due to high restrictions, businesses required approval from up to 70-80 government agencies to obtain licenses to operate in the country. The licenses were difficult to get, which led to increased corruption in the bureaucracy. See 'Explained: What was licence raj and why is India better off without it?', *Business Standard*, 9 August 2023.

meant going to a relative's house where boarding, lodging, and food would be free. Savings were a big part of the middle class budget. After liberalization, all this changed. With new opportunities and job creation, middle class income increased, and the shift to consumerism set in.

In a recent interview on *Lallantop*, author Sara Rai recounted an interesting anecdote: 'When I was a kid, someone asked me once what I wanted to be growing up. My reply was "to be poor"... because money was considered bad in our house. That was the thinking, that was the perception, that was the value system we were growing up with.'[8]

Rai comes from a highly distinguished background. She is the granddaughter of Munshi Premchand, one of the greatest Hindi writers of the twentieth century, whose works showcase the plight of the common man, especially those belonging to the lower-middle and working classes. However, what makes this anecdote most interesting is that it highlights the thought process of the literati of the early twentieth century that mostly came from the lower-middle and middle classes—simple living and high thinking. They celebrated frugality, the path shown by the Mahatma, and before him, scores of other saints. Money was important, but the accumulation of wealth was not approved of. In other words, the life of the average Indian was simple.

The sources of income were limited (the economy was closed and jobs were mostly in the public sector), which in other words meant restricted income. A large portion of this restricted income was spent on covering just the basic needs, such as food and housing. Once that was taken care of, only then was the discretionary income spent on education, clothing, travel, and entertainment. A large chunk of the population was impoverished, which meant that the economic disparity between the poor and the middle classes was much lower. In terms of wealth, such as salaries, assets, investments, etc., most of the middle class was more or less on the same scale.

Though problems were aplenty, the 'contentment quotient' was high because choices were few, and people who could exercise a choice didn't feel the need to do so. For example, students would either take the bus or walk down to the school or college. Private schools were very few, and the bulk of the students went to government-run schools. Only a handful of middle-class people owned a vehicle, or other luxury items such as a television or refrigerator. Telephone was a rarity.

Recalling his school days, Anand Subramanian, a retired bank officer, says, 'You lived in a cluster where everybody would go to the same school, wear the same uniform purchased from the same shop. At best, everybody had the same two-wheeler. Most didn't have that either. Everybody took the school bus; there was no other mode of transportation. And for everybody, the big luxury was a Gold Spot. Nobody had the pocket money to buy anything, so it was out of the question. There wasn't anything for anyone to compare. The kinds of clothes you wore were all the same. It was a very homogenous sort of cluster. Differences were not large…and socially it was a good thing because people were together. As there was no choice (local brands), there was no comparison or competition.'[9]

Subramanian makes a valid point. As the economic disparity between the middle and lower classes was low, there was no social disconnect between them. Controlled prices and equal distribution (ration system) acted as unifying factors between classes. Society was more closely knit. As the economy opened, a culture of consumerism started developing among the middle classes. Anyone who had a decent education flourished. Aspirations grew with per capita income. Maslow's hierarchy states that an individual's behaviour is controlled by five categories of human needs: 1) physiological needs, 2) safety needs, 3) love and belonging needs, 4) esteem needs, and 5) self-actualization needs. Out of these, the first four fall under the basic needs category, and only when these are met can the self-actualization need be fulfilled. Though Maslow's theory has largely been rejected in the past by many scholars due to the limitations of its methodology (for instance, critics argue, that it does not take into account the dynamic factor of human needs or it has an inherent cultural bias or lacks empirical grounding) it does provide a holistic approach to understanding human behaviour in general and middle class, in particular. In fact, the latest research conducted by psychologist Ed Diener of the University of Illinois, reveals that Maslow's theory is largely correct. He put the theory to the test in different countries all over the world and concluded that the needs that Maslow listed were still relevant and universal. What it needs, say experts, is a little enhancement by integrating contemporary elements such as creativity and evolution, relationships and mating, and self-transcendence and future generations.[10]

The order of the needs, however, is not rigid (as Maslow admits), as it is based on external factors and individual preferences. For instance, for the upper-middle class the need for honour is probably more important than the need for love. Or, in the case of the lower-middle class, physiological needs take precedence over the need for belonging. By the seventies, the five-stage hierarchy had expanded to become an eight-tier model, bringing cognitive, aesthetic, and transcendence needs into its ambit.

One sees a tremendous push for self-actualization across all categories and sub-categories of the middle class. This change was driven by two factors: first, liberalization encouraged private players, including foreign investors, to enter the market, which created job opportunities in several verticals. And second, increased competition led to the growth of the manufacturing sector, which, for the first time, presented a choice to customers.

Though not all sectors of the economy saw gains (while the agriculture sector was grossly neglected, manufacturing saw only a marginal increase), the tertiary sector, also called the service sector, and the quaternary sector, which included businesses based on intellectual activities such as education, IT, entertainment, etc., saw remarkable changes in the first decade or so.

In 1994, the government passed the Air Corporations (Transfer of Undertakings and Repeal) Act, which paved the way for private players in the aviation sector. The first to enter the aviation market was Jet Airways. The deregulation also attracted foreign investment, for instance, ModiLuft was a joint venture by industrialist S. K. Modi and Lufthansa, though the airline proved to be a failure and ceased operations in 1996. However, many private airlines have entered this segment since. Similarly, the automobile industry saw a boom as companies like TVS and Hero Honda (in the two-wheeler segment) were started in competition to Bajaj Auto.* Today, the consumer durables market is flush with labels, both domestic as well as foreign, and the customer is spoilt for choice.

So, how did these changes pan out for the middle classes?

One, they created new employment opportunities, especially for the lower-middle and middle classes; and two, they deeply influenced the consumption pattern and consumer behaviour of these classes, thereby driving economic growth.

While delivering a lecture on the middle classes of the past and present in Lucknow on 20 January 2023, Rajesh Misra commented that 'when economists say that the growth of the economy was due to the emergence of the private sector or corporates, they are wrong'. According to him, if seen in class terms, 'globalization resulted in the casualties of the working class, while the corporate bourgeois class gained a lot and, in all this, the middle class played a big role. Globalization led to middle class social mobility. It also changed the nature and characteristic diversity of the middle class'.

The Income Tax Department website provides annual data on each income band and the number of people filing income tax. A comparison between present-day data and decade-old data shows a remarkable increase in the number of tax filers, which means there is an overall increase in middle-class wealth, though in pyramid

*Bajaj Auto was established in November 1945 as M/s Bajaj Trading Corporation Private Limited. It initially imported and sold two- and three-wheelers in India.

form. On the one hand, increased purchasing power of the middle classes is changing age-old notions related to expenditure, and on the other hand, it is altering their economic and social behaviour.

The triple dose of liberalization, privatization, and globalization gave a boost to the GDP growth rate and led to an increase in the country's per capita income. The economic push came not only from foreign investments but from a growing breed of start-ups, too, which were a result of rapid technological development in the country.

This provided an impetus to local businesses by creating opportunities, besides encouraging competitiveness, in multiple sectors such as the automobile industry, telecommunications, research and development, etc. The most significant outcome of liberalization, however, was the expansion of the services sector, especially the information technology industry. One good example is that of Infosys.

The growth of Infosys from a small IT firm to India's second largest software exporter, with a market capitalization of over 6.5 lakh crore, has been hailed as the success story of liberalization. The company was founded by N. R. Narayana Murthy in 1981 along with six other engineers, his colleagues from Patni Computer Systems. Today, it is seen as an embodiment of middle class aspiration and grit. What makes the Infosys story worth recounting is the impact it has had on the middle classes of India.

The Infosys Story

In the 1980s, starting a company was extremely difficult. There were too many processes, and to top it all, securing a loan for a software business was next to impossible. Thus, the initial years of Infosys, prior to liberalization, were fraught with difficulties. 'Banks did not understand software and wanted physical collaterals. We had none, as you know, so term loans and working capital loans from banks just did not exist for our industry,' Murthy recounted.[11]. According to him, it took two to three years and around fifty trips to Delhi for them to acquire the license to import a computer, and by then technology had advanced; manufacturers in the US had released the new version of the disk drive which had 50 per cent more capacity and was priced 30 per cent less.

He explained that during his visit to the Department of Electronics to update the model numbers in the license, the officers advised him against the move suggesting a 'possible inordinate delay' in getting the approval.

It took another year for Murthy to get the model numbers revised in the license, and due to the bureaucratic delay, India was 'at least two generation behind and paid 30-40 percent more for an inferior product'.[12]

The change in the company's fortunes came with the reforms. The success of Infosys had a ripple effect on the economy as well as society. Infosys's success created a demand for professionals from verticals such as information technology and communication, hospitality, healthcare, and education. It brought about a sea change in the education sector too, as institutes included additional subjects like computers and management courses in their curricula. As the demand for these courses increased, several institutions imparting technical and skill-based education mushroomed throughout the country. This boom in the service sector created a plethora of job opportunities for the middle classes.

'Assume that for every job we create in our industry, we create five jobs to support this industry,' says Infosys co-founder Nandan Nilekani. 'That means, in effect, Infosys creates a quarter of a million jobs. The economic impact of that in terms of job creation is significant. The whole idea of economic reforms, which was to reduce the dead hand of government on enterprise, let Indian entrepreneurship bloom, has really been redeemed by us.'[13]

Today, the company, headquartered in Bangalore, has more than 3 lakh employees.[14]

Another interesting development that needs to be highlighted here is the triple boom in technology—Y2K or the year 2000, dotcom boom, and technical advancements in the telecom sector globally—led to a change in the way business was done. In addition to the existing traditional business model, an alternative was created by Infosys that presented India as an outsourcing global hub. The new business model treated the 'whole world as a network of people and finds ways to reallocate work on that network in an optimal fashion. All our customers are going through major change'. The changes were motivated by globalization, technological advancements, and the more number of young people in India and China as compared to the west. The other reason cited was: 'Supply chain technology has made outsourcing to China possible, information technology and telecommunications have made outsourcing to India possible.'[15]

Infosys's unique business model has moved thousands of people from the lower- to the upper-middle class or upper class rungs. In 1994, for the first time in the economic history of India, a corporation introduced an employee stock option plan (ESOP). The plan had two components. The first was performance-oriented, which included peons, drivers, and office boys (founder members were non-eligible), and the second was based on the loyalty and longevity aspects of an employee.

The company has played a huge role in generating wealth for the middle class through its policies. Stories of class IV Infosys employees (those engaged in functions such as housekeeping and security) becoming millionaires are legendary. What made the Infosys ESOP special, according to Murthy, was that the company worked on 'Mahatma Gandhi's principle that every decision should be taken keeping in mind the betterment of the poorest employee'.

> Several peons, who have probably kept their shares are worth at least 10 to 15 crores. My colleague, Kris Gopalakrishnan ensured that every employee who was not part of the 1994 and 1998 ESOPs had at least 10 shares in the company as late as 2008, when he was the CEO. As of date, Infosys has given away 19 percent of outstanding equity, amounting to Rs 1.3 lakh crore today, to its non-founder employees.[16]

These developments from Infosys created a sort of ripple effect as many other companies like Wipro, ICICI Bank, L&T, and Dabur among others followed suit. In 2000–2001, when business process outsourcing (BPO) pioneer Raman Roy was setting up Spectramind, its human resources head offered share ownership to 500 of its employees.[17]

In the eighties and early nineties, the overarching philosophy of the middle classes was that accumulation of wealth led to moral corruption. Infosys shattered this notion, which is why its story needs to be retold every once in a while. Here was a corporation that not only created wealth but was instrumental in distributing it among its employees as well. The ideological takeaway for the middle class from the Infosys business model was that wealth creation was not wrong so long as it was done responsibly, which meant that the sharing of wealth was almost as important as creating it.

It is not that corporations like Tata, Birla, or Godrej do not have employee-friendly policies. They have been at the forefront of India's development since Independence. However, what needs to be seen here is: a) the middle class was buoyed by the fact that a few middle class entrepreneurs could create a highly successful business venture like Infosys; b) there was a change in the mindset regarding the creation of wealth at this time.

The basic goal of a business or corporation is to generate profit, it was true in the sixties, seventies, and eighties, and it is true today. However, corporations also use part of that profit for developmental work, and have employee welfare and corporate social responsibility (CSR) schemes as part of their business model.

The period post liberalization saw tremendous growth in the service sector (not so much in manufacturing). And this growth was led by the middle classes. Manufacturing required many permissions and licences, apart from huge capital, manpower, and availability of land and other resources. As opposed to this, the challenges for the service sector were almost negligible. A license, some hardware, and one's intellectual prowess were enough to start a business. Most of all, the technological advancement fostered an industry where a middle class person, who had the intellectual prowess and was a genuine entrepreneur, could actually become an entrepreneur. Here, India had a big advantage as it had intellectual capital in abundance. In short, it was a marriage between intellectual prowess and global requirements.

Thus, 1991 became a landmark year in the economic history of India. The drastic measures taken by the government to revive the economy led to the emergence of a new middle class (the previous such boom was under the British Raj, as we've seen). This new middle class was based largely in urban areas (metros, tier-two and tier-three cities) and was guided by the diktats of a free market economy, which made it highly competitive by nature, consumerist in behaviour, and aspirational in outlook.

The rise of the middle class has been both the cause and effect of India's economic growth. When income increases, people want to spend more. Increased purchasing power triggers the desire to buy things, which in turn leads to increased spending, though spending habits and consumption patterns change according to one's income.

A 2003 survey by *India Today* magazine reveals that the middle class has 'moved from functional living to a lifestyle of fulfilment'.

> So sweeping—and complex—have been the changes in the spending volume and pattern that the traditional classification of consumers based on income levels (lower, middle and high incomes) has lost some relevance. Instead, experts suggest classifying consumers into four new categories: value conscious, fashion driven, time savers and those who enjoy shopping. Consumers from any income class could fall into any of these four categories. So, even a high income earner could be a value conscious shopper whereas a consumer from the lower income class could be fashion driven.[18]

A middle-class man's basic needs are already taken care of. He has a certain level of comfort in his life, whether it is owning a vehicle, smartphone, computer, or other consumer products, which gives him the freedom to use the discretionary income for his aspirational needs like branded consumer goods, travel, entertainment, etc. A study of the buying patterns of this class has revealed a few interesting aspects: a) buying is no longer need-based and b) it does not depend entirely on the affordability factor.

An upward demand graph indicates that, in the past few decades, the emphasis of the Indian middle class has been on maintaining a standard of living reflective of their 'middleclassness'. But who sets this standard? If the number of advertisements being flashed on a daily basis on television channels, newspapers, internet, and social media are any indication, one would say the media. The middle class is being bombarded with brands, each promising a better life than the other. In essence, this visual imagery is generating a need where there is none. For instance, we have been washing fruits and vegetables in salt water for generations to remove dirt and chemicals. Now we have products that claim to 'naturally clean the vegetables and make them safe for consumption'.

Political scientist Leela Fernandes maintains that 'idealised discourses of the new middle class' have started impacting the consumption practices of individuals both in metropolitan cities as well as smaller towns. She quotes the following example of a shifting pattern of consumption in Gujarat in her research:

> Middle-class status demands a level of consumption that is in tune with the times, and the increased expectations that upward mobility and new consumer styles have brought. When Dharmesh explained to me that one reason Jitesh wants to have a refrigerator is that guests notice it if they don't get ice in their water when they come to visit his house, he touched upon a sensitive point. The 'noticing' is a matter of devaluation. An important reason goods like refrigerators have become 'requirements' is the fact that the maintenance of status among peers requires them.[19]

She maintains that commodities are viewed by the middle class as 'cultural' and 'social' capital that individuals must obtain to elevate themselves up the social ladder. Several groups of middle class might actively try to 'emulate the consumption practices associated with the liberalizing middle class', with families stretching their financial limits to acquire certain commodities as 'symbols of the culture of liberalization'.[20]

Which is why, perhaps, there has been a steady rise in credit culture in India in the past decade or so. Traditionally, India has been a debit card market. However, with new products and services entering the market incessantly with credit options, more and more middle class individuals are availing of this facility. A PWC report providing data on credit card usage states that 'credit card issuance has grown significantly in India at a compound annual growth rate (CAGR) of 20% in the last four years. The number of credit cardholders increased from 29 million in March 2017 to 62 million in March 2021. It has further grown by 26% and 23% respectively, in 2019 and 2020'.[21] However, this credit culture seems more in tune with the urban middle class, as rural India still prefers the traditional mode of transaction.

The picture is clear—markets are flooded with products, with every conceivable brand available to consumers, the demand curve is shooting off the charts, and malls have become a new haven for the middle class—but is it complete?

While the media presents a rather rosy picture of the growth of the Indian economy, what it omits is the grave inequality that has crept into society as a result of liberalization.

In July 2013, while on a visit to India, political activist and philosopher Noam Chomsky was interviewed by the erstwhile news magazine *Tehelka*. When asked what baffled him the most about India, he was categorical in saying that what struck him most was 'the indifference of privileged sectors to the misery of others'.

> You walk through Delhi and cannot miss it, but people just don't seem to see it. Everyone is talking about 'Shining

> India' and yet people are starving. I had an interesting experience with this once. I was in a car in Delhi and with me was (activist) Aruna Roy, and we were driving towards a demonstration. And I noticed that she wasn't looking outside the window of the car. I asked her why. She said, 'If you live in India, you just can't look outside the window. Because if you do, you'd rather commit suicide. It's too horrible. So you just don't look.' So people don't look, they put themselves in a bubble and then don't see it. And those words are from somebody who has devoted her life to the lives of the poor, and you can see why she said that—the misery and the oppression are so striking, much worse than in any country I have ever seen.[22]

A decade later, the picture remains the same. In fact, the demonetization of currency in 2016 and the rather hastily implemented Goods and Services Tax (GST) have aggravated the crisis. 'As talk has grown of India's new Tryst with the Market, the number of people relegated to the margins of our society has also grown dramatically. The convergence of the economics of inequality and the politics of majoritarianism has made India a more divided and unequal society than at any other time in its recent history,' writes Harsh Mander.[23]

Chanda Kathuria, a retired commerce professor from Mumbai University, has been associated with social work through her trust Shikhar Youth Foundation. She echoes the sentiment that the economic growth in the country has been very lopsided. 'The state has given them (the middle classes) a lot of opportunities, but the impact of all these policies in rural and urban areas has been different. In urban areas, these policies have been implemented to a large extent and have been acceptable to society to a large extent.'[24]

Chanda has been working in the Palghar area, which is about two-and-a-half hours from Mumbai by road. She shares her experience thus:

> Women over there are still performing the basic role of taking care of the house and family. All those policies we talk about—new education policy etc.—have not reached there. There are 4-5 villages that have just one school. It's just a small, barren school building with one classroom. Children from all the villages come there to study and they need to be motivated to come, just as people are motivated to get their Aadhar cards made. The school has only one teacher who takes care of everything. I asked her, 'What about college?' She said, 'Nobody goes to college.' In answer to my question 'why,' she replied that the government was not focused on these areas much. They still want to be this self-sufficient group—grow rice, eat rice and be satisfied. So, they are stuck with their basic needs, even in the middle income group, though there's hardly any. The facilities and the reforms have not reached them. Or the efforts have not been made to make them available to them. In the first standard there are some 80 students, the number reduces to 25 in the fifth standard, and by the time they clear their 10th and are ready for college, there are only 1 or 2 students left. Travelling to college is also not easy.

The situation is better in tier-two and tier-three cities, which are catching up with the bigger cities, though the pace is extremely slow. Another interesting fact is that different regions of the country have different levels of progress and so the middle class in these areas also differs in size. For instance, in Bihar, the middle class is very thin, whereas in the south it is very thick. The density of the middle class can be judged by using markers such as education and modern occupations. According to the latest census, at 61.80 per cent, Bihar has the lowest literacy rate in India. It is also the least developed state.

In the last six years, however, the Indian middle class has seen a significant downturn, especially in the lower-middle- and middle-middle class segments. The dual impact of demonetization, which was introduced by the BJP government in 2016 to put a check on black money, and the implementation of GST in 2018, put scores of small-scale entrepreneurs in jeopardy. The liquidity crunch saw many small businesses shut down.

The Covid-19 pandemic dwindled the middle class further, as compared to other Southeast Asian countries, especially China. Together, India and China constitute more than one-third of the world population. According to PEW research, the middle class in India is 'estimated to have shrunk by 32 million in 2020 as a consequence of the downturn, compared with the number it may have reached absent the pandemic. This accounts for 60 per cent of the global retreat in the number of people in the middle-income tier (defined here as people with incomes of $10.01-$20 a day). Meanwhile, the number of people who are poor in India (with incomes of $2 or less a day) is estimated to have increased by 75 million because of recession due to Covid-19. This, too, accounts for nearly 60 per cent of the global increase in poverty. The change in living standards in China is more modest than in India. The largest impact in China is the estimated addition of 30 million people to the low-income tier (incomes of $2.01-$10 a day). The number of people in the middle-income tier likely decreased by 10 million, and poverty was virtually unchanged'.[25]

Nevertheless, the impact of the pandemic was not uniform on the middle classes. Small shopkeepers, lawyers, and self-employed professionals such as teachers, architects, chartered accountants, artists, and others were the most vulnerable segments of the middle class, facing significant financial stress as a result of restrictions and lockdowns. In fact, their condition was much worse as many could not avail themselves of government schemes under which free 'rations' and monthly fund transfers were extended to the poor.

A May 2021 report in the *Times of India* quotes the Centre for Monitoring Indian Economy estimates that over one crore Indians became jobless in the second wave of the pandemic. '[The] most unfortunate part is that in the last 18 months, the Indian government or the state governments did not give the desired thought to this vulnerable and hard hit middle class…they are never perceived to be the vote bank by any political party as they are not organized and have no platform to collectively bargain for their benefits,' writes journalist Bhartendu Sood.[26] In an article published in *The Wire* on 26 April 2023, Professor Nilanjan Banik explains the reason why the middle class in India is not flourishing as it is in other Southeast Asian countries such as China, South Korea, and Vietnam. The key, according to him, is that in the last couple of decades of the twentieth century, these countries saw a shift of their labour force from the low-income agricultural sector to the high-productive manufacturing sector, resulting in a push to their GDP growth.[27]

Most electronic products such as mobile phones, air conditioners, refrigerators, and computers are manufactured in these countries, resulting in their transition from low to middle- and high-income economies.

> Although, thanks to reforms and the consequential high growth rates in GDP, India was able to reduce poverty—from 40% in 2004 to 10% in 2019—however, the drop in poverty merely resulted in an increase in the low-income population. Data from the recently published India Consumer Economy 360 survey points towards a fall in income growth for the poor and middle-income households, whereas that of the high-income households surged…The number of ultra-high-net-worth individuals (with net assets of $30 million or more) has grown by 11% year-on-year in 2021, the highest percentage growth in the Asia-Pacific.[28]

The Periodic Labour Force Survey (2021–22) provides the following statistics:

- At 45.5% agriculture remains the largest source of employment, followed by construction at 12.4% and trade and hospitality industry 12.1%.

- Unemployment level was stagnant at 8.8% since 2017.
- Only 1.3% had technical education and 0.7% had diploma/certificate graduate level in vocational education.

Low productive labour force, near-stagnant wage growth, rising healthcare and education costs, and only marginal employment creation against a burgeoning young population—the middle class is feeling the squeeze, no doubt, and that is reflected in its behaviour as the fight for resources has intensified over the years and has taken political overtones.

15

Structure and Composition of the Middle Class

The absence of any structured definition of the middle class makes it difficult to classify what constitutes the Indian middle class and how the different groups it contains affect its behaviour. In the Indian context, the task becomes doubly difficult as society is already segregated on the basis of caste, though there is a significant overlap between caste and class. Both caste and class operate in a distinct manner, though. A caste is an ascriptive identity. It cannot be changed and is hierarchical by nature. A Brahmin's son will be recognized as a Brahmin. Class, on the other hand, is based on meritocracy. It can be changed by changing the external components associated with it. For instance, a person belonging to the poor class can increase his income by getting educated or trained in a particular skill and upgrading himself to the lower-middle class strata. Or a lower-middle class person can become an engineer and promote himself to the upper-middle-class bracket. Thus, class is mobile. Most importantly, class is not just an urban phenomenon; it is very much a social indicator in the rural sector too. For that matter, caste is not limited to rural areas. Caste-based divisions can be seen in urban areas too. Post-liberalization India has seen a significant increase in its middle-class ranks. A growing population and inclusion of diverse social groups in the middle-class bracket have changed its composition significantly. These groups have different orientations and represent diverse interests and goals. The most immediate outcome of this plurality is a conflict of interests. The social welfare policies adopted by the government, such as free education and reservation for the socially backward classes, in both the education and employment sectors, have pushed many distressed groups up the social ladder. While on the one hand, increased caste consciousness among people has created deep divisions in society, on the other hand, it has given an identity to the depressed classes, who were not considered part of the chaturvarna system before 1947. They constituted the fifth varna, and were referred to as Avarnas or Panchama since ancient times. Post-Independence, they came to be known as Scheduled Castes and Scheduled Tribes. After the abolition of the caste system in 1950, provisions were made under the Constitution to grant reservations in legislatures for the SCs and STs. Thus, class consciousness has made the depressed classes aware of their social status, and has brought them under a single umbrella to fight for their rights.[1] Over the years, the Indian middle classes, which were initially divided along regional, social, and religious lines, have further branched out into various sub-groups representing generational as well as gender identities. Each of these groups differ from the other in terms of social standing, income, and education, and their social and economic aspirations, political ideologies, and cultural needs vary a great deal, often resulting in a clash of interests. There is a constant tussle between different social groups at every level.

As the middle class is the main driving force behind the economic, political and social development in India, it becomes imperative to study the changes it has undergone after liberalization in its composition and structure. Political scientist Leela Fernandes maintains that the new Indian middle class is a political construction of a social group that advocates economic liberalization. By 'newness' she does not mean the upward mobility of the lower classes into the middle class bracket, rather, she is referring to a 'process of production of a distinctive social and political identity that represents and lays claim to the benefits of liberalization'.[2]

'At a structural level,' she says, 'this group largely encompasses English-speaking urban white-collar segments of the middle class who are benefiting from new employment opportunities (particularly in private-sector employment). However, the heart of the construction of this social group rests on the assumption that other segments of the middle class and upwardly mobile working class can potentially join it'.[3]

This makes the boundaries of this class highly flexible, and as people from different social segments can equip themselves with the required features such as education, skills, cultural capital, etc. to gain access to this group, the politics associated with this new class can have far-reaching political and economic consequences. Take, for instance, the Dalit middle class. To be recognized as a class, the Dalit middle class had to not only acquire the kinds of capital required but also subscribe to a common ideology, which had an immense impact on the Dalit movement.

Age-old caste and religion-based inequalities continue to mar the Indian job market, both in the public and private sectors. In her book on contemporary India's middle classes, Fernandes writes:

> Research on India's highly successful information technology industries has shown that access to new economy jobs in places such as Bangalore has been highly restricted to upper-caste Hindus (Radhakrishnan 2011; Upadhya 2007). While Muslims in India tend to represent a significant portion of India's urban population, both governmental reports and academic research have documented the growing political and economic marginalization of large segments of the Muslim community. Local ethnographic research has shown that while Dalits and Muslims use a variety of strategies, such as, education to gain access to middle-class status, members of these communities often experience long-term unemployment (Jeffery *et al.* 2007).[4]

A 2017 study by researchers Sandhya Krishnan and Neeraj Hatekar reveals that between 1999–2000 and 2004–05, there was no significant change in the size of the new middle class. Within the new bracket, the middle-middle and upper-middle layers expanded, but the percentage of the lower-middle class drastically declined while that of the poor increased. The rural sector showed a similar trend, where the number of the poor people surged, and the middle-middle and upper-middle classes witnessed marginal decline. Urban India, on the other hand, showed a marginal decline in the number of the poor, whereas the urban new middle class increased due to the growing numbers of the middle-middle and upper-middle classes.[5] The study highlights the growth of the middle class and the heterogeneity in its occupational structure. According to the research, which is based on the National Sample Survey Office (NSSO) data, 2004–05 to 2011–12 saw a major change in the class composition in both urban and rural sectors. The middle class saw a sudden increase in its number, which almost doubled. The rural sector witnessed a decline in the numbers of the poor from 70 per cent to 50 per cent, and the middle-middle and upper-middle classes increased from 5 per cent in 2004–05 to 13 per cent in 2011–12. Interestingly, it was the lower-middle class that saw an 'unprecedented' growth, the study reveals, mainly in the $2-$4 category (daily per capita consumption expenditure range for different classes in India using economist Abhijit Banerjee and Esther Duflo's definition), as numerous people moved upward from the depressed segments to join the lower-middle-class ranks.[6]

In 2019, the *Hindustan Times* published a report that supported the findings of Krishnan and Hatekar. The report, based on research by Swati and Ramesh Ramanathan, founders of NGO Janaagraha, states that the Indian middle class constituted around 33 per cent of the population in 2014. The researchers contradicted the popular belief that the middle class in India was largely urban, stating that it was the rural middle class that was the largest category at 13.7 per cent. 'Adding the trader middle class-rural, and the rising middle class-rural, the overall size of rural middle classes is 2/3rd of India's total middle class. In the urban areas, the Urban Private Middle Class has increased from 0.4% to 2.7%, making it the fastest growing segment,' reads the study, which is based on the National Electoral Survey (NES) conducted by Centre for the Study of Developing Societies (CSDS)/Lokniti for the years 1999, 2004, 2009, and 2014.[7] If one goes by the National Council of Applied Economic Research (NCAER) classification, households having an annual income between ₹2 and ₹10 lakh fall into the middle class bracket. As per the given range, a recent survey by People Research on India's Consumer Economy (PRICE), a not-for-profit research centre, has revealed that the Indian middle class has grown from 14 per cent in 2014–15 to 31 per cent in 2021–22. The survey states that 'one in every three Indians is "middle class" with an income ranging from ₹5 lakh to ₹30 lakh per annum. This number is expected to double by 2047, placing two out of every three Indians in the category'. Another survey by Ejaz Ghani and Homi Kharas highlights that almost 55 per cent of the Indian population is expected to enter the middle class bracket in the near future. With new social groups joining this segment and new political identities being created, there is diversification of interests and fissures within the segment.

Based on the data at hand, one can conclude that rapid economic development since 1991 has resulted in an increasingly 'broad' middle class in India. The use of the term 'broad' instead of 'large' is deliberate. Liberalization has created avenues that have enabled people from different segments of society to join the middle class ranks in the rural as well as the urban setting, leading to a massive growth in their numbers. The reason is two-fold: education and a growing service sector. A third reason, which is largely a result of the first two, is rapid urbanization.

Education is, as is well known, an essential prerequisite for class mobility. The Indian middle class places a huge emphasis on education, as it is their only recourse to upward mobility. Part of the middle-class income goes into educating the young. Easy access to education in tier-two and tier-three cities and in the neighbouring villages has helped people acquire the desired skills required for the various job opportunities made available to them by the ever-expanding service sector. Among all sectors, it is the service sector that has been the most dynamic in the Indian economy and has shown the fastest growth since liberalization. The economic survey of 2021–22 reports that the sector contributed over 50 per cent to India's GDP and is highest in terms of labour productivity.

Now the question is who constitutes this dynamic class?

To begin with, according to scholar E. Sridharan, the Indian middle class incorporates many classes into itself.[8] The Indian middle class space has been, since olden times, dominated by the 'twice-born' or upper-caste Hindus. There were many reasons for that. Foremost among them was that the caste system did not leave enough scope for the lower castes to gain access to education, even as late as the 1970s and 1980s. This made it difficult for them to move up the social ladder as a class. The 1991 reforms brought much needed change to the Indian economy. The liberalization and, more importantly, globalization of the economy led to social transformation as well.

Swami Ramanathan and Ramesh Ramanathan say otherwise though:

> At an overall level the upper castes are over-represented in the middle classes; OBCs are fairly represented; Scheduled Castes and Scheduled Tribes are substantially under-represented, and Muslims are marginally under-represented. Disaggregating further, OBC share is higher among Rural (2-wheeler), Trader (2-wheeler) and Rising Middle Class, and substantially lower among Urban Private Sector Middle Class. While SC/ST shares among Rising Middle Class are closest to their share in overall population, they are virtually non-existent among Trader and Urban Private Middle Class. The share of Muslims is higher among Trader Middle Class than in the overall population, and Muslims generally have higher representation among the urban middle class than the rural middle class.[9]

Meanwhile, others divide the thick layer of the Indian middle class using four parameters—location, education (school and college), occupation, and vehicular ownership—using these as a strong indicator of middle classness.[10]

On the basis of this, the middle class can be segregated into five segments: rural middle class, trader middle class, rising middle class (school/college educated but whose fathers were illiterate), public sector middle class, and urban private sector middle class.[11] While the first three categories are self-explanatory, there is a technical difference between the last two. The social standing of a bureaucrat (mid-level) drastically differs from that of an executive in a private firm.

These segments are further segregated into categories and sub-categories, each of which has its own political leanings, social goals, and cultural ideologies that differ from the other, though at a macro level they might be pursuing a common goal. For instance, all middle classes aspire for upward mobility, irrespective of caste, religion, or gender. In reality, though, socially backward castes, minority communities, and women are struggling for their basic rights to freedom of expression, education, and employment.

Social and political changes have also contributed to new groups joining this highly ambivalent and political class. Take, for instance, the Dalit middle class. Dalits are considered the lowest rung of the caste hierarchy, they were outside the chaturvarna system. The change came in the past four to five decades, when many from the community started their upward journey of social and economic mobility.

Sociologist G. Srinivas maintains that the Dalit middle class is quite unique as compared to the middle classes of other communities, as, traditionally, Dalits were not part of the middle classes. The emergence of this class is seen as a consequence of the reservation policy, which came into being towards the end of the 1980s under the V. P. Singh government.

Srinivas talks at great length about the contribution of the Dalit middle class to the Dalit Movement and how it was different from the 'Indian' middle class. 'The Dalit middle class comes from a different caste—SC,' he said. 'Most of them have availed modern education and employment. Therefore they have attained these income levels which are comparable with middle class. But that itself doesn't make them Dalit middle class. To become Dalit middle class individuals, who come from different castes recognized as SCs, have to find a common ideology that binds them together.'[12]

It goes without saying that the Dalit ideology is inspired and shaped by Dr B. R. Ambedkar's ideology and politics. It is under the umbrella of this ideology that Dalits, across all sections, fight against caste inequality and mobilize by construing a common culture of their community and also articulating a politics for future generations. The awareness of who they are, their problems, their role in changing caste inequality, and their common political ideology, this is what defined the class—a Dalit middle class. 'In essence, mere economic mobility (incomes comparable to the middle class) is not enough to categorize Dalit individuals as middle class. They have to have a political ideology too,' Srinivas tells us.

It is in this context that the Dalit middle class plays a huge role. While it is discovering its roots in history and construing a common heritage, it is also becoming more vocal on various social platforms, shaping Dalit consciousness, and presenting Dalits as a community. They are part of the Indian middle class, of course, but their social reality and political consciousness make them a separate identity within this social group.

The emergence of the Dalit middle class in the latter part of the twentieth century has been instrumental in providing much needed thrust to the Dalit movement. Today, elections are fought on the basis of caste and religion. Srinivas is categorical when he says that 'without the Dalit middle class, the Dalit movement, the Dalit literary movement and Dalit political mobilization would not have been possible. Most of the Dalit organizations are founded by the Dalit middle class. When we think of the Dalit movement, we see it as a mass movement, a large number of people gathering. But who is mobilising them? It is the Dalit middle class.'

Still, discrimination continues to be rampant, at workplaces or in their neighbourhoods. In the lower-middle classes, especially in the rural areas, it is more public. For example, earlier this year, a Dalit groom was assaulted for riding a horse in the Sohalla village in Agra by a group of upper-caste men. A similar incident happened in Salt, in Almora district, where the wedding procession of a twenty-seven-year-old employee of a private firm in Himachal Pradesh was stopped by upper-caste women. He was asked to get off the horse or face a repeat of the Kafalta incident of 9 May 1980 in which fourteen Dalits were lynched and five of them were burned alive when the groom refused to dismount. Recently, the Kaliamman Temple in Veeranampatti, Tamil Nadu, was closed down following an altercation between people from a dominant caste and Dalits over temple-entry restrictions.

The Wire highlights the challenges faced by Bahujan journalists in the newsrooms, which are dominated by people from the upper castes. One of the participants states, 'I found [the] lack of enough DBA [Dalit, Bahujan and Adivasi] folks in the newsroom to be alienating. There was no open discrimination per se, but certain things bothered me. Like some jokes that a lot of people found funny seemed unpleasant just to me because of my caste background.'

As per Srinivas, such existing discriminatory practices among the middle class in general, at workplaces or in the neighbourhood, is also partly the reason why middle-class Dalits gain this consciousness.

An interesting point of view put forth by Y. Srinivasa Rao is that the educated Dalit middle class has 'failed to become a middle class in the real sense'. According to him, it is not just the upper classes that ignore the Dalits, the emerging educated and upwardly mobile middle-class Dalits, who have been benefiting from the entitlements provided to them under the Constitution, are also unmindful of fellow Dalits belonging to the lower class.

Rao says that this class 'despite being educated, is deeply religious, ritualistic and socially and culturally orthodox' and works against the Dalit consciousness. In the process of upward mobility, they have acquired the cultural, social, and ideological behaviours of caste Hindu middle class.

> In other words it works as a counter to the interests of Dalits in two ways: one, its perceptions, religious orthodoxy, its conformity to discriminatory social customs and norms in Hinduism provide needed armoury for the caste Hindus and Hindutva ideologies to counter the anti-caste and anti-religious criticism by conscious Dalits (most of which is the product of such Dalits in the intelligentsia). And second, its perceptions and social behaviour could also be used by the Manuvadi ideologues to justify their viewpoint that Dalits are an integral part of Hinduism and that anti-Hindutva criticism is the conspiracy of a small minority of middle-class Dalits influenced by foreign ideologies. Distancing itself from the responsibilities of paying back to the community or even from the basic identity may not be a problem to general Dalit society. But its comfort with religious orthodoxy and conformity to social customs that are against Dalits is quite dangerous, and it does not realize this. At a time when Hinduism and Hindutva are becoming a greater danger, its religiosity and its submissiveness to orthodox Hindu social norms need to be examined for the purpose of making this category a more responsible and positive one.[13]

Dr Bhimrao Ambedkar had recognized this problem in the fifties, and was concerned about its impact on the Dalit movement. In his historic speech delivered on 18 March 1956 in Agra, he conveyed his disappointment with the educated Dalit middle class, thus:

> Our society has progressed a little bit with education. Some persons have reached high posts after getting education. But these educated persons have betrayed me. I expected that they

> would do social service after getting higher education. But what I see is a crowd of small and big clerks who are busy in filling their own bellies. Those who are in government service have a duty to donate 1/20th part of their pay for social work. Only then the society will progress otherwise only one family will be benefitted.[14]

Another major social development after liberalization has been the emergence of the Muslim middle class. Earlier, Muslims were presented either as victims or as perpetrators, or they were perceived as a monolithic, deprived community. References to the Muslim middle class were extremely rare. However, as government records show, the picture has changed in the past decade or so. The social climb has been slow and hard, but it is there, unmistakably.

According to the National Family Health Survey, while the percentage of Muslims in the highest wealth category of the country was still the lowest, its overall share had gone up from 17.2 per cent in 2005–06 to 18.8 per cent by 2015–16. The data also displays the percentage of Muslim men who had studied till higher secondary, which doubled in 2016, and though the educational status of Muslim women improved much faster than the men, their number remained slightly below 15 per cent. The number of graduates was a dismal 5–6 per cent, including both men and women. Another survey (Indian Human Development Survey) reveals that after 2000, Muslim households have been spending at least three times more on vacations (not including hajj) and social functions.

Journalist Ashwaq Masoodi talks of the growing need among Muslim men and women coming from the lower-middle or poor backgrounds to get educated. Professor Hilal Ahmed, from the Centre for the Study of Developing Societies in New Delhi, says, 'We have a very small rich Muslim class, a tiny middle class, a big lower-middle class, the artisan class, and finally a big poor and the marginalized class. But when we look at Muslims in the country, we only tend to look at the last two classes, and have ignored the existence of some, and the slow formation of the other classes within.'[15]

Ahmed defines the emerging Muslim middle class as one different from the post-Partition Muslim elites, who believed in exclusivism, and the elites of seventies and eighties, who adopted a protective attitude towards Urdu, Aligarh Muslim University (AMU), and the Babri Masjid. 'This new Muslim class consists of semi-urban and urban educated Muslim professionals and upwardly mobile semi-rural elites. Unlike Muslim elites of the 1960s and 1970s, who came primarily from erstwhile Muslim-dominated urban centres like Hyderabad, Lucknow and Delhi, these new Muslim professionals belong to lower middle class Muslim neighbourhood of metro cities, small towns and qasbas. Delhi's Zakir Nagar, Mumbai's Byculla, Hyderabad's old city, Kochi, Ranchi, and other small towns with Muslim concentration are the sites that are gradually producing an upwardly mobile set of Muslim individuals.'[16]

During the campaign for the 2014 Indian general election, Prime Minister Narendra Modi introduced a new category, the neo middle class, urging lower class aspirants to join the ranks of the traditional middle class. The BJP election manifesto read:

> India has a large middle class with immense understanding, talent and purchasing power. In addition, a whole new class has emerged. Those who have risen from the category of poor and are yet to stabilize in the middle class, the 'neo middle class'. This class needs proactive handholding. Having moved out of poverty, their aspirations have increased. They want amenities and services of a certain standard. They, thus, now feel that Government facilities and services are not up to the mark, and hence resort to the private sector for things like education, health, and transport. This is obviously costly, putting the neo middle class into a daily dilemma. As more and more people move into this category, their expectations for better public services have to be met. We have to strengthen the Public Sector for providing efficient services to our citizens. In particular attention will be paid on government providing:

- Educational scholarships and educational facilities.
- Medical insurance and quality healthcare services.
- Middle-income housing.
- Efficient public transport systems.

Modi's resounding victory in the 2014 Lok Sabha elections has been, according to some political analysts, due to this rather sizeable section of society which was largely the result of rapid urbanization that took place post the 1991 reforms. Political scientist Christophe Jaffrelot says that 'class-based voting patterns have contributed to the success of Narendra Modi, not only because he has capitalized on the support of the middle class, traditionally pro-BJP, but also because he has attracted large sections of the emerging "neo-middle class", an aspiring social category born out of the economic growth of the previous decade. The BJP has benefited from the differentiation of the OBCs in socio-economic terms. Its upwardly mobile layer expected from Modi jobs and "development" in general'.[17]

This, in essence, was the right-wing party's answer to the Congress' 'aam aadmi' rhetoric. Previous governments had mainly focused on the poor and marginalized sections of society, whereas the middle class, especially the 'neo middle', had by and large been ignored. The BJP had found, in its numerical strength, a ready base of loyalists. Since its inception into the middle ranks, this class has emerged as a fierce supporter of brand Modi.

In recent years, a new community has surfaced on the social front in India that has altered the social and political framework—the LGBTQIA+ community.

The subject of homosexual relationships has been highly sensitive in India. It is not that these relationships did not exist in the past, they did, but they were brushed under the carpet.

In 1942, Urdu novelist Ismat Chughtai had to face an obscenity trial for her literary work *Lihaaf* which was published in the Urdu literary journal *Adab-i-Latif*. The story was about a neglected wife in a Muslim feudal society and was suggestive of homosexuality.

Chughtai was asked to apologize, which she refused. She won the case after her lawyer proved that the story was merely suggestive and that nothing offensive was found in it. Her other work, *Angarey*, remained banned for several decades, though.

Loosely based on *Lihaaf*, Deepa Mehta's *Fire* (1996) was about two lonely, neglected middle class housewives who find solace and love in each other's company. Though the film was passed by the censor board without any cuts, it saw violent protests by Hindu right-wing groups.

Post liberalization, India witnessed the emergence of the pride movement, members of which mainly belonged to the upper and middle classes. On 2 July 1999, queer rights activist Pawan Dhall participated in the first pride walk along with fifteen other marchers in Kolkata.[18] With the decriminalization of Article 377, the community has grown in numbers exponentially in urban areas over the past few years as more people have become vocal about their sexual orientation. According to globally recognized Kinsey scale, India has the largest LGBTQ+ community in the world, around 135 million.[19] Pushpesh Kumar, who teaches Sociology in Central University of Hyderabad, talks about sexual minorities and how, among the issues related to caste, class, ethnicity, and social movements, the issue of sexuality gets left out. He also critiques the queer movement for ignoring the issues of caste and class. 'While working class gays and lesbians are almost invisible, upwardly mobile middle class and upper class pride members have experienced new affluences and new freedom like any other member of the urban middle class and have been vocal against anti-sodomy law, providing a strong support base to the queer movement in India'.[20]

Kumar raises a pertinent issue that class controls access to cultural resources: the very fact that those from the working class have to bear the dual burden of class and sexuality. They, according to Kumar, form the invisible segment of society that needs to be studied. In contrast, several middle- and upper-class LGBTQ+ members have affluence and freedom to be vocal about their identity, rights, and preferences. Thus, as Kumar mentions, access to cultural resources does influence articulation and cultivation of one's identity.[21] Kumar is right when he says that sociology needs to incorporate the queer movement into its scope of social movements. Contrary to popular belief, queerness is not an imported concept from the West. It has very much been a reality in India since ancient times. The *Kamasutra*, written by Vatsyayana sometime between 400 BCE and 300 CE, also has references to homosexuality. Another hugely popular ancient Indian legacy, which indicates the prevalence of homosexuality in India, are the temples of Khajuraho in Madhya Pradesh. Built between 950 and 1050 CE, during the reign of the Chandela dynasty, these temples are famous for their overtly erotic sculptures, exhibiting sexual fluidity between homosexuals, which scholars believe is reflective of society then.[22] The queer community acts like a social class, comprises individuals from different religions and castes, is highly vocal about its rights, and is focused on fighting for a common goal—equal rights and recognition.

However, despite growing acceptance, especially in the metro cities, queer people still face discrimination and bias in their day-to-day lives, at educational institutes, workplaces, and public spaces.

'Whether it is East or West, there is a problem of acceptance,' says Ivan John. 'Indeed, with the striking down of Article 377, being gay does not make me a criminal any more. But that doesn't mean my life is hunky dory because I still have to deal with family members who are unsupportive. I still have to deal with colleagues who raise an eyebrow. I still have to deal with students who say, "Oh there he comes." And the prejudices and discrimination, the violence and the extortion rackets continue. So, it's not as if things have suddenly changed. Yes, now that the law has been read down, it is a big deal. It's like saying that equality is in the Constitution, it's a promise but does it mean it's happening? It's a goal, it's a struggle to get to that goal.'[23]

The fear—'what will people say?' dictates the behaviour of most members of society, and is often used as a weapon to make non-conformists toe the line, whether it is to discourage inter-caste, inter-religion, or homosexual relationships. The worst sufferers are those belonging to the queer community. Often, they have to hide their identity from the family itself, as, in most cases, coming out means going through emotional, physical, and mental trauma.

The confusion, guilt, shame, and other such negative emotions have a deep impact on children in growing years. They need counselling and support, which is hard to come by, especially in the lower- and middle-middle classes. As a result, these children either become depressed or start to rebel. In either case they end up losing themselves.

As Payal Dhar writes:

> As in many conservative societies, gender roles in India are strictly demarcated. In many places and situations, mixing between boys and girls is discouraged, and sex and sexuality are taboo topics outside of marriage. This means that children, and especially LGBTQ+ children, often grow up with no terminology to explain their identities. The internet is beginning to change this, at least for more affluent youngsters, but, in my experience, having the vocabulary to describe who you are does not necessarily come with understanding oneself.[24]

However, despite much social ridicule, the queer community has managed to gain a foothold in politics since Shabnam Mausi Bano, a transgender person, became an elected member of the Madhya Pradesh State Legislative Assembly in 1998. Apsara Reddy is another transgender woman who worked as a journalist with *The Hindu, BBC World Service, New Indian Express*, and *Deccan Chronicle*. In 2019, she joined politics and was appointed the National General Secretary of All India Mahila Congress.

In 2015, Madhu Kinnar won as an independent Dalit candidate from Chhattisgarh, and was the first transgender person to become a mayor. A cook by profession, Tamil Nadu's M. Radha, was the only transgender person to contest the 2019 Lok Sabha elections from Mylapore in Chennai, and later the 2021 Assembly elections. However, she lost on both the counts due to financial restraints and lack of political support.

The fight for these political aspirants remains tough. There has been a substantial increase in the queer community's vote bank (45 per cent since 2014), prompting the Election Commission to create a 'third-gender' category, however their representation remains dismally low due to persisting discrimination.[25]

The change is laborious, one can say, but it is taking place. Well-known LGBTQA+ activist and author Harish Iyer who joined the Congress party in 2019, has said, 'Political parties in India are slowly peeping out of the closet and talking more prominently about LGBTQ rights.'[26] Iyer was one of India's first openly gay persons to join a political party. He feels there is more awareness and acceptance of the community among Indians, especially the youth, and now even politicians are taking up issues related to LGBTQ rights.

16

Characteristics and Behaviour

Since it came into prominence post 1857, the middle class has been constantly evolving and increasing in volume. It was a thin layer, comprising mainly administrators and professionals such as teachers, lawyers, doctors, and small businessmen, sandwiched between the elite and the lower bulk of the population in the British Raj. And now, it has become the main driving force of the Indian economy, constituting members from varied backgrounds engaged in primary, secondary, and tertiary occupations. The middle class has massively expanded. As its composition changed over the years, so did its character, behaviour, and aspirations. However, it has some inherent traits or characteristics by virtue of its location, which falls between two great classes, the bourgeoisie, and the proletariat, that make it a social class.

Middle class interests are always guided by two factors: stability and security. That remains unchanged whatever be the situation. To ensure this, the middle class alters its behaviour according to the given situation. The Indian freedom movement is a prime example of this. The new middle class that emerged as a result of British colonialism, which 'was Indian in blood but British in taste', did not participate in the freedom struggle initially. In fact, the Marwaris and traders of Calcutta celebrated the British victory against the Marathas. Anand Kumar maintains that the 'middle class was double-faced, with one face towards the freedom movement, and it would align itself with it off and on, while the other was towards the British Raj. It was more interested in partnering with the British, to get a foothold in the British power system. It was only after it became apparent that the British could no longer remain in India that they started participating actively in the freedom movement, to safeguard their interests in Independent India.'[1]

The year 1991 marked a distinct change in middle-class behaviour. The reforms aimed at improving the economy of the state impacted the middle class deeply, turning it into a consumerist entity, an increasing number of shopping complexes with an ever-increasing number of consumer brands being a testimonial to that. The ensuing economic aggression is mirrored in its attitude towards society and politics where this class has become extremely vocal, especially on social media platforms, which have amplified its power.

With liberalization and globalization, and the emergence of a neo middle class, the nature of the middle class underwent a change once again. It is not limited to the country and its economy but has started becoming global. 'We are the number two country (after China) sending students abroad to study. Silicon Valley is America's Bangalore. As the Indian middle class went from parochial to global, its nature started changing from communal to nationalist…from communal to worldview. With all these developments, now the middle class started influencing the economy directly as well as indirectly,' says Misra.[2]

A major component defining the middle class globally, in modern times, is its consumerist behaviour that also signifies its penchant for upward mobility. Studies have shown that the 'wants' of the middle class extend far beyond their basic 'needs'. This drives demand leading to the development of a competitive market. After liberalization, the aspirations of the Indian middle class, too, have grown manifold, so much so that, today, it is driven more by aspirations than ideology. It desires the same social status as that of the upper class and wants to own the same luxuries that they enjoy, which is why it has emerged as one of the biggest and most lucrative markets for consumer goods in the world, attracting foreign investment. The advertisements crowding the airspace or jostling for prime-time viewership feed an aspirational image of the middle class to the masses—from the right family size to the best investment plan.

However, these aspirations are set differently, based on affordability. For instance, an upper-middle class student might go abroad for studies, while a middle-middle class student might settle for a good private college. Similarly, an upper-middle-class person will go for high-end brands or a foreign vacation or a top-of-the-line car, whereas a middle-middle class individual will settle for a comfortable car or a nice, pocket-friendly family vacation within the country and a lower-middle-class person will aspire to take the place of the middle-middle class. As Kumar says, it is the middle class craving for material things that forces it to behave the way it does. 'Before 1991, the basis of defining life was different. Democracy…freedom, these were the middle class values. Consumerism and materialism became the pillars of a new perspective for the middle class emerging after 1991. For the past 200 years, the middle class craved for things like shoes, vehicle, watches, liquor, clothes, etc. Today, it is submerged (indulging) in that. It is searching for happiness and peace in these things.'[3]

It is this consumerist behaviour of the middle class that is the primary force shaping the social, economic, and political environment of the country. On the economic front, increased consumption has led to an increase in demand, thereby giving a push to market economy. The middle class is now spending more on luxury goods than saving. For instance, a person owning a Mahindra XUV 300 or a Honda Amaze, cars that cost in the range of ₹8–10 lakh, works towards the ₹10–25 lakh bracket, which includes brands like Hyundai Creta, Tata Safari, Toyota Innova. Brands have become status symbols, which the middle class strives to achieve. Socially, the middle class is under a constant fear of 'missing out' and that reflects in its actions as it tries to imitate ideas, behaviours, and experiences of the upper class. So, a foreign vacation once a year has become a must and buying the latest gadget or picking up new tastes and habits has become a sort of goal for the middle class.

Irrespective of the period, pre- or post-Independence or after 1991, the middle class has certain typical attributes that dictate its actions. Being highly ambitious and aspirational is foremost among them. Most middle class individuals have adequate income to live a comfortable life but not enough to afford a life of leisure. This instils in them the desire to grow professionally and earn more. And this is also the reason why a lot of emphasis is on education and children are taught to value hard work and perseverance. A typical middle class individual sets a goal and then strives to achieve it and once that goal is achieved, the bar is raised. It is this nature of the middle class that makes it highly competitive too.

Another important attribute of this class is the unwillingness to challenge the status quo. 'You are beset with problems and challenges of life, at the same time you may not always be part to fighting against the system,' remarks John. 'I would think that is important because you want to play safe…don't say much because then you can get into trouble. And that continues even till today. Don't upset the cart because you want security, stability and if you rock the boat too much, you might just lose it.'

Where its interests are concerned, the middle class can be quite self-centred. Its unwillingness to 'rock the boat', so to say, is a clear indication that it holds its well-being above everything else. A simple example being its reaction to economic liberalization. The middle class resented state intervention and control over the economy, however, it did not want it to end as the public sector provided the necessary security and stability it so desperately desired.[4] A third, and perhaps the most problematic, trait of the middle class is the duplicity it shows when dealing with social issues. The great Indian middle class may talk or espouse brilliant ideas or dream big, but these ideas or dreams don't get actualized in the real world. 'So, you may talk about women's rights etc. but when it comes to your own child you might say she is only a girl and so she doesn't have to study after class twelve or she does not have to leave the village, let her be at home because she must get married. Thus, you might be educated, but your mindset is old. These are the contradictions of the middle class. We might espouse great ideas and values and talk about them and shove it down our kids, but do we really practice it in our everyday life? We live in this contradiction. Which is, of course, the problematic area.'[5]

In the present times these contradictions have become more pronounced, despite better education and awareness about things in general. A middle class individual may take a stand and participate in discussions or argue about what is right, but he may not necessarily put that into practice. A contemporary example of this is the raging debate on veganism. The trend which was started by the upper classes is now being followed by the middle classes quite fervently. Messages and video clippings of celebrities endorsing veganism and talking about its 'positive impact on the environment' have inundated WhatsApp groups lately. While being vegan is not wrong, the duplicity is in the claim that they are protecting the environment, whereas the fact is that their consumption of energy remains the same and so does their love for gadgets.

John believes that the Indian middle class lives with contradictions. And all that talk of equality and rights is only superficial. 'By and large how many people are really internalizing what we talk about, what we fight for, whether it is social justice, cleaner environment, or scavenging? We treat our own house help inhumanly. The language we use for them is inappropriate. We are all aware about LGBTQ+ rights, but again the acceptance is not there. The usual reaction is "I don't want my child to be taught by someone who is a lesbian". These are the contradictions—we say one thing but believe in something else.'[6]

This duplicity is also evident in its relationships with other religious and ethnic groups. While the slogans 'Beti Padhao, Beti Bachao' and 'Sabka Saath, Sabka Vikas' have become catch phrases for political parties to garner votes and create a positive image of the country globally, statistics tell a different tale altogether. As government data shows, crimes against women have increased significantly, so has communal and caste-based violence. The National Commission for Women (NCW) received nearly 31,000 complaints of crimes against women in 2022, most of which were related to emotional abuse of women, followed by domestic violence and dowry harassment.[7]

In March 2022, Minister of State Home Affairs Nityanand Rai shared a report by the National Crime Records Bureau (NCRB) with the Parliament stating that '857 communal or religious riot cases were registered in 2020, 438 in 2019, 512 in 2018, 723 in 2017 and 869 in 2016. In addition to that, 51,606 rioting cases were registered in 2020, 45,985 in 2019, 57,828 in 2018, 58,880 in 2017 and 61,974 in 2016, he said in the written reply. The MoS added that no separate data on mob lynching is maintained by the NCRB'.[8]

The Delhi riots in 2020 were a result of continuous communal propaganda, aided by the hate and bigotry-enthused reportage of the mainstream media, which instigated attacks on the Muslim community.[9] Eye-witness accounts and evidence suggest that the attacks on the minority were allegedly intentional and pre-planned where Muslim homes and shops were targeted after ascertaining that the victims belonged to the minority community. The scale of violence was so high that it led to the displacement of Muslims and possible ghettoization. The role of police and judiciary has also been questioned in the case. But the most disturbing aspect has been the complete apathy shown by the majority middle class.

Similarly, the absolute silence of the middle classes on the gruesome acts that took place during the 2002 Gujarat violence (women being raped and children being burnt alive as reported by some)[10] raises concerns about the kind of society we live in. Revati Laul, a political analyst who covered the Gujarat riots in 2002 and later wrote a book on it titled *The Anatomy of Hate*, maintains that the 'problem is not with Kejriwal or Modi. The problem is with our middle class that is constantly making right wing Hindutva-vadi leaders succeed one after another whether it is in the government or in the Opposition. This is a mirror of who we are as a middle class'.

Revati's book isn't only about the carnage and destruction, it also explores what made the middle class partake in it and how it is coping with the after-effects. One of the protagonists of her book, Pranav, who was pursuing masters in social sciences when the riots broke out and was actively involved in the violence, is now working with an NGO de-radicalizing people who are at the periphery of hate and is trying to 'unravel the process he had been through'. The other, Dungar, who comes from a tribal background, came forth with his story, despite the fact that he had lied in court and caused his witnesses to turn hostile, knowing full well that a confession to a journalist might land him in jail, because, as he told Revati, 'I don't want my children to grow up without knowing the guilt and the fear, the lack of respect, the lack of sense of self that I have had to live with, and the things I have had to do. I want my children, the next generation to see this, so that they can grow up differently.'[11]

The point Revati is trying to drive is that, more than the individual, it is the middle class action as a collective that one should be mindful of. Herd behaviour is an inherent trait of the Indian middle class and it comes into play in times of heightened religious and nationalistic sentiments, as was witnessed during the national movement and in the case of the Babri Masjid demolition.

The sheer size of the middle class puts it in a prominent position in society and makes it powerful enough to influence public discourse. In some instances, it has resulted in positive action being taken as well; take, for example, the Nirbhaya case. The brutal assault and rape of the twenty-three-year-old woman, on the fateful night of 16 December 2012, shook the nation. What made this horrific act even more gruesome was the violence attached to it. The incident moved the masses. 'Justice for Nirbhaya' became a kind of movement which was led from the front by the middle classes. This was probably the first time when the blame was put squarely on the perpetrators and not the victim, though some sexist voices did question the woman's choice of company and the lateness of the hour. However, these were drowned out by the cries for justice that upheld women's rights to freedom and safety as massive protests erupted on the streets of the capital. Mounting public pressure, on social media as well as physical demonstrations, forced the administration, which was dragging its feet in the matter, to act quickly. By 22 December, all six culprits had been arrested by the police. The speed with which the police took action shows the power of the middle class in steering public opinion.

Similarly, the anti-corruption movement, started by social activist Anna Hazare, which brought the issue of corruption to the forefront, resonated deeply with the middle classes. Here, too, the middle class sentiment translated into action when the tide of public opinion turned against the ruling United Progressive Alliance (UPA) government and led to its defeat in the 2014 Lok Sabha elections.

While these incidents highlight the role the middle classes have come to play in mobilizing public opinion on social and political issues, they also reveal the true nature of this class, that is, it is governed by an intrinsic value system stemming from its composition, which directs its involvement in social causes.

The bulk of the Indian middle class is formed by upper-caste Hindus, who are extremely caste conscious. Consequently, it showcases double standards where its interests are concerned. This is why, perhaps, there have been almost no public outcries when women from Dalit or poor backgrounds or belonging to the minority community are sexually assaulted by upper-caste men.

Take the 2020 case of a nineteen-year-old Dalit girl from Modasa, Gujarat. The girl was gang-raped and subsequently murdered by four men. As in the Nirbhaya case, there was a great deal of violence. Her body was found hanging from a tree. The Special Investigation Team of CID (Crime), constituted to investigate the matter, ruled out any foul play. They concluded the girl was neither raped nor murdered. The SIT claimed that it was a case of suicide and that the girl was romantically involved with the prime accused. Deputy Inspector General of Police (DIG) Gautam Parmar stated in a press conference held in Ahmedabad that 'other than injuries on the neck caused by the dupatta used for hanging, no other injury was found on victim's body. The injuries found on victim's body in the post mortem are said to have caused by bark and branches of the tree. No semen or saliva was found on victim's body to prove rape, gang rape or unnatural sex (sodomy). Moreover, call records show that the victim had called Bimal Bharwad herself so kidnapping has been ruled out.'[12] According to him the post-mortem finding of fluids from vagina and rectal prolapse had occurred due to decomposition of the body. There were many lacunas in the SIT report, and apart from the prime accused all the other men were released.

The nature of crime in both the Nirbhaya and Modasa cases was similar. Both crimes were brutal and in both cases the victim did not survive. Yet, the Modasa case did not generate any mass protest. In fact, it failed to garner much attention. The only reason could be that Nirbhaya belonged to the higher Bhumihar community whereas the girl from Modasa belonged to a poor lower caste.

According to a 2020 article in *The Diplomat*, 'After the Nirbhaya case, no considerable public outcry had erupted until a few months ago, when a 27-year-old veterinarian was raped and burnt to death in the southern city of Hyderabad. The Indian middle class once again could 'connect' with the victim, who was neither economically poor nor belonging to a 'lower-caste' or minority community.'[13] The article states that 'when given a choice to empathize with strangers, and share in their experiences, people tend to avoid empathy because of its perceived cognitive effort (emotional hard work). We empathize easily and naturally only when we have a sense of social, cultural, and economic affinity with a victim'.[14]

In the matter of corruption, too, there have been no discussions in the media or other forums, or even simple questioning on the central government's failure in dealing with corruption. According to the 2022 Corruption Perceptions Index by Transparency

International, India is fortieth on a scale of 0 (highly corrupt) to 100 (clean). The report states:

> In India (40), considered the largest democracy in the world, the government continues to consolidate power and limit the public's ability to demand accountability. They detain more and more human rights defenders and journalists under the Unlawful Activities Prevention Act (UAPA).[15]

Here again, one witnesses the double standards of this class. Most of the middle-class population is Hindu, and the majority has voted the BJP to power. Hence, for them questioning the government is out of question. Misra provides a simple analysis: by nature, the middle class has always sided with the powerful, 'working as a base for the establishment of rule'. It acts as an administrative tool for the government. This was true in colonial times, and it is true today. If one studies the history of the middle class in India one would find that this class has always been complacent when it comes to countering state policies. In colonial times, it sided with the imperialists till it became evident that independence was inevitable. It was only then that it threw its might behind the movement. The same submissiveness was displayed in the seventies when Indira Gandhi declared Emergency.

With an increasing percentage of the population shifting from the working class to the middle class, the dynamics of the latter have changed. The Indian middle class has become divergent, and while it has become more adaptable to the changing economy and society to remain relevant, it has also experienced a significant change in its character. The biggest influencer is caste, which affects its working as a social and political agent.

Misra believes that the middle class is responsible for caste consciousness in a big way because it can not only argue for identity but articulate it as well. Moreover, 'it can trace the history of exploitation and explore its history of relationship with other castes. Thus, the middle class can very easily express caste consciousness.

Therefore, one can say that the role of the middle class is not limited to promoting nationalism but extends to creating caste consciousness, regional consciousness and linguistic consciousness, too.'[16]

The plurality of the Indian middle class affects the behaviour and character of its various groups significantly. While the socially focused values, such as freedom, justice, etc. of the groups remain the same, their personally focused values, like materialism, hedonism, etc., differ greatly depending on their income and level of education. For instance, the aspirations of an upper-middle-class individual differ greatly from those of a lower-middle-class person. Aspirations are related to self-worth. An upper-middle-class background indicates access to good education and training, which enables a person to aim higher, go for overseas employment, or indulge in hedonistic pleasures. Conversely, a lower-middle-class person's limited reach to such facilities leads to shorter goals. He looks for a secure, well-paying job and is less inclined to spend on materialistic pleasures. 'They fear that if they lose patriarchy, caste, and communalism they will lose a lot,' explains Anand.

When it comes to the rural sector, one notices that the middle class is far more pronounced today than it was 25–30 years ago—it has grown in numbers and has distinct characteristics. Yet, caste and religion play a prominent role in a rural setting even today. 'The act of caste as a factor in the rural area is significant when compared to urban life,' says John. 'You may not necessarily follow many things in toto while you are an urban dweller but when you go back to the rural setting, you suddenly put on the rural hood and you behave in that way as is expected in that environment. Incidentally, the middle class, which is far removed from the rural environment and the shackles of caste or landlord ownership, goes back to the old customs when it comes to the issue of casting their vote or marriage.[17]

As we've seen, regional differences also play a major role in defining the character of the middle class. Unequal development of the country has resulted in an uneven distribution of the middle class. For instance, in states like Bihar and Uttarakhand, lack of education and modern occupation has yielded a very thin middle class whereas in the South, where emphasis on education is immense and multinational companies have a larger presence, it is a very thick.

A report says the reason is that the 'youth in Bihar have been brought up to join a salaried existence, preferably stable and secure, in an organization. Entrepreneurship, innovation and private initiative have not only been denied to the state from other parts of the country and world, but the youth of Bihar have also failed in offering that to their land.'[18] The middle-class Bihari is not a risk-taker. Bihari youth aspire for a government job not only because it guarantees security but it is also seen as a mark of prestige in Bihari society. In contrast, the Gujarati middle class is a go-getter. In 1969, Karsanbhai Patel quit his government job to start his detergent business. He went door-to-door selling the product. Today, he is one of the richest businessmen from Gujarat and his product, Nirma, is a household name.

The history and geography of an area shapes the character of the people living there. Rajasthan, Punjab, Haryana, Delhi, and Uttar Pradesh have had a long history of violence. These were the areas where political upheaval has been the most, be it invasions, wars, or battles. The social, cultural, and political practices of the people have been influenced by this history. For instance, according to historian Satish Chandra, the highly rigid social custom of purdah in the North, which continues till date, started from the beginning of the thirteenth century to protect women from invaders.

'The growth of purdah has been attributed to the fear of the Hindu women being captured by the invaders. In an age of violence, women were liable to be treated as prizes of war,' he writes in the *History of Medieval India*. This also explains the absence of purdah system in the South. A 2019 Lokniti study reveals that 'over two-fifths of both Hindu women and Muslim women observe purdah even in their personal spaces, i.e. from the men of their family (42% and 45%, respectively), almost half of them comply with the age-old practice when their relatives are around (48% and 49%, respectively). In public spaces, however, Muslim women appear more likely to comply with the practice.[19]

Talking of present times, the hegemonic space in Indian society is occupied by the new middle class that emerged post liberalization. This young, metropolitan, mostly upper-caste Hindu middle class, which copies its western counterpart in terms of consumption and lifestyle, prefers private services to government when it comes to education and health. Even its career choices differ from the old middle class, in that it prefers private white-collar jobs to government jobs. Increasing capitalism has altered their behaviour towards other social groups in society. As this class is upwardly mobile, it tries to identify itself with the upper class by adopting their mannerisms and tastes. At the same time, it is apathetic towards the lower class and disassociates itself from it completely.

However, most of the current crop of middle-class youth, especially from the lower-middle class, are academic underachievers. They have high aspirations but little in terms of skill. This impacts them in two ways: first, they learn to compromise, so much so that it becomes second nature to them; and second, they become easy prey to the politics of hate.

The other most significant characteristic of the middle class is its emphasis on identity. It lives to protect its identity, which could be based on region, religion, or gender. Identity plays a major role in shaping the character of the middle class. For example, Dalits could attain social mobility only after they became class conscious, for then they could fight for their rights. Their identity helped them avail themselves of privileges otherwise denied to them, like education, jobs, and healthcare.

A study on self-perception carried out by economists Milan Vaishnav, Neelanjan Sircar, and Devesh Kapur in 2014 showed that middle class is 'clearly an aspirational identity'. The economists argue that aside of a social identity, the middle class wants a more neutral identity—an 'aspirational identity'.[20]

Lebanese-French author Amin Maalouf believes that identity is not made up of a single component; it has multiple constituents. But therein lies the problem. The middle class, invariably, sticks to a single identity, which often leads to violence—as is happening in contemporary Indian society.[21]

That, according to academic Vipul Mudgal, is a result of multiple identities striking in different ways. 'Earlier, nobody would say I am a Haryanvi. That identification with the province or with the state was not there. We have multiple identities at all times and there is an attempt to subsume many of those identities into a tight Hindu identity and nationalism is a part of that project.' And anyone who does not resonate with that identity is considered anti-national.[22]

In metropolitan cities, the class divide is the greatest. The middle class in these cities are highly dependent on domestic help, yet, when it comes to their rights, they are discriminated against. In cities like Delhi and Mumbai, domestic help get only two leaves in a month. In most houses, they don't even have access to basic facilities like toilets.

There are many factors influencing the character and behaviour of the middle class: economic, social, religious, and political. Even its location impacts the way it reacts to situations and interacts with the other classes. It has an inherent duality of character that allows it to adapt to changes yet keep traditions alive. All in all, the new middle class is not driven by ideology as much as by consumerism, aspirations, and identity.

17

Politics and the Middle Class

The middle class has acted as an agent of political change in India. The first instance of this was when they provided leadership to the national movement and drove the agenda of independence. Since then, it has, time and again, directed the political discourse in the country and has fought for issues impacting not only its own interests, but those of the working classes too. It could be a local matter or a national issue, the middle-class opinion is expressed vociferously and freely.

Over the past few decades, however, the middle class seems to have withdrawn from political processes in India, to the extent that even their participation in the electoral process is minimal. Though the Indian middle class is highly critical of the system, politicians, and politics, it is the least active when it comes to casting votes. In the 2019 general elections in Odisha's Bhubaneswar, the voter turnout was 46 per cent, out of which only 10 per cent were from the middle class. Those who do vote are more attracted by the charismatic appeal of Prime Minister Modi than the issues plaguing society.[1]

Sabyasachi Basu Ray Chaudhury, professor of political science presents an interesting perspective as to why the middle class is attracted to the Hindutva ideology of the BJP. He believes that neoliberalism is interlinked with the rise of Hindutva, and that the neoliberal economy has, in fact, 'created more space for Hindutva'. At the core of this observation is the Gujarat model of development brought about by Modi, wherein the middle class, the elite, and the dominant upper castes have been the beneficiaries. Chaudhury maintains that the middle class of today has 'found in militant nationalism a new self-esteem'.[2]

Today, a discussion on politics can lead to mental harassment, broken relationships and, in some cases, even physical violence against those taking an anti-government stance. Trolling and doxing on social media are a classic example of that.

'I have quit my school's WhatsApp group. Every time I criticized the present government over rising prices or unemployment or intolerance, I was called an anti-national by a certain person who has been a US green card holder for the past several years,' laments Rama Iyer, a homemaker living in Mumbai. Born and raised in Mumbai, Rama, a computer engineer who volunteers as a teacher in an NGO, reminisces about her college days when she could discuss politics and religion without the fear of being called an anti-national. She has a simple question for the 'person': if he cares that much about the country, why doesn't he come back and contribute to the GDP?

She has a point.

So, then the question is, at a time when a single statement can create havoc in one's life, how safe is it to discuss or reflect upon today's politics and politicians? For that is one of the prime roles of the middle class, to critique the government on its policies and decisions, and to help keep democracy intact. Citizenship comes with rights and duties. The middle class is very conscious of its rights but how aware it is of its responsibilities needs to be explored.

'Of course, we all looked forward to democracy after Independence,' says Habib, 'but the universal adult franchise comes with a responsibility because using your vote with responsibility is a major challenge. In today's India, though we talk of these rights, how to use them is a big question. If you are an aware citizen, a citizen who knows, particularly from the middle class, how to use this franchise, then there is no problem. But today, majority of people are not even aware of those rights. That's why the voting percentage goes hardly beyond 50. You are not aware that as a citizen you have a duty to go and vote. Vote for anyone you like, but you have to be a participant in the process.' He believes this is where the middle class has the maximum responsibility owing to their large and growing population. 'And they affect the politics of the country this way or that way. So, they play a major role.'[3]

The fact that the responsibility of taking the country forward lies with the middle class has been made amply clear in the past too. Modern education in India is the best example of the social change brought about by the middle-class intelligentsia. Upper class dominates economically, politically, and socially. Hence, it has no incentive to bring about any change on these fronts. On the other hand, the lower classes are economically and socially not equipped to fight for their rights. The upper class exhibits power which gives it an edge over the other two classes. Power reduces justice and is a threat to democracy, which makes the political activism of the middle class crucial as it demands greater political accountability. It was this activism that made freedom a reality and gave equal voting rights to women.

In the present Indian scenario, however, one finds the middle class increasingly following the politics of majoritarianism. Politically, the middle class is divided on the issues of identity and nationalism. Each social group has its own definition of nationalism, which differs from the others, leading to rising intolerance in society. Mudgal holds the view that 'the combination of nationalism and some form of religious fundamentalism and populism and autocracy' can be seen in many countries around the world.

At one level, it is a clash of identities, not only between different social groups but within a person as well, and this is giving rise to religious fundamentalism, not only in India but the world over. Author Aamir Malouf's hypothesis is that an identity is made up of several components like religion, class, status, region, and one's experiences. The problem occurs when the person sticks to just one component, disregarding the others. That leads to disharmony.

Since the BJP came to power in 2014, under the leadership of Narendra Modi, the main topic of conversation among people has become religion. From what not to eat to what not to wear, every aspect of an individual's life is discussed. The BJP is accused of using religion as a tool during campaigning, although it fought the 2014 elections on the main issue of corruption.[4]

Modi's appeal to the masses has been tremendous. He has achieved the stature of a 'Mahapurush' among the middle classes. 'Modi hai, toh mumkin hai...(Modi is there, it's possible)'—this is the kind of mass hysteria his image evokes.

Personality cults are not a new phenomenon in Indian politics. They have always existed as people have reposed their faith in individuals rather than a political group. A simple example that can be cited is the Muslim League. The League gained acceptance among the Muslim middle class because of Muhammad Ali Jinnah. And it was leaders like Gandhi, Nehru, Subhash Chandra Bose, Sardar Vallabhbhai Patel, Krishna Menon, and Ambedkar who drew the middle classes to the freedom movement. After India's independence, political stalwarts like Indira Gandhi, Jyoti Basu, K. Kamaraj, J. Jayalalithaa, etc. won elections based on their charisma and personal ideology rather than the party's doctrine.

The problem with cult politics is just that: in the hands of an autocrat, it can create havoc. Indira Gandhi did that in the seventies when she declared Emergency. She curtailed the freedom of the press, suppressed free speech, and put all voices of dissent behind bars. Even then the middle class had not raised its voice against her. Modi, too, came to power riding on his popularity and, going by the number of sedition cases filed against people, there is speculation among political analysts that there is an undeclared emergency in India today.[5] And, but for a few, the middle class has largely been silent.

Why does a class remain silent when a particular community is being persecuted by the state, in clear violation of its democratic rights? This, especially when, as per the diktats of sociology, the same class should be talking about social equality and justice for all—for that is what it stands for.

This is because the middle class does not question the state, even if it takes decisions detrimental to the growth of society as a whole. It surrendered its right to question at the time of Emergency itself. According to Anand Kumar, 'It is a very insecure middle class which can't resist the market and state forces and lives a very hypocritical existence. Their own thinking is very radical but when it comes to expressing it in public, they remain quiet. Middle class is very nervous when it comes to identity. They think that if they leave their traditions behind, they are not sure whether the new identity as a secular, rational, modern professional will be stable or not.'[6]

The level of fear depends on who the opponents are and what is at stake. During the freedom movement, the opponent was an outsider and the question at hand was of attaining freedom. Also, it was only a section of the middle class that took part in the movement. Those working for the British stayed clear of it and kept the government machinery functional. In independent India, the opponent is a fellow national. That makes it a difficult choice for the middle class to act against.

In pre-Independence India, the stakes were low and the goal was universal. Now the stakes are high as the middle class has achieved much more politically, socially, and especially economically.

After liberalization, the middle class has emerged as the largest consumer of luxury goods. It not only derives comfort from material gains but also views them as status symbols. Owning a car or an air conditioner has become a necessity, rather than a luxury, to be called middle class. The multinational culture has given a boost to the private sector in India which has, on the one hand, opened new vistas for the middle-class youth, and on the other hand, created job insecurity among them. Thus, financial stability has become quite inconsistent for the middle class and to maintain their middle-class status, people generally avoid confrontational situations, especially if the opponent is the state. Which is why, when there is state action against any particular individual or community, the middle class abstains from commenting.

For instance, when the Jharkhand government signed MoUs

with around 150 companies in 2000, the tribal people of Khunti-Gumla district rose up to protest the acquisition of their land. The middle class was not part of that protest. Adivasi and indigenous farmers have played an important role in conservation of natural resources. Special provisions have been made in the Constitution to protect tribal culture and the land inhabited by them. Yet, in the name of development, their rights are frequently infringed upon by the central and state governments and private players. The question is how many people are even aware of their struggles let alone fight for their rights? Almost negligible.

Thus, the middle class has, in a way, surrendered its right to protest in favour of the gains it perceives are necessary for maintaining its status in society.

Diversity is another major factor that makes the middle class indifferent to the problems existing in society today. Middle income groups in India do not form a 'class' in the traditional sense of the word, rather they are different middle-class categories based on their socio-economic status. In other words, in India, ethnic identities are stronger than middle class identities. Hence, we find that the middle classes have more dissimilarities than similarities. These identities often cloud people's judgement of right and wrong. This is why when a state-sponsored bulldozer drive wreaks havoc on the properties of a particular community,[7] there are no protest marches by the middle class. Or, when men of a particular community are lynched over rumours of cow slaughter, the middle class chooses to ignore the reports.

Even during the protests against the implementation of the Citizenship Amendment Act, though the majority of the middle class supported the movement, especially the student community, yet, when the state machinery retaliated, the middle class retracted. It did not question the government about the brutal attacks on the students.

As per an *Outlook India* report, a timeline of the events shows how the state machinery went about crushing the anti-CAA movement.

> December 15, 2019: The day witnessed horrifying attacks on the students by the police of Aligarh Muslim University, Aligarh, and Jamia Millia Islamia University, Delhi. Rapid Action Force and CRPF attacked the students peacefully protesting against the Citizenship Amendment Act with tear gas, and rubber bullets and unleashed lathis on them leaving 60 students injured. In the aftermath, the fingers of two students had been cut off and one was left with an amputated arm. In this chaos, 26 protesting students had been detained.
>
> The same day, hundreds of Delhi police officers forcefully entered Jamia Millia Islamia University and confronted the students with batons and tear gas. There was a brutal lathi charge on the students. Over 200 people, mostly students, were injured. The attacks on students on their university campuses triggered nationwide protests with Human Rights Watch urging India to launch a probe into the attacks.[8]

Yet, there was no collective action on the part of the middle class to take the government to task for taking such an extreme step. In fact, there was no public reaction to the killing of Muslims and destruction of their properties in the Delhi riots of February 2020, where political leaders openly called the protesting women traitors and incited the masses to 'shoot the traitors'.[9] Similarly, the arrest of sixteen prominent citizens in 2018, including activists, lawyers, scholars, and artists, after caste-based violence in Bhima Koregaon, a village in Pune district, failed to unite public sentiment in favour of the activists. The activists were arrested for 'allegedly' having Maoist links. Again, there was no voice raised for their cause by the middle class.[10]

Politics of Majoritarianism

Lately, one finds the Indian middle class turning more towards majoritarianism. The political fallout of this development is the marginalization of minorities. The social and political implications of this trend have been quite detrimental to the democratic values of the country.

Majoritarianism entitles the majority group in society a pre-eminence that ensures their interests are protected at the others' expense. This 'representational democracy' creates trust deficit in society leading to the hegemony of the majority over minority communities.

It is this lack of trust that one sees in the three countries of the UK, US, and India that are cited as the most prominent examples of universal suffrage. The lack of trust is not just in the political system but between different sections of society. A significant factor underlying this lack of trust is the sharp rise in polarization in all these countries. A comprehensive analysis of the role of polarization in endangering democracy and ushering in majoritarianism has been provided in the edited volume, *Democracies Divided: The Global Challenge of Political Polarization*, where the editors, Thomas Carothers and Andrew O'Donohue, have echoed a very similar opinion. They make an interesting point: 'A growing economy would ease polarization. Yet we found that in some places, such as India, it actually made things worse. Indeed, the growth of India's middle class has led to rising support for polarizing Hindu nationalist narratives.'[11]

How aware is the middle class of this dangerous trend of representational democracy needs to be studied in great detail. More so, because India is the biggest and most varied democracy in the world. The heterogeneity of the Indian middle class affects its ideology, preferences, and political thought. Usually, there is a direct correlation between economic development and higher political participation of the middle class with a democratic approach. But in the Indian context, democracy takes different forms as the middle class uses its cultural and social capital in contradictory ways. On the one hand it promotes modernity, while on the other, it acts as the custodian of tradition; it covets freedom yet bows down to authority; and it talks of equality while continuing with social hierarchy.

Its political attitudes are governed by its location in religion, caste, class, ethnicity, region, etc. Which is why, perhaps, it supports identity politics—even the new global middle class, with its modern outlook indulges in identity politics. The idea of democracy is perceived keeping one's interests in mind.

Not many people in India, especially the middle-class youth, know the distinction between true democracy and representational democracy, nor do they understand the value of it. The reason, according to Habib, is lack of information. 'They do not read history...what has happened to other countries...what happened to us. The middle class plays a major role in society. They should realize what we got after Independence and what our neighbour got. See what majoritarianism and religion has done to the fellow country. We broke away in the name of religion. And see where they have gone. And what we have done to ourselves. We have institutions nurtured over the years. Now many of those institutions are under threat, including our parliament and courts. Those are institutions that we need to cherish, which a country like Pakistan couldn't do. We should realize what they have done to their country in the name of religion. They have destroyed themselves.'[12]

Yet, majoritarianism, feels Habib, is a passing trend as nothing is permanent ever, 'because history is not linear, it always has jerks and breaks'. Today, majoritarianism and right-wing politics is not just confined to India; it has become a global trend, with countries like Hungary, Turkey, France, and Netherlands, which never had this issue before, facing a similar challenge.

Looking at the past, one is hopeful of the sentiment. Indeed, world history has seen phases of democracy (ancient Greece) being replaced by oligarchy, representational democracy (Rome) being replaced by monarchy, and monarchy being replaced by socialism (Russia and China). But to restore true democracy in India, there is an urgent need to separate religion from politics.

There can never be true democracy in a country where religion-based politics is practised. According to Sudhakar, political scientists are of the view that India is becoming an ethnic democracy where identity is defining political direction. The BJP has a systematic action plan to build a brigade which appeals to people through social media. And it's not just the party, but people aligned to the BJP as well, who use misinformation to influence the middle class.[13]

Consequently, instances of public lynching and violence against minorities have increased manifold. Hate speeches and anti-Muslim slogans, attacks on churches and mosques, open discrimination against minorities have become common occurrences.[14] In the Delhi Vidhan Sabha elections, in 2020, BJP leaders called on the people to 'shoot the traitors', openly targeting Muslims.[15] Since 2014, most of the elections have been fought not on development issues but religion. On its part, the educated urban middle class either remains quiet or is in cahoots with the perpetrators, leading to a widening social divide between the communities.

In most cases, the minority middle class keeps quiet but when important issues like the CAA come to the fore, there is retaliation, as happened at Shaheen Bagh in Delhi. Still, most of the minority middle classes play it safe. 'A lot of minorities like the Christians and the Sikhs are apolitical,' says Sudhakar. 'Wilson college doesn't have a political position, it plays safe. ...Before the 2014 election, Principal Fraser of St. Xavier's College, Mumbai, wrote a letter to the alumni saying now many of you seem to be fascinated by the Gujarat model of development but the social parameters, women, education have actually become worse there. A lot of them attacked him for being political, but he stuck to his ground saying that he was a teacher and if he believed something needed to be questioned, he would do it.'[16]

Still, colleges are increasingly becoming apolitical. As a result, students, too, seem to be losing interest in politics. While in places like Delhi, Kolkata, and Bihar, political consciousness among students is still high, the rest of India seems to be devoid of an active student political body. Mumbai University has not had a student body election since 1997-98. 'So, students have no sense of accountability, standing for elections with or without political parties. The idea of political participation itself is gone. Earlier, every college would have a student wing of different political parties. They would recruit, they would try and make people stand…see that there was something happening.'[17]

However, the current crop of students gives much hope that it is possible to realize that elusive dream of social equality yet. Their participation in the anti-CAA protests was indicative of that. To a generation that projects itself as global citizens, social divisions appear insignificant. And though a lot of youngsters are also online trolls, what is interesting is that many youngsters, who otherwise come from extremely conservative and highly (religiously) polarized backgrounds, hold quite a liberal position. Sudhakar maintains that this shows that 'there is still space for conversation, influencing people, asking people to think. That space is important. When I went there (anti-CAA protests), I saw so many college students, and a significant number of them were non-Muslim. That kind of gives me hope'.

Today's middle class youth, especially Generation Z, in urban areas, are the first 'digital generation' having access to a variety of digital platforms which helps them stay connected to all forms of self-expression making them liberal and diverse in their outlook. And this diversity is reflected in their self-expression. It also affects their politics. They form a sizeable vote bank for political parties. Hence, getting them to vote for a particular ideology is not easy as many of them are moved by causes of social justice and corruption more than religion—MeToo and CAA being prime examples of that. Though restricted to the urban areas, these movements saw massive participation by the youth.

Nationalism vs Patriotism

In the wake of violence during the Non-Cooperation Movement, when nationalistic fervour was at its peak, Rabindranath Tagore expressed his apprehensions and concern regarding possibilities of aggression inherent in it. In recent years, it is this aggressive nature of nationalism that has come to the fore.

Increasing influence of the middle class in politics has redefined the concept of nationalism. But as in the case of democracy, here too, each group projects nationalism according to its needs. Which, according to Keshav Chaturvedi, a former journalist, author, and communication and content strategist narrows it down to three big clashes: the Hindu right-wing, which talks of a homogenized Hindu rashtra—one nation, one people, one religion; Muslim nationalism, which states that Islam will live on in India on its own terms; and communist nationalism, which envisions a non-religious, casteless, and classless society.[18] In the past decade, Hindutva has not only compromised the secular nature of state but has also resulted in creating a national identity based on communal lines. There has been a slow and steady saffronization of public spaces, education, and social practices, and a deliberate undermining of the Muslim rule in India. From renaming cities and roads to rewriting history to equating dissent with anti-nationalism, the BJP has redefined nationalism and linked it to Hindutva as envisioned by the RSS, creating different middle class identities in the process.[19] So, you have a middle class Hindu nationalist, a middle class Muslim nationalist, a middle class Dalit nationalist, and so on. The problem here is that the idea of nationalism differs from community to community and each of them uses it to its own advantage, which makes its relevance questionable.[20]

So, then the question arises, does that not act as a roadblock in the larger goal of taking the country forward?

The answer is simple. Anything which is narrow, which doesn't take larger interest of the country, of fellow citizens into account is obviously harmful. As Habib points out, one needs to have a broader view and understanding of nationalism and nation both. And there should be acceptance of fellow citizens belonging to different linguistic groups, religious groups, and caste groups. 'These are serious issues for us because that is where the middle class must play an important role as it is an educated class.'[21]

Habib believes people don't understand the difference between patriotism and nationalism. 'When they call themselves a nationalist, they believe they are talking about the interests of India. They don't realize that they are talking not just about India, they are talking about an aggressive position of a country vis-à-vis somebody else. Nationalism cannot exist without an adversary, whereas patriotism is not adversarial.'

Sudhakar agrees that people confuse nationalism and patriotism. Nationalism means love for the identity and patriotism means love for the country. 'But the question is how do you define a country?' he asks. It is a valid point. The concept of Hindu rashtra promotes Hindu nationalism and ignores the rest. Similarly, in the case of nationalism, we find definitions which are diametrically different from each other. For instance, Rabindranath Tagore's nationalism was inclusive whereas V. D. Savarkar's was exclusive.

The problem, today, is that the middle class uses the terms nationalism and patriotism interchangeably. Most people have no idea that the two are strikingly different from one another. In its discourse, the ruling party presents nationalism as a political construct equivalent to patriotism, and the middle class identifies with that construct. This form of hyper-nationalism requires one to constantly prove that he/she is a nationalist, which the middle class does day in and day out. And this kind of nationalism is highly exclusive. It rejects, or overlooks, social groups that do not align with the ideology of the ruling party. Hence, we see minorities at the receiving end. And this hyper-nationalism being nurtured by the state has, over the years, replaced patriotism. The resulting social disintegration and chaos has not only affected the unity of the country but has also affected its development process.

At a time when India is trying to emerge as a major player in global economy, this kind of hyper-nationalism can be detrimental to its image. This is where the middle class can play an important role, by correcting this anomaly. For that, it must first make sense of what the two terms actually mean.

In his book *Indian Nationalism: The Essential Writings,* Habib argues that it is not nationalism but patriotism that is the need of the day. 'Patriotism is something which is confined to you as a citizen of a country where you don't need to compete with somebody else, with your neighbour. You don't need an enemy to be a patriot.'

Nationalism was a borrowed expression from Europe. It is highly context-specific and while it worked well for the European countries, all of them having one religion, one race, and one language in those days of early nineteenth century, it had to go through a 'churning' before it was adopted here, simply because of the diversity of the region. 'We needed to define nationalism in a very composite way: composite nationalism, integrated nationalism. In the past 9–10 years we have defined nationalism in a very crude majoritarian way, as if religion is central to nationalism, national identity,' says Habib.

Madhukar Upadhyay presented a third view. He feels that nationalism and patriotism both have negative connotations. Nationalism, because it is divisive, and patriotism, because it is linked with patriarchy. 'Nationalism is wrong because it divides society and limits people to manmade boundaries and patriotism is wrong because it promotes a patriarchal society. People generally don't link patriotism with patriarchy, so they think it is positive.'[22]

A look into the etymology of the word patriotism shows that it is indeed linked to patriarchy. However, over the years, this link seems to have been broken, and patriotism has become gender neutral and inclusive.

By calling themselves nationalists, people believe they are talking in the interest of India. As Professor Habib says, nationalism needs to find enemies, if not foreign, then enemies within. 'So, we find enemies within India, in the name of religion, in the name of caste, in the name of class. That's what nationalism does. It cannot exist without an adversary. It has to be adversarial. Patriotism is not adversarial.'

How it has affected the social milieu of India can be gauged from the fact that the minority voice has quietened down in the past few years. The minority middle class is not voicing its political opinion publicly. It is not their fellow citizens, but the reaction of the state that they fear, maintains Habib.

It is not that the minorities are uniformly virtuous. There are people holding extreme views among the minorities as well, whether it is a Muslim minority or a Sikh minority, but the majority of them want to live in peace. The same goes for Hindus. 'Had the majority of Hindus been bad, life would have been difficult. It's only a small section that creates trouble and indulges in hate mongering. And it's creating trouble because it believes that the state is behind them. Once the fear of punishment gets into their minds, they will disappear; not that they didn't exist before—they were there, a small section was always there, but they have become more vocal.'[23]

A similar view has been presented by Sucheta Mahajan, who feels that nationalism has adopted different meanings today. 'For me nationalism would be keeping the interest of the country safe, and it would mean, as Gandhiji used to say, those policies of the state which are for the poorest person. So, the idea of social justice is very much part of my idea of nationalism. For others it can be xenophobia, and it can be very aggressive, it can be against minorities. You can have a very majoritarian nationalism that is in operation these days.'[24]

The middle class talks passionately about Bose and Bhagat Singh as being great revolutionaries, but it forgets that they were intellectuals in their own rights. 'It is a great disservice,' says Habib, 'to restrict them to any particular region. They were national leaders representing the people of India.' He puts forth a simple question: if religion is so central for the middle class, then, believing in Bhagat Singh and his martyrdom as it does, when he says he is an atheist, would his nationalism be questioned?

Here again, it is important to understand the role of history. History should guide us, inspire or warn us, but it certainly should not make us judgemental. Most people, especially the educated middle class, make the mistake of judging political decisions taken some fifty to sixty years ago and then acting on or reacting to them. We forget that history is context-specific and should be read keeping the same in mind. When people with vested interests quote history, they go by their convenient interpretation of it whenever the need arises. So, while there is much talk of Babur invading India, not much is said about Akbar breaking ties with the Ottoman Caliphs, thus signifying that Hindustan was his home. Or that Shah Jahan's eldest son, Dara Shikoh, translated the Upanishads and the Gita into Persian.[25] Thus, the perception that is created among the middle class is of a marauding, ruthless race that ruled over Hindus for over 200 years.[26] That's the RSS propaganda the middle class has internalized without questioning the reasoning behind it. The fact that Hindus have remained in the majority throughout and, in fact, have increased in numbers is completely overlooked.

Dr Vipul Mudgal gives an interesting insight into the rise of the 'intolerant Hindu'. According to him, currently, there are multiple identities striking in different ways in India and there is an attempt to subsume many of those identities into a tight Hindu identity and nationalism is a part of that project.

'The combination of nationalism and some form of religious fundamentalism and populism and autocracy is going on in at least 20 countries of the world. So if such a thing is happening in my neighbourhood, in my country, it's happening in Turkey and Venezuela, in Austria and France, in Hungary, in so many other countries then I think there must be something more than meets the eye. Not only because there is the rise of intolerant Hindu polity. I think it is something bigger than that. I think contemporary capitalism, neo-liberal capitalism, is looking for, or wanting to, reshape the world.'[27]

Nevertheless, it is an established fact that the middle class has retracted from political participation. A lot of it is due to the fact that, as Mudgal points out, we live a highly 'atomized' existence, which, he believes, is also very apolitical and anti-political.

Despite instruments like RTI (Right to Information), there is a revulsion against public participation. The reason, he believes, is that people participate when there is a cataclysmic event, like the India Against Corruption movement. 'The root of that was in the scandals of corruption that happened. It was a big corruption. I think people are not moved by small corruption. Within this society, there are instruments which need to be used but which are not being used by the middle middle class at least.'[28]

It is true that the only way to fight corruption is through these social instruments, but the middle class doesn't seem too aware or too confident or, for that matter, too inclined to use them to fight corruption or to hold the political parties accountable for their actions.

18

Educating the Middle Class

Education had been a largely ignored area in pre-Independent India, especially for middle and lower class women and those from the backward castes. And it was only when social reformers like Raja Ram Mohan Roy and Jyotiba Phule stressed on the need to educate Indians, especially women and backward castes, that due importance was given to it. While Roy instilled in Bengalis the importance of education through his Brahmo Samaj, Jyotiba, who came from a lower caste himself, laid the foundations of the Satyashodhak Samaj in Maharashtra. Like Roy, he believed that the only way to eradicate social ills was through enlightenment of women and lower castes. 'Without education, wisdom was lost; without wisdom, morals were lost; without morals, development was lost; without development, wealth was lost; without wealth, the Shudras were ruined; so much has happened through lack of education,' he philosophized.[1]

The Industrial Revolution had facilitated the need for investment in education and development of professional skills, which had led to the creation of human capital, of which the middle class was a dominant component. Increased human capital was a necessity for any country to develop, and it could only be achieved through education.

Education leads to social and financial empowerment; it equips a person to think rationally and makes him open to change. An increase in human capital promotes innovation, productivity, equality, social well-being, and increased participation of people in economic and political activities. Overall, education is a pre-requisite for the creation of a middle class. Hence, it is important to understand how accessible modern education is to the masses, in what manner it is being imparted, and what kind of output it is generating.

For a country like India, where caste- and religion-based inequalities are deeply entrenched in the social fabric, education is often seen as an equalizer. The leaders who fought for India understood this. They also understood the dynamics of the emerging middle class and the role it could play in the socio-economic framework of the country. Hence, it was necessary to restructure the education system of India post Independence. Constitution-makers were well aware of the fact that the democratic processes and the progress of the country were largely dependent on an educated electorate. Thus, under Article 29 (1), emphasis was given to 'Equality of Opportunity in Educational Institutions', and it became the joint responsibility of the state and the central governments.

Whether education has been an equalizer or not is rather debatable. However, it definitely is an important pre-requisite of the middle class. Professor Krishna Kumar, the former Director of National Council of Educational Research and Training (NCERT), feels it plays a dual role of being a catalyst of change and a 'preservationist'.

> This idea that education is a leveller is in that sense a very innocent idea. If social inequalities are entrenched in a society and are institutionalised in some of its most powerful formations, then our expectations from education will need to be backed by very strong and sustained effort if we wish to persist in our hope that it will act as a leveller. That is the broad theoretical statement with which we need to proceed. Has education performed a levelling role in our society more than it has performed a reproductionist role? I would say it is a mixed picture...Now, this statement needs to be nuanced by referring to specific regions. In certain regions of India, especially in the latter half of the 19th century, education did create a ripple which was capable of creating a considerable tumult in an otherwise very strong and stable social order.[2]

Kumar says education 'rarely acts in isolation'. It 'contributes' to the efforts being taken to bring about change. Which is probably why we have different literacy levels in different regions and in different communities. The reform movements of the nineteenth and twentieth centuries have resulted in higher literacy rate in West Bengal and the southern and western states of India. In contrast, Uttar Pradesh and Bihar fare poorly. The change has been too little, too slow, and too unequal. Caste barriers and gender discrimination have deprived a large section of the population from getting educated.

Today, India's total literacy rate is 77.70 per cent (2021–22 data). On the other hand, China at 99.83 per cent, as per the data provided by GlobalData, has almost achieved its goal of zero illiteracy. A comparison with China is important to gauge the effectiveness of our policies vis-à-vis that of China, given that the two countries started their journey towards growth almost at the same time and both adopted a similar approach to education in the 1950s: focus on higher education and emphasis on science and technology.

A study conducted by a Finland-based think tank, United Nations University's World Institute for Development Economics and Research (UNU-WIDER), states that it was the educational reforms carried out in the 1990s that put China twenty years ahead of India. China laid emphasis on overcoming illiteracy by focusing on elementary education, while India continued with its focus on higher education in science and technology. It was only in 2009 that India introduced 'free and compulsory education' under the Right to Education act.[3] Most scholars attribute the failure of primary education in India to Nehru's education policy, which laid more emphasis on higher education in science and technology. While praising Nehru for his role in the growth of technical education in the country, Amartya Sen lamented his lackadaisical approach to primary education in 2011. 'Nehru had the understanding of primary education and was committed to it, but in terms of channelising resources, priorities or planning, there was a big failure,' he said.[4]

While the criticism is justified, it would only be fair to see the larger picture and keep the socio-economic conditions of the time in mind. India was a nation in ruins when it got independence. The treasury was nearly empty, poverty was at its peak. Partition had left the society wounded and religious sentiments were running high. Under such conditions, it was crucial to give the youth of the country a direction and channel their energy into nation-building to stop them from going astray. The idea is not to provide a clean chit to the government, but to reestablish the fact that pulling a country out of a quagmire of chaos when the world has all but written it off requires a concerted effort on a war-footing. The Indian government did make this effort. It had to build a nation out of ruins, and at the same time face the challenges put forth by the developed nations in world politics, the biggest challenge being the Cold War. Border disputes with China and Pakistan, which continue to this day, were a constant threat to the security of the nation, and the two wars with China in the sixties made matters worse.

The educational advisor to the Government of India makes a sort of declaration in his 1950 report, brought out by the Ministry of Education, that 'at a time when the Government was already pre-occupied with the post war problems of food shortage, scarcity of all consumer's goods, rising prices and unemployment, they had suddenly to face the problem of the rehabilitation of millions of people displaced in the aftermath of the partition. Such factors were bound to have their repercussions in all spheres of national life, and education could not escape. In spite of all adverse factors, progress in education was, however, maintained though the rate was slower than one could wish'.[5]

According to the report, 'the total enrolment in all the educational institutions in the country rose by almost 14 lakh to approximately 1 crore 50 lakh during the year (1950). Of the latter, around 1 crore 14 lakh were men students and 36 lakh were women students. Of the total number of students under instruction in the recognized institutions during the year, 78.6 percent were studying in the primary stage, 17.4 percent in the secondary stage and 1.6 percent in the university stage. The percentage of students studying in professional subjects was 0.9 during 1947-48. Of the total increase of ₹10 crore, approximately ₹8 crore 84 thousand were spent on institutions for men and ₹1 crore 17 thousand (approx.) on institutions for women. All kinds of institutions shared the increase. The share of primary schools was the largest.'

The report further states that the 'basic system of education was recognized to be the national system of education and steps were taken by the Provisional Governments to carry out the recommendations of the Central Advisory Board of Education. Financial difficulties and paucity of trained teachers, however, held up progress... As regards the number of basic trained teachers, special steps have been taken by all the Provincial Governments to increase their output partly by training new recruits and partly by giving refresher and short-term courses to the existing teachers.'

To fight illiteracy, the challenge was not only to create an infrastructure of schools and public libraries, but, according to Upadhyay, to 'arrange for the required number of trained teachers', too, in a short time frame. For this, several teacher-training institutes needed to be built. Focus on scientific research and technology was also equally important if India was to find solutions to its various problems.

American scholar Hugh B. Wood, writing in 1955, reported that in order to make universal education an accomplished fact 'India would need to construct three million classrooms and train three million teachers. This training will require the construction and staffing of 1500 new teacher's colleges of the size now prevalent. If the job was to be done in ten years, conservatively, to finance such a project would increase educational expenditures tenfold'.[6]

Thus, primary education in India, in its initial years, was affected by a multitude of factors, not just state neglect. It was, however, gross neglect of elementary education on the part of the state in the seventies and eighties that delayed the process of mass literacy programme in India. And while India continued to emphasize science and technology at the higher education level in the seventies, China shifted its focus to elementary education. In the late nineties, China brought key changes in its education policy, which included shift from rote learning to quality education, changes in curriculum, better infrastructure, incentivizing teaching in rural areas, to name a few.

India's education system has proved to be a failure on many fronts. Its accessibility, its affordability, and its relatability are highly questionable. The concerns have increased manifold from making education easily accessible and affordable to the masses to ensuring that it makes people 'learned' and not just 'educated'. The latter deserves more attention because India's growth depends on the youth and what we instil in them through education today will decide the future of the country. Despite the Right to Education Act, India still suffers from problems of illiteracy and unequal access to education. And they are not limited to the poor and marginalized; the middle class is also facing multiple challenges as far as higher education is concerned.

Caste discrimination in education continues to be a harsh reality, especially in higher education. Whether it is the upper, middle, or the lower segment, life for a Dalit is plagued by challenges. And admission to a prestigious institute like the Indian Institute of Technology (IIT) does not guarantee elevation of social status. In most cases, alienation starts right after admission when the ranks of the competitive exams are shared. The stamp of 'quota' makes a student an outcast, and most certainly undeserving of being an IITian.

Darshan Solanki's case presents a harrowing tale of mental anguish and broken dreams of a first-generation Dalit IITian. On 12 February 2023, Darshan, a first year BTech student, died by suicide by jumping from the seventh floor of his hostel building. Swapnil Gedam, a PhD scholar and member of the Ambedkar Study Collective (ASC), informs *The Wire* that the 'alienation endured by the Dalit and Adivasi students on campus is only comparable to Dr B. R. Ambedkar's theorization of "social boycott". When a Savarna student dies, the discourse is around his/her mental health. But when a Dalit or an Adivasi student is pushed to end his life, he is invariably looked at as a "loser" who couldn't deal with academic pressure'. Incidentally, the chargesheet filed by the SIT also mentions that 'Solanki's poor academic record along with the threat issued by his batchmate' prompted him to take such a drastic step.[7] Darshan's family issued a press release, after addressing a press conference, narrating how he was harassed on the campus. 'On knowing Darshan's caste, they ostracized him, reduced their interaction with him, and humiliated him for belonging to the SC category. Darshan had confided to his sister Janvi that when his peers learned that he is from the SC community, they would call him out and say… 'dalit aaya..dalit aaya' (look, the Dalit is here) when he would try to join them during group studies or meal hours,' reads the press release.[8]

Darshan's is the latest in the long line of tragedies of Dalit students who aspire for a better life. Most of these students are first-generation achievers. Rohith Vemula is another such case. Rohith was a PhD scholar at the Hyderabad University, and was fighting for Dalit rights under the banner of Ambedkar Students' Association. He, along with four other Dalit students, was thrown out of the hostel and his fellowship of ₹25,000 was suspended following a complaint filed by the students' wing of the BJP, Akhil Bharatiya Vidyarthi Parishad (ABVP). Both Darshan and Rohith belonged to the lower-middle class, were from the Dalit community, and both ended their lives due to caste-based harassment. An *Indian Express* report, dated 2019, cites a 2014 survey that appeared in IIT-Bombay's student magazine on the presence of caste-based discrimination among students. Aptly headlined 'We don't need segregation', the survey revealed that '56 per cent of students belonging to categories like SCs, STs and OBCs believe discrimination exists in the institute, albeit in a discreet manner. In recognition of the need for more substantial service of counselling, a counselling care centre was set up in 2015. RTI records dating December 31, 2018 revealed that out of 1,034 sanctioned faculty posts, only five were filled by faculty belonging to SC and none from ST.'[9] Another grey area is women's education. Though significantly improved, it is still not up to the mark. The National Statistical Office (NSO) pegs female literacy across the country at 70.3 per cent, as compared to global average female literacy rate of 79 per cent (as per UNESCO). As per the data made available by the National Sample Surveys, conducted by MoSPI, gender gap in literacy rate went down from 18.2 percentage points in 2007–08 to 14.4 percentage points in 2017–18. Gender gap was 16.5 percentage points in the rural and 9.4 percentage points in the urban areas.

Also, this education is not really transformative. Despite getting educated, many middle-class women remain trapped in age-old customs and traditions. For instance, in most Hindu households, widows are not allowed to partake in any auspicious work during weddings even today as they are considered to bring bad luck.

Most often, education, including higher education, does not translate into careers where women are concerned. Middle-class women take up a job for supplementary income rather than making a career out of it. As opposed to a job, which is only about earning money, career is an amalgamation of values, passion, and a sense of purpose. It is a long-term endeavour that requires patience and perseverance.[10]

Unfortunately, this conditioning has persisted even in families with two or three generations of working women. In India, a career is not seen as mandatory for women, even among the most advanced and educated classes. A career is an indulgence until one 'settles down' in marriage. In a country strained for resources, there are thousands of women who are taking a homeward turn, putting their elite education and hard-earned experience to waste.

The education system of India is also reflective of its society. Its four boards, International Baccalaureate (IB), Central Board of Secondary Education (CBSE), Indian Certificate of Secondary Education (ICSE), and the state board, represent the three layers of society: upper, middle, and lower. Upper class and elite students opt for the prestigious IB schools, which are expensive and exclusive. These schools follow international curriculum with a focus on creating global citizens. The CBSE and ICSE boards mostly cater to the needs of the middle classes. The CBSE board prepares students for competitive exams and is economical compared to the ICSE board. The ICSE board, on the other hand, stresses on developing analytical skills of the students. These boards have English as the instructional medium. Students coming from the lower and marginalized classes select the state board, as it is more economical than the other boards and is widely available in public and private schools.

The result of this segregation is that it creates social gaps by eliminating the need for social interaction between the lower and the upper classes. Children learn from their environment. Lack of interaction with children from humble background keeps them oblivious to the hardships of life. They do not know what deprivation is and are not able to socially relate to the deprived.

The Indian middle class puts great emphasis on educating their young. While the rising cost of education is an area of worry for most people, including the middle classes, most concerning is the quality of education that is being imparted. The productivity of education depends on its usage. As Nehru said, 'Only through right education can a better order of society be built up.' A logic-based curriculum would promote critical thinking required for an aware public. Which is also the reason why the educational policy of the first elected government of independent India stressed on the development of science and technology.

Krishna Kumar maintains that education seldom leads the way. 'How education will be used depends on a pre-existence of an enlightened leadership. Otherwise, you may want to use education but you don't understand how education works. In that case, you won't be able to utilize the potential that good education offers to a society to increase its inner intellectual capacities, to reform itself, or sometimes to transform itself.'[11] He stressed on the need for a 'One Nation One Education Board'. His argument being that a uniform education system with a common syllabus had many advantages. 'It will ensure equal opportunity to all students throughout territory of India in spirit of Articles 14–16. It will promote fraternity, unity, and national integration among students of different education boards. It will curtail the menace of linguism and regionalism as well as the feeling of being rich or poor. Also, it will ensure that all the students have a level playing field for what they aspire to be.[12]

He cites a study of the past ten years' data, which revealed that despite free and compulsory education under the RTE Act, students in state-funded public schools, particularly minority schools, 'do not appear fairly well (equipped) and at ease with the children of the same age group and same classes pursuing their studies in the CBSE affiliated convent and private schools'.[13]

Whether a uniform education system is required or not is a debatable issue. What can't be argued is the fact that the present education system does create, and promote, class-based divisions in society. Students from higher- and middle-class backgrounds generally prefer to interact with students from similar backgrounds.

The revised National Education Policy (NEP), 2020, seeks to erase this disparity and make critical changes in the education system aimed at curtailing the dropout rate, making education affordable, modifying pedagogical and curricular structure, and ensuring holistic and sustainable development of students to turn them into global citizens.[14]

However, since the announcement regarding the implementation of the NEP, which has been accepted in parts in some states and rejected wholly in some, the coaching industry has grown exponentially, raising education costs significantly. Some of the credit for this can be attributed to Covid. As per a study conducted by Pune-based Infinium Global Research, India's coaching industry is currently generating a revenue of ₹58,088 crores, and 'the growth trajectory of this industry is set to soar significantly, with projections estimating a market value of ₹1,33,995 crores by the year 2028. This exponential growth showcases the immense potential and prospects of the coaching industry in India'.[15] Much of this demand is due to the career choices of the middle class. When it comes to education, middle class Indians have set preferences. Even today, careers in India, especially in the middle income group, is not an individual's choice. It is a family matter. The family decides which course the student should graduate in. In the south, the options are engineering, medicine, or chartered accountancy, whereas the northern parts focus on the civil services. In the past couple of decades, most middle-class families have preferred sending their children abroad for higher education. A 2022 study has estimated that more than 57 per cent of the Indian middle class is inclined towards overseas education. That means a hefty educational budget. Many of these families take education loans to fulfil this goal.

This rising trend for foreign education is a clear indication of the shortcomings of the Indian education system. One of the major problems is lack of correlation between knowledge and implementation. Indian education system has always been theory-based, even in boards like ICSE, which claim to impart practical and analytical education, especially in science and technology.

Habib feels that in the past couple of decades, there has been enormous degeneration of educational institutes, universities, and scientific enterprises. 'If you talk about the past few years, like I have spent twenty-five to thirty years in CSIR (Council of Scientific and Industrial Research), that institution has degenerated to a huge extent. It's not that everything happened in those ten years, it was happening even before. But the degeneration is quicker, faster; the pace has increased. And the quality has come down, and that is true of other scientific enterprises and universities. It is true of social sciences too. If you go to any science lab in a public university, it is not in good shape at all. And that has something to do with this whole public and private sector. The investment from the state has come down. Science needs investment, it needs laboratories.'[16] In the past decade, Master of Business Administration (MBA) has emerged as a preferred career choice, even for engineering students. Akshat Joshi, a student counsellor in Varanasi, feels that students are now opting for management-based careers for the financial security they provide. 'With the introduction of CUET (Common University Entrance Test), the seriousness towards class twelve's boards has taken a hit. Those who are scholars, or achievers—for them it doesn't matter. Median range of students—their mindset has changed. Now they focus on competitive examinations. Earlier, majority of students would get into science. Now that has changed. Post BTech students, whether they are from IIT or any other reputed college, are going for MBA or CAT. In my institute, we prepare students coming from different streams for CAT. They see management as a backup; if nothing else works out then management will at least ensure a secure job with a hefty package.'[17]

Of course, the different rungs of the middle class in India respond to challenges differently. In the urban space, upper-middle-class youth aspire to become global citizens and pursue higher education with this goal in mind. They have financial resources and prefer overseas education and the job opportunities it presents. The middle-middle class, though aspiring for a similar goal, often compromises, owing to lack of funds. Those who can avail an education loan are still able to fulfil them, the rest settle for a cheaper option within the country. Lower-middle-class youth, interestingly, seem to be contented as far as their educational achievement is concerned. In most cases, they do not aspire for higher educational goals.

Here, as per Keshav Chaturvedi, it becomes a matter of perspective. 'While this is true from our perspective, from their perspective they have come way ahead from where they were fifteen years ago. And, just as for our kids, experience-gaining is more important than material-acquisition; for them, material-acquisition is the new aspiration. And they go for only that much education that fulfils that aspiration.'

In the rural sector though, the story is a little different. Deepika Joshi runs a private school, Sunny Valley Academy, near Varanasi, where children from neighbouring villages come to study. 'Sometimes, children from lower classes turn out to be more intelligent, though they are not as in touch with the outside world as the middle-class and upper-class children are. They don't have access to the internet. Whatever they are taught in the school, they concentrate on that and try to do the best in that.'

A very marked difference between the lower-middle and other rungs of the middle classes in the context of education, as per Joshi, is that only those parents in the lower-middle class are interested in sending their kids to school 'who really want them to learn something'. According to her, 'They have access to government-run primary schools but as education there is not taken seriously, they work hard to put their children in a private school like ours. They have a dream that their child should speak in English. These are the people who could not get educated themselves but want their kids to study. And they do everything for that.'

Different segments of society live distinctly dissimilar to each other. Their expectations and goals are drastically different. So are the challenges and the solutions. For instance, children of the elite do not depend on examinations to succeed. They work outside the system with networks and 'family connections'. To them, success lies in developing soft skills and gaining a 'holistic' educational experience that is focused on 'social-emotional development, creativity and problem solving'. The middle class, on the other hand, considers education a necessity for their social and economic upliftment. Success, for them, is largely exam-oriented. This is why private K12 tuition and education technology-related products have such a huge market in India. However, these tools of learning promote content memorization more than learning. As ed-technologist Nidhi Hebbar writes, 'Children in India's middle class face immense pressure and competition from a very young age, narrowly focused on entrance exams in a sliver of industries deemed reputable—at the expense of their curiosity, creativity, and critical thinking: the very skills we know are necessary for today's global workforce.'[18] For the lower classes, education is often expendable. Their primary concern is to earn enough to cover their basic needs of food and healthcare. Lack of infrastructure in government-run schools and a dearth of trained teachers, along with uninspiring and outdated curricula, all contribute to stifle the creativity and curiosity of these children.

Thus, in its current format, education in India is far removed from being a leveller. In fact, it acts almost in a contrary fashion as the heterogeneity of Indian society manifests itself in its education system. The Right to Education Act makes learning compulsory for everyone and works on the premise that all learners, irrespective of their backgrounds, must get quality education. However, as quality varies depending on the population (the quality of education also depends on the gentry of the particular area), the goal of social equality has become all the more difficult.

19

Struggles of Middle-class Women

For centuries, women in India have been judged by the code prescribed in *Manusmriti*, a scripture defining a code of conduct for Brahmins, supposedly written by sage Manu sometime between the second century BCE and third century CE. The book details how an ideal Hindu woman should look and behave; it also shows a woman's place in Hindu society. Here are a few shlokas from the original text:

> Let him wed a female free from bodily defects, who has an agreeable name, the (graceful) gait of a Hamsa or of an elephant, a moderate (quantity of) hair on the body and on the head, small teeth, and soft limbs. (Chapter 3; 10)
>
> Her father protects (her) in childhood, her husband protects (her) in youth, and her sons protect (her) in old age; a woman is never fit for independence. (Chapter 9; Shlok 9.3)
>
> For women no (sacramental) rite (is performed) with sacred texts, thus the law is settled; women (who are) destitute of strength and destitute of (the knowledge of) Vedic texts, (are as impure as) falsehood (itself), that is a fixed rule. (Chapter 9; 9.18)

The RSS ideology is based on the *Manusmriti*. It considered *Manusmriti* as the Hindu Law, which states that: 'A woman who controls her mind, speech, and body and is never unfaithful to her husband attains the worlds of her husband, and virtuous people call her a "good woman".'[1] One of the most influential RSS figures, Madhav Sadashivrao Golwalkar's adarsh Bharatiya nari (ideal Indian woman) embodies these virtues. In a paper presented to the

Centre for Women's Development Studies in 1987, Ish N. Mishra, a retired assistant professor of the Department of Political Science, Hindu College, University of Delhi, talks about the RSS attitude to the question of women in these words: 'Balasaheb Deoras, chief of the RSS after Golwalkar, justifies the exclusion of women from the RSS structure on the grounds of domestic responsibilities: "How can women participate in Shakhas (the daily meeting and the drill) when they have domestic responsibilities?"'

Mishra quotes an anecdote which provides an insight into the mind of Golwalkar: 'When a group of women activists asked for suggestions on a literacy campaign amongst women, Golwalkar advised them to "first and foremost inculcate noble Sanskras (set moral values) in them (women). Then only think of literacy".'[2] The examples of adarsh Bharatiya nari that the RSS quotes are based on mythological characters like Sita and Savitri—women who are embodiments of purity and devotion; epitomes of duty and sacrifice; and role models for the Indian women to follow. Not too many women have been able to challenge these set norms publicly to reach the pinnacle of their careers, one of them being the first and only woman prime minister of India, Indira Gandhi. 'My father was a statesman; I am a political woman. My father was a saint; I am not.'[3]

These words of hers carried a lot of weight, not because they were uttered by a prime minister, but for the message they delivered: Don't put women on a pedestal.

That has been the problem in India. A woman can get elevated to the status of a Devi, but she does not enjoy equal rights accorded to her by the Constitution. The bar of expectations is set very high. She is the custodian of family honour, values, and traditions. The burden of carrying forward the family lineage falls on her shoulders. She has to be virtuous and an embodiment of selfless love and sacrifice, characteristics that equate her to a Devi, where she gets stuck for life. But, bound by honour and traditions as she is, she cannot exercise free will in matters concerning her life.

While the sacrifices made by women have been glorified in mythological literature, what is often ignored, or hidden from the public, is their strength of character and bravery. Sita was a strong-willed woman, not afraid to face the hardships of a forest life. Most importantly, she exercised her will in taking all the major decisions of her life right from following her husband into the forest to deciding not to go back to her husband. Similarly, when there is talk of Savitri, there is no mention of the fact that she fell in love with a man she met in the forest and, against the wishes of her father, who was a king, married him, despite being told that he would not live for more than a year. These incidents in the lives of these two women show an independent streak, which goes against the traditional image. Right from childhood, girls are brought up to follow the ideals set by the agents of patriarchy.

Upper-class women may not necessarily fit this mould. The dynamics differ. But they, too, struggle for an identity of their own despite being highly educated and receiving support from the availability of different resources. Lower class women, on the other hand, have neither the resources nor the qualifications to push the boundaries imposed on them. Middle-class women, though well educated and financially empowered, choose to toe the patriarchal line.

Liberalization brought with it the much-needed change in the social status of middle-class women as their literacy rate went up. According to the National Family Health Survey (NFHS-5), 2019–21, the male-female gap at the all-India level was 11.7 percentage points, with male literacy at 83.2 per cent and female literacy at 71.5 per cent,[4] as compared to Census 2011, when the literacy rate at the all-India level for males was 80.9 per cent and for females, it was 64.63 per cent.[5]

Since it came to power at the centre in 2014, the Modi-led government has introduced several measures to encourage women's participation in the economy. It has fast-tracked projects involving substantial investment and increased public expenditure on schemes like Prime Minister's Employment Generation Programme (PMEGP) run by Ministry of Micro, Small and Medium Enterprises, Mahatma Gandhi National Rural Employment Guarantee Scheme (MGNREGS), and Pandit Deen Dayal Upadhyaya Grameen Kaushalya Yojana (DDU-GKY) schemes run by Ministry of Rural Development, and Deendayal Antyodaya Yojana-National Urban Livelihoods Mission (DAY-NULM) run by Ministry of Housing and Urban Poverty Alleviation. Pradhan Mantri Mudra Yojana (PMMY) gives a special rebate of 0.25 per cent to women borrowers. In 2018, almost 75 per cent loans (9.02 crore out of total 12.27 crore sanctioned loan as on 31 March 2018) had been extended under the MUDRA scheme to women entrepreneurs.[6] The push for education and participation of women in the economy has borne fruit. The latest data shows a 35 per cent jump in white-collar jobs for women from February last year.[7] Companies are extending benefits such as maternity leave, even menstrual and childcare leaves to women workers. Women have started entering fields which were traditionally considered to be male bastions. Though still not a part of the Indian Army's artillery and infantry divisions, women officers are being inducted in all combat roles in the air force and navy. Squadron Leader Avani Chaturvedi became the first woman combat pilot in the Indian Air Force in 2016. In 2020, Flight Lieutenant Shivangi Singh became the first and only woman pilot to fly the Rafale fighter aircraft. Smart, intelligent, and confident, these women achievers have become role models for many middle-class women across India, just as Mary Kom and the Phogat sisters are.

However, unfortunately, for the modern Indian woman, along with social and economic empowerment, came the unbearable burden of being a superwoman. The problem is that middle-class women have added new roles to their existing portfolio. This is why you would find women cutting vegetables in the Mumbai local on their way back from office or making breakfast and lunch for the whole house before leaving for office. Added to this is the expectation to be an ideal wife, mother, daughter, sister, and daughter-in-law.

In her book, *Lies Our Mothers Tell Us*, author Nilanjana Bhowmick says, 'Society has conditioned us to believe that the domestic is our primary realm, and everything else must come second. This toxic pattern keeps repeating itself in the middle-class households across India. But we—middle class women—rarely talk about this phenomenon, except in passing. It's easier to wear the cape of a superwoman and accept the accolades rather than exposing the reason for the dark circles under our eyes, the incessant anxiety, the suppressed anger.'[8]

Despite a modicum of financial empowerment that women have achieved post liberalization, social and intellectual empowerment remains a distant dream for most of them because of the highly patriarchal nature of our homes. In fact, traditional influences of patriarchy seem to have become more pronounced. Gender discrimination, both at home and workplace, sexual harassment, and absence of pay parity continue to plague women's growth in society.

In recent times, attempts have been made through cinema to create awareness about these issues. While *Dil Dhadakne Do* talks about gender discrimination in an elite family, *English Vinglish* showed a middle-class woman's fight to gain respect in her house, *Thappad* made a strong statement against domestic violence while *Lipstick Under My Burkha* dealt with a middle-class older woman's sexual desires.

The annual report released by the National Crime Records Bureau (NCRB) last year shows a 4 per cent jump in crime against women at 445,256 cases in 2022, up from 428,278 cases in 2021. In majority of the cases, the perpetrator was the husband or his family. The report titled 'Women and Men in India 2022', published by the Ministry of Statistics and Programme Implementation (MoSPI), incorporates data from thirty-six states and union territories as well as central agencies and states that 'in the six-year span from 2016 to 2021, nearly 22.8 lakh crimes against women were recorded in India. Of these, about 7 lakhs, or 30 per cent, were reported under Section 498A of the Indian Penal Code (IPC). Section 498A pertains to cruelty by a husband or his relatives against a woman.'[9]

Stereotypical depictions of an ideal Indian woman in TV soap operas have made matters worse for middle-class women by reinforcing patriarchy. The biggest target audience of these soaps are middle- and lower-middle-class, as well as lower-class women. Their idea of an ideal woman is inspired by these soaps. An ideal woman is shown to be traditional in outlook, virtuous, religious to the point of being superstitious, and subservient to her husband, whereas a modern, career-oriented woman, who may excel at work but falls short of expectations in household duties, is often portrayed in a bad light.

Such portrayals deeply impact the psyche of the women. Thus, ill treatment is borne with grit because family honour is to be protected at all costs and questioning patriarchy is taken as a sign of rebellion against the head of the family.

Clearly, it is not just women who need to be educated about gender equality and their fundamental rights in society; men, too, must be a part of that. When a man 'allows' a woman to pursue a career, or invest in a business venture, it is patriarchy at play. The very idea that the woman needs permission to do so points to patriarchy.

In contemporary times, most middle-class women are aware of their rights, yet, equality at workplaces is still a distant dream. Anamika Prasad, a political science lecturer from Delhi University, says that in her college, the demarcation between a man's job and a woman's job is clear. Of course, the narrative is set by men despite women being equally competent. 'In my college, the highest positions are held by women but there is one ultimate decision-maker who is a male,' informs Prasad.[10] Women who question authority and pose an alternative to the given solution (invariably approved by a male) are not 'liked'.

Some of the biggest obstacles to women's progress are the narratives set by men. These narratives play an important role in social conditioning. For instance, a woman is considered the prime caregiver of the family and so the expectation is that she must prioritize family over career. Which is what most middle- and upper-middle-class women end up doing. They leave their jobs post marriage or childbirth. The choices of lower-middle-class women are directed by money; they have to make both ends meet, so, for them, these narratives or societal norms don't matter as much.

According to Prasad, a successful woman is seen as a threat to a man and successful, bold, and loud women are so much of a threat that a narrative is constructed that such women are not correct for Indian society. 'We have been trained (by parents) since childhood to be role models as successful career women, mothers, breaking boundaries, glass ceilings, and what not. However, men have not been trained by their parents, by their environment to accept the reality of successful women,' she says. 'That is a definite barrier, I feel. They might like a successful mother or a successful sister but find it hard to live with a successful wife.'[11]

The narratives created around a single woman usually centre around her 'single' status, that she must not have found a good match, or there must be something wrong with her. The fact that it could be by choice is not even considered. Another lecturer (name withheld on request) from Delhi University, who is a divorcee and quite vocal in her college, says that she has been a victim of such narratives. 'I have been called loud, undisciplined, and morally corrupt. Whatever the reason (for my divorce), they will say that "her husband must have left her because of her nature". I have been a victim of these narratives because I voice my opinion. If you talk, you are not a woman acceptable to Indian society and Indian men,' she says.

Surprisingly, the same is not true for a married woman with children. If she exhibits some of these features, then it's acceptable. The sad truth is that these narratives are built by men and seconded by some women.

Prasad feels the narratives mostly affect the middle- and upper-middle-class-women as societal norms are firmly attached to them.

Thus, despite being educated they have not been able to progress. Lower-middle-class women, on the other hand, are using education for their upliftment. 'My beautician works till 8-9 in the night while her husband looks after the child. This I will not associate with the middle- and upper-middle classes. I don't see my colleagues doing that.'[12] The reason is that the mobility of the lower-middle class is associated with money; hence, for them, social stigma takes a backseat.

Even in decisions such as marriage, unlike middle- and upper-middle-class households, girls from lower-middle class buckle under family pressure only if they are not financially independent. If they are earning well (not highly educated but skilled), then they get married to a boy of their choice.

Middle-class women in India have jobs, not careers. In India, the main purpose of providing good education to daughters is to secure a good match. After marriage, the woman plays different relational roles of wife, mother, and daughter-in-law, and career takes a backseat.

There are numerous factors responsible for this. Foremost among them, says Prasad, is a lack of awareness among girls about a second career option. Families see limited work opportunities for girls and most girls view teaching as the ideal choice as it helps them achieve work-home balance. They do not have a second career option. Also, many a time, it becomes difficult for a girl to get a job after migrating to another city post-marriage.

Divorce lawyer Vandana Shah feels that middle-class women are not progressing because they have taken on themselves to be protectors of the so-called moral rights. 'So, what happens now is that I have to instill the right cultural values, but in today's day and age what really are the right cultural values?'[13]

Cultural norms change with time as cultures evolve, with their elements disappearing, multiplying, merging, changing, and new elements adding on to them. The evolution reflects in our foods, clothing, language, lifestyle, etc. Unfortunately, of late, this change seems to have become stagnant; in fact, one even sees a sort of regression here. 'I don't remember my mum wearing the bindi as often but there was never this emphasis at home that you must wear bindi. Bindi was an adornment, now it has become your identity,' says Vandana.

Middle-class women, both in urban and rural areas, have made significant progress in terms of education and awareness in the past decade or so. The concern lies in how it translates into their lives.

As statistics reveal, women's education in India has shown significant improvement, but unfortunately it is focused more on improving grades rather than improving minds, which is why women still face exploitation and abuse, be it at office or at home.

Ivan John maintains that the solution lies in imparting 'education that transforms, not just education in itself and for itself, but that transformative power of it'.

But the education needs to be holistic, and for both men and women. For things to change at the ground level, the male mindset needs to undergo a transformation. Only then can the boundaries be broken.

One would think that middle-class women in the film and television industry would be more progressive. However, that is a misconception according to Zoya (name changed on request), a costume designer who has been associated with the industry for the past 26–27 years. 'In fact [the film] industry is the one that's not at all liberal,' she says. 'It's very strange. We make all these films, shows and ads, but in reality, we are still clinging to our old patriarchal mentality. These women are all over Instagram and social media. They talk about Gandhi, J. Krishnamurthy, freedom, democracy but do they actually follow? No. It's all a pretense.'[14]

Most girls entering the industry are educated. They are well-groomed, financially independent, and aware of their rights, yet when it comes to decision-making, especially in matters of marriage where the family is involved, they go by the family diktat. Even here, education has not been able to transform mindsets, feels Zoya.

Zoya comes from a middle-class Muslim family. She and her siblings were brought up by her mother single-handedly as her father was in the Gulf and rarely visited them. Her mother ensured that Zoya and her sisters got educated and had careers. She went against the wishes of the family and supported her decision to work in the industry. However, she feels things have changed for the worse in the past few years. 'They have become so rigid. My mother has started wearing the naqab! It disturbs me to see her like this,' she says. And this change is not due to the political situation, she clarifies. 'This political situation was always there, so this change is not because of that. We have been through Hindu-Muslim riots. It should have happened then.'

Like all young girls, Zoya fell in love but as the boy was a Hindu, there was resistance from both families. The couple decided to live together. They have been living together for more than 25 years now. Meanwhile, Zoya adopted a girl child. However, neither the partner nor the daughter have been accepted by her mother. Even her convent-educated cousin has been critical of her life choices. 'No one in my family knows that I am in a live-in relationship,' she says.

Issues like female infanticide and honour killing are as much a dark reality as are marital rape and acid attacks. According to a recent United Nations Population Fund (UNFPA) report, almost 4.6 crore females were 'missing' in Indian demography in the year 2020 mainly due to pre- and post-birth sex selection practices stemming from gender inequality. As per the report, India accounts for almost one-third (32.1 per cent) of the total 142.6 million missing females in the world.[15]

One would question why, despite the feminist movement of the seventies and eighties, these issues continue to plague our society. The answer is not straightforward. When there are different versions of the same ideology, each having a different focal point around which the movement is constructed, their effect gets diluted. That is the sad truth of the feminist movement in India. India's heterogeneity has resulted in the emergence of multiple feminisms, just as it has given rise to multiple patriarchies. Feminism in India has been a response to historical and cultural realities, and has changed according to the level of consciousness, perception, and action of individual women, and women as a group, over a period of time.

Most of the women associated with the movement belong to the middle classes. Upper-class women, though not fully liberated, are not the same as the middle class. They are educated and have financial security that takes care of their basic needs and extravagances. For lower-class women, the issue of survival is of the utmost importance, which makes them resilient. They face extreme oppression and abuse but lack the resources required to fight them. Thus, the responsibility of leading from the front falls to middle-class women.

When it comes to education and empowerment among women, particularly middle-class women, the progress varies from community to community. The process of empowering women started early in the Hindu community whereas in Muslim and Dalit communities it was exceptionally delayed due to religious and caste factors. While the Muslim community did not emphasize women's education much, Dalits were deprived of this fundamental right altogether. However, in the past decade or so, Muslim middle-class women have made great progress in the fields of education and employment in urban areas. In the Dalit community though, the process is extremely slow. For Dalit women it is a three-pronged battle against caste, class, and gender discrimination.

One major question that most Indian feminists fail to address is the issue of caste-based discrimination. They see caste as a socio-economic category rather than an independent identity. The bitter truth is that when it comes to caste, upper-caste women are as biased as the men. Even today, a lower-middle-class Dalit woman is not hired as a cook in most upper-caste kitchens. Upper-middle-class Dalit women don't have it easy either. They, too, have to bear with snide remarks and jokes about their caste on a daily basis. In her memoir *Ants Among Elephants*, author Sujatha Gidla, recounts her college years where she received the same disdain from 'Brahmin Christians' as she did from upper-caste Hindus.[16]

Within the media landscape you would find a large number of women journalists who are Muslim, and they are doing some exemplary work. 'Some of them actually do fine reportage within the social Muslim construct—i.e., they embrace their identity by wearing hijab and dressing conservatively,' says Ghazala Wahab, journalist and author.[17]

But that, according to her, is only a part of the middle class. Women in the lower-middle and lower classes are still struggling. School and college dropout rate is very high among them for various reasons. 'Security comes into play, identity comes into play. Take Karnataka, for instance, when the restriction on hijab came, almost 150 women were pulled out of educational institutes by their families. And here you find women being victimized, both by the state and their families.'[18]

The issue of hijab has evoked contrasting views among educated and accomplished Muslim women.

Wearing a hijab or a burqa out of one's own free will is one thing. The problem occurs when it is imposed on others by people in the name of religion and culture. In a city like Mumbai, it becomes difficult for a middle-class or lower-middle-class girl, living in a Muslim dominated area, to stay immune to Zakir Naik's brand of orthodoxy, try as they might. Conversations with young Muslim girls revealed that most of them had to wear a burqa when stepping out of the house. Not doing so leads to harassment by the local youths, they said.

Activist Noorjehan has been fighting for Muslim women's rights for over a decade now. In the battle against patriarchy, whether it is for securing women's right to enter the inner sanctum of Haji Ali Dargah in Mumbai, or crusading against the practice of triple talaq, she has often found herself alone. Neither non-Muslim feminist organizations nor middle-class Muslim women have extended their support to her.

The root of the problem is that women, across class, caste, and religion, are not aware of their rights, neither legal nor constitutional, which makes any talk of gender or caste or religious equality redundant. Women may have become educated and may have achieved financial independence, but do they have the right to exercise their free will?

The answer is an emphatic no.

Divorce lawyer Vandana Shah feels that middle-class Indian women have, in fact, not fared well over time. Despite awareness and education, women put up with physical and mental abuse because they don't want the stigma of 'divorcee' attached to their name. There's still a discomfort around divorce in India. In her own case, her relatives would advise her not to tell anyone about her ongoing divorce in family functions.

Surprisingly, one of the issues related to divorce which no one talks about, she feels, is that it can bring an upper-class woman suddenly into a middle-class bracket. She recalls a case where a woman married into a jeweller family, living in a posh Mumbai area, got divorced. The husband proved in the court that he did not have money and she was granted only ₹700 as alimony. It is only when the children threatened to disown their father that he gave her the money. Abuse is another area where women have been at a receiving end, and not just middle-class women. There is very little awareness about abuse among women, in general. Most women are not even aware of the mental abuse they undergo. 'I had a client coming from Grant Road. Her husband had never called her by name in their twenty-five years of marriage. He would address her as "bitch", and she was okay with that. It was only when her father-in-law physically abused her that her brother brought her to me. She was still in denial, saying that the father-in-law pushed her in anger, and that she had not sustained any injury.'[19] What is ironical is that in most cases of abuse, the perpetrators are other women.[20] Vandana's ordeal started within months of her marriage with her in-laws criticizing and putting her down all the time. Verbal abuse soon became physical, and then one day she was thrown out of the house in the middle of the night. In all this, her mother-in-law was as much a perpetrator of the abuse as the father-in-law and husband were.

The dichotomy of the middle-class women, whether to be the custodians of culture and traditions or the harbinger of social change, has become a roadblock to their progress. These women are aspirational and inspirational and yet they are not free of the mental shackles of patriarchy.

20

Interaction with Other Classes

In his social theory of class, Karl Marx has divided society into two classes: the dominant class (bourgeoisie), which controls the means of production and distribution; and the working class (proletariats), which produces and provides services to the dominant class. These two, according to him, are in a constant state of conflict. As for the middle class, he believes that it does not exist in the real sense. His argument is that in times of class conflict, between the bourgeoisie and the proletariat, the middle class would not play any role. In fact, it would dissolve into two sections, one joining the bourgeoisie and the other the proletariat.

But the Marxist theory doesn't hold much water in the capitalist society of today, where the middle class not only exists but plays a crucial role in maintaining a balance in society and is increasingly expanding. The very location of the middle class, sandwiched as it is between the upper and the lower classes, makes it a mediator between the other two classes, and there is a marked difference in how it interacts with them.

In the context of India, the role of the middle class is more expansive. Along with heading working-class movements,* and fighting for their rights, the middle class has also become a custodian of Indian culture and traditions. Now, this presents a contradiction in the middle-class relationship with the working class, and exposes its hypocritical nature at several levels. To understand the 'how', it

*From Bal Gangadhar Tilak to B. P. Wadia to Datta Samant to George Fernandes, almost all the leaders instrumental in spearheading workers' movements in India were from the middle class. Besides, they were educated and could articulate the needs of the working class well.

is imperative to first understand what 'culture' actually stands for in the Indian context.

Culture is an ambiguous term with no set definition. It is an umbrella term used to signify behaviours, philosophies, ethics, morals and mannerisms, customs and traditions, and religious, socio-political and economic activities. According to sociologists Robert M. MacIver and Charles Hunt Page, it is the 'realm of styles, of values, of emotional attachment, of intellectual adventures'.[1] So, when the middle class says it is an upholder of Indian cultural and traditional values, it means that it strongly believes in the social hierarchy that forms the basis of Indian culture, and gives hegemonic status to the 'twice-born' over the rest. Hence, it is a firm believer in the caste system. This becomes evident in the social interaction between the middle and the lower classes which, essentially, comprise the socially backward and Dalit sections of society. The upper class doesn't face such an issue because a) there are hardly any backward or Dalit individuals in this category and b) the factors influencing upper-class behaviour are different and work on a different plane altogether. Here, economics gets more weightage than any other factor.

That being said, history is proof that most of the working-class movements have been led by the middle class, be it the 1917 Champaran Movement led by Gandhi or the 1974 nationwide railway strike under the leadership of George Fernandes or the National Domestic Workers' Movement started in the eighties by Dr Jeanne Davos in Chennai.

'Middle class is an interest group in our understanding of sociology,' says Anand, 'and they define their relationship with other interest groups on the basis of ideology and issues.'[2] Ideology and issues can unite or divide different interest groups. For instance, on the issue of inflation, the middle class stands united with the working class, whereas it is against the farmers' protest on the issue of minimum support price (MSP). On the other hand, on the issue of admissions to university and paper leaks, it is the middle-class youth that are agitating because it concerns them, the working class is not that affected by it.

In terms of ideology, the Hindu middle class and the Hindu working class unite on their prejudice against Muslims, though their reasons differ. The Hindu middle class feels that its identity is threatened and the Hindu working class feels that there is more competition in the job market. Thus, the middle class displays a duality when it comes to interacting with other interest groups. On the one hand it lends support on issues that impact its own interest, while on the other hand, where the issues are not aligned to its own interests, it shows indifference.

The upper-middle class tries to align itself with the upper class or elite and tends to ignore the working class. At the far end is the lower-middle class, which is closer to the working class economically but considers itself socially and culturally superior. The middle-middle class aspires to be in the rich club, yet, at the same time, doesn't want to let go of its traditions. It is this class that has held on to the cultural practices and social values despite being upwardly mobile.

The working conditions of the lower-middle class are similar to those of the working class or poor. Government school teachers are one such example. Economically, they are no better than wage earners as their salaries are the same as that of a working-class employee. However, their cultural and social conditions are much different. They are more educated than the lower class, their social status is higher, and they are hugely impacted by the upper-middle-class consumption patterns and try to imitate them.

Elucidating the role of the middle class, Mohapatra states that, in India, the middle class 'represents a body of people who carry forward the voice of the working class, asking for justice and equality in society. They are engaged in different occupations, speak different languages, but they have a common vision of transforming society. Middle class is becoming the voice for the working class. It is waging a war for justice, democracy, equality, and at the same time it is also fighting against economically dominating upper class. Hence, middle class has become a catalyst for social change in India'.[3]

While that may have been true in the India of the sixties, seventies, and eighties, in recent years, the middle-class equation with the working class has changed significantly. It no longer believes in collective action. This change was first noticed in the Great Bombay Textile Strike of 1982. According to scholars, the failure of the strike was more 'political than structural. At each moment, it would have been theoretically possible for the Communist parties in India to resist very differently than they did, and their refusal to lead the working class with slogans and the organization of solidarity allowed the (working) class to be decimated'.[4] Economic liberalization has also played a big role in defining the attitude of the middle class towards the working class. Increasing consumerism made the middle class more individualistic. That, according to Anand, changed its equation with the working class. 'Earlier you would become a member of the trade union or make associations. The emphasis was on collective action whether it was a question of caste or women's literacy or fighting against superstition. Today, collectivism is no longer there. The politics of collective interest has taken a backseat. The middle class has backed out from trade union.'

Another, and perhaps the most defining, factor dictating the terms of relationship between the two is that, inherently, the Indian middle class is non-egalitarian by nature. This reflects in its daily interaction with the working class, although it espouses the idea of equality. Most middle-class households employ domestic help to do menial chores around the house. The working conditions for them are quite tough. They get only two days of leave per month, work on minimum wage, and have no job security. The threat of getting evicted from work without prior notice dissuades them from fighting for their rights. Added to that is the treatment meted out to them. In most households, they are expected to sit on the floor. They are not allowed to use the toilet while working in the house and, if they live with the family, they have their own separate toilet.

Even the plates they eat from are separate. This, despite middle-class women actively raising issues of women's empowerment and rights.

Prior to liberalization, the economic gap between the middle class and the working class was less. The question of status did not figure in the interaction between the two. But increasing economic gap has made the middle class more status conscious. In fact, some housing societies in upscale areas of metro cities have separate lifts for domestic workers.

Despite being a socialist republic, India still has a deep social divide so far as caste is concerned, though more in tier-two and tier-three cities as well as rural areas.

Misra believes that the middle class is not very conscious of equality as its class goal or class interest. 'Equality may be a value for society at large...but it is logically not appropriate for the middle class because it is not a homogeneous class either economically, culturally, socially, or even politically. It is a heterogeneous class and heterogeneity is also in terms of inequalities.'[5] In his view, the middle class has never been an advocate of equality, though it may use it as a form of camouflage to attain certain objectives in the name of equality. But when the question of providing equality comes up, as some kind of a reward distribution to the whole society, the middle class doesn't support that argument. The working class, on the other hand, he feels, is highly conscious of equality owing to its economic, political, and social existence. For the working class, equality is not merely a value but a kind of support in the three parameters. 'Therefore, in the whole human history you will find, particularly in the nineteenth century, all over Europe and other parts of society, that the working class struggled for political rights; it was not the middle class.'[6]

Of course, the ideologies of equality are always thought over and articulated by middle-class intellectuals.

In early nineteenth-century Britain, voting rights were enjoyed only by the rich. The British middle class had become quite powerful by then, and under pressure from them, the Reform Act of 1832 was passed by the Parliament allowing the bourgeoisie to vote. However, women and the working class was excluded from this. It was only later in 1918 that the Representation of the People Act was passed granting voting rights to all men over the age of twenty-one, and by 1928, women were finally given the franchise on the same terms as men.

The India story has been quite different. Here, the middle-class duplicity lies in providing leadership to working-class movements on the one hand and extending intellectual support to the ruling class on the other. 'For example,' says Misra, 'in the Indian situation, you see the middle class always supporting the arguments of fascism at every level: local level, family level, caste level, community level, and national level, but, at the same time, it also, as a civil society leader, lends support to democracy and democratic argument.'

The upper class and the middle class have a love-hate relationship. The middle class loves to imitate the upper class attitude and lifestyle, but is envious of its privileged position in society. Since it can't match the upper class either politically or economically, or, for that matter, socially, it invariably takes a moral high ground, considering itself to be the protector of Indian culture and tradition, and of the Indian value system, something that the elite are thought to be lacking in.

The elite in India make up 1 per cent of the total population. They are the trendsetters in society. Their children study at foreign universities; they don't go on vacations, they gain 'experiences'; their leisure activities include playing golf, or shopping, or attending art auctions. The actions of the upper class are guided by what American economist and sociologist Thorstein Veblen calls 'conspicuous consumption'. Explaining this theory in *The Theory of the Leisure Class* (1899), Veblen argues that the upper class reinforces its social status by displaying its wealth using luxury goods and services. According to him, utility goods have two distinct characteristics. The first is its 'serviceability' and the second is its 'honorific' aspect. 'Since the consumption of these more excellent goods is an evidence of wealth, it becomes honorific; and conversely, the failure to consume in due quantity and quality becomes a mark of inferiority and demerit,' he writes.[7] Thus, the motivation to buy luxury goods, like the Falcon Supernova iPhone 6 Pink Diamond, the world's costliest phone, serves the dual purpose of providing connectivity to the world and exhibiting the affluence of the consumer. About the upper class's apathetic behaviour towards the lower class, Deepanshu Mohan, Associate Professor of Economics and Director of the Centre for New Economics Studies in OP Jindal Global University mentions how 'Veblen's work distinguished between two motives for consuming conspicuous goods: "invidious comparison" and "pecuniary emulation". "Invidious comparison" refers to situations in which a member of a higher class consumes conspicuously to distinguish himself from members of a lower class. "Pecuniary emulation" occurs when a member of a lower class consumes conspicuously so that he will be thought of as a member of a higher class. In modern terms, these motives are the essence of what explains elite consumption behaviour amongst both upper and lower classes (including in India). Members of higher classes voluntarily incur costs to differentiate themselves from members of lower classes (invidious comparison), knowing that these costs must be large enough to discourage imitation (pecuniary emulation).'[8] It is this lifestyle that the middle class tries to emulate. It carries the values of the rich, and as Mohapatra says, so long as they accept the culture of the upper class, consensus will be maintained. There is a sort of interdependency between the upper class and the middle class. The middle class aspires for a luxurious life and pines for social recognition. It enjoys the privileges extended to it by associating with the elite. Conversely, the upper class wants to be seen as one with the middle class because of its significance in society and its various achievements right from the freedom struggle to the political transformation of India. In fact, many people from the upper class, as well as lower class, identify themselves as middle class. The reason is that the middle class has always been considered as an achiever. Historically, the middle class has had a lot of socio-political significance: it brought the freedom movement to fruition, it resulted in the political transformation of India, and it supported democracy, while the elites remained largely absent from the scene. However, while the middle class emulates the rich, Indian elites aspire to be in the global elite club. And since the middle class has also started vacationing in 'touristy' destinations like Singapore, Barcelona, Paris, or Switzerland, in a bid to distinguish themselves from them, the Indian elites have shifted their focus to more expensive locations like St. Moritz or the Bora Bora islands. They display exclusivity in their preferences, be it in clothes, sports, entertainment, travel, or food. Nevertheless, the fact remains that the elite can't afford to ignore the middle class completely. For one, it provides a buffer between them and the working class, and two, the cultural capital of the middle class far exceeds that of the elite. And so, they display their Indianness by association. When Nita Ambani says that she has middle-class values,[9] she is propagating the same message.

Thus, as per Mohapatra, it is this interdependence that gives a dual nature to the middle class. 'If the middle class takes up a new body of values, looking into the plight and sufferings of the working class, they will be questioning the upper class. So, the middle class gives rise to the persistence of inequality, yet, at the same time, it is also challenging the persistence of inequality.'[10]

21

Middle Classes Around the World

In a world of increasing interconnectivity, the role of the global middle class becomes extremely significant. The emergence of the middle class in the West, post industrialization, as a consumer class resulted in massive development and economic growth sweeping across Europe and America in the twentieth century. By the beginning of the twenty-first century, developing economies such as India, China, and Latin America also started witnessing the emergence of a promising middle class.

Post-World War II, as western societies underwent an egalitarian reconstruction, the middle class that emerged was based on certain parameters that gave it a definitive character. To begin with, despite a capitalistic outlook, the post-war middle class rooted for welfare schemes and the expansion of public services. Another very distinct feature of this middle class was that it was wage-based rather than wealth-based, as was the norm in previous decades. This wage-earning middle class depended on a stable income to maintain its middle-classness, which was much higher than that of the working class. A steady income ensured a steady rise in the standard of living over time, leading to an affluent society. Wage moderation meant the promotion of equality, which resulted in sustained economic growth. The rebuilding of European nations after the war was done keeping the larger socio-economic goal in mind. The thrust was on a 'democratic, social and developmental form of capitalism', or simply welfare capitalism.[1] This was the period when education and occupation ranked higher than wealth. For instance, when US president Franklin D. Roosevelt, asked Vannevar Bush, the director of his wartime science office, about the role science should play in the post-war era, he recommended that government funding of scientific research 'should continue to support three important government missions: national security, health, and the economy'.[2] Thus, high levels of economic growth and production ushered in what is known as the Golden Age of capitalism, which saw an unprecedented growth of the middle class.

In contrast, third-world countries, or the developing nations as they are now called, were non-industrialized and economically challenged and had the Herculean task of rebuilding the nation, especially in the case of India, after throwing off the yoke of colonialism. The middle class in these countries was miniscule and still fighting its way through poverty and illiteracy.

However, there has been a marked difference between the middle classes of developed nations and developing nations, like India, in terms of aspirations and commonalities. According to Anand, the main difference lay in how they perceived nationalism. In some countries, the primordial identity of religion, language, and race became more attractive and interesting. 'The European middle class slowly became more civilizational on the nationalism platform. Instead of France and Germany, it went towards creating European Union. It shared universal values of socioeconomic progress, of scientific achievements, of technological developments, and of environment protection. The Indian middle class, on the other hand, moved towards decolonization and asserting its own identities by accepting scores of traditional identity principles in an uncritical way.'[3] In simpler terms, it became more varied and heterogenous as opposed to the European middle class, which became a homogenous mass. Another major difference has been in the problems faced by the middle classes in both developed as well as developing countries. In developed economies, the middle classes are concerned with income polarization, unequal distribution of wealth, and economic stagnation. The state policies there are centred on the same. On the other hand, in developing countries the middle class struggle, apart from the issues of income polarization and unequal distribution of wealth, has been to rise above poverty, illiteracy, and disease and be a part of the rising global middle class, which has been the most significant economic development on the world stage in the past few decades. The middle class is the backbone of economic growth and democracy. It drives the demand for quality consumer goods and good governance, and mandates investment in sectors such as education and health.

In the seventies and eighties, expanding markets, growing competition, and increasing consumerism sent the aspirations of the European middle class soaring. Over the past few decades, however, as consumer capitalism grew, it led to a major socio-economic shift in the West. The Council of Europe, in its Parliamentary Assembly report (2021), notes that despite growing prosperity, 'disparities in income, wealth, educational achievement, health status, nutrition, living conditions, occupations, social identity and participation in society have kept widening between and within countries. These inequalities not only negatively affect individuals and communities, but also restrain overall economic development, undermine social justice, and hurt the functioning of our society'.[4] The pandemic only magnified these inherent social inequalities, resulting in reduced social mobility and greater polarization. While economies became less resilient to external shocks, socio-economic polarization increased the risk of social unrest and political instability. The report further states that the Assembly was highly concerned about diminishing social mobility and 'extensive inter-generational transmission of inequalities'.[5]

Looking at market trends, scholars believe that the middle class in developing nations, especially India and China, are witnessing growth whereas developed nations like US, UK, and Japan have been witnessing a 'shrinking' middle class. According to available statistics, currently, two-fifths of the global middle class resides in Brazil, Russia, India, and China (BRIC), while the developed countries are home to only a quarter.[6]

The Organisation for Economic Co-operation and Development (OECD) 2022 survey reveals that there is a 'hollowing out' of the middle class in the US as a result of 'low intergenerational movement and rising income inequality accompanied by a rise in polarization of income distribution'.[7] The pandemic has also contributed to the shrinkage of the middle class. A 2020 PEW analysis report states that the number of people joining the middle class ranks was shorter by 54 million than what was predicted prior to the pandemic.[8]

However, the claim that the middle class in developed countries has been shrinking was contested by a recent report published by the European Commission. It is, in fact, the working class that has faced tremendous economic loss in the past four decades. Taking the Luxembourg Income Study as base, the report, tracking the growth of class-based employment and income of six developed nations, US, France, Germany, UK, Poland, and Spain, in the past four decades, highlights that 'over this period, employment of the upper-middle and middle class strongly expanded, while the skilled and low-skilled working class shrank everywhere. Working-class households also made consistently smaller income gains than middle-class households in all countries except Poland. Real labour income of the working class declined in Germany, stagnated in the US and grew by less than one percent annually in France and the UK'.[9] Be that as it may, there is no denying that there has been a significant increase in income disparity and polarization among social classes. Loss of employment due to automation has been cited to be a major reason for the decline in the middle class by many scholars. However, *The Journal of Chinese Sociology* published an article that provides an interesting view. It states that there is a need to 'understand' social stratification in the context of 'wealth-based domination' instead of an occupation-based one, as has been the norm.[10] In the decades following World War II, wealth was considered secondary to education and earnings by the middle class. 'Rewealthization'*, on the other hand, leads to abundance at the

*Derived from the French word *repatrimonialisation*, it signifies the return of inherited wealth to primacy. This has had a considerable impact on social stratification in western societies.

top of the social order, leading to dissatisfaction and frustration in the classes below.

Author Louis Chauvel considers rewealthization to be the defining trend of the squeezed middle class. He writes: 'In the Golden Age of wage-based middle-class societies, when earned incomes were the major source available for consumption or savings, middle classes had a relatively homogeneous self-definition in terms of socioeconomic wellbeing. The relative prestige of neighbourhoods, house sizes, and cars were relatively well determined by the purchasing power of households' earnings. In a wealth-based society, each social stratum, even in the middle class, shows an inner polarization between extremely wealthy members who can afford a standard of living of much richer social groups, and others who must consider the consequences of their limited wage realities (Leicht and Fitzgerald 2013; Temin 2017). For instance, it is common in prestigious universities to see academics of different wealth backgrounds, many live like standard petty-bourgeois, and others own luxury properties in one or several global cities.'[11]

A declining middle class is not just a western phenomenon. The world's third largest economy, Japan, too, is witnessing a declining middle class post-pandemic. Known as the 'hundred-million middle-class' society once, Japan is battling rising unemployment induced by the pandemic. According to a 2022 report, 'from 2020 to 2021, estimates stated that one in six people living in Japan lived in relative poverty'.[12] Post pandemic, open work has become scarce, says the report. As consumer spending plummeted and retailers shut down, most women, who worked part-time or as non-regular employees to balance work with childcare, lost their jobs.

Owing to the sheer size of their populations, both India and China are touted as the future of the world consumer market. The World Bank predicts that 70 per cent of Chinese will achieve middle class status by 2030, driving consumption to the tune of $10 trillion in goods and services. India, on the other hand, stands to outdo both China and the US due to its burgeoning population, which has surpassed that of China. Reports state that, by 2030, India and China will come to represent approximately 'two-thirds of the global middle class and 59% of middle-class consumption that is expected to tally $64 trillion'.[13]

India and China started on their journey of growth and development almost simultaneously. But, after the economic reforms of the nineties, China raced ahead of India to emerge as a regional power. China's middle class is defined as a three-person household earning US $14,844 to US $74,221 per year. The rapid transformation of the Chinese economy has had a significant impact not only on Asian but also on world politics. Nevertheless, China's recovery post pandemic seems to be sluggish, to say the least. *The Guardian* reported on 23 July 2023 that China's GDP had improved by merely 0.8 per cent, ringing alarm bells in Beijing. And while, till a few years ago, the Chinese Communist Party was coming down heavily on high-profile private companies, now it wants to make the atmosphere 'bigger, better and stronger' for entrepreneurs. One might say that in China's smooth porcelain finish, cracks are beginning to appear.[14]

'Modern and urban China is increasingly becoming a Westernized society and the one-child norm has precipitated the matter. What would have taken 100 years has now been compressed to 30 years. So, the demographic crisis has come much earlier than it would have in the normal process of westernization,' says Sujit Dutta, a political scientist and expert on the subject of China.[15] Chinese society had reached a dead end under the old totalitarian system. In terms of both poverty and illiteracy, China was behind India. India's GDP per capita was higher than China in the seventies, and more or less equal in 1988–89. China's shift from communism to capitalism was gradual. In 1979, Chinese Premier Deng Xiaoping began a modernization campaign by opening doors to foreign investors, allowing the private sector to operate in the country. In the same year, it adopted the one-child norm to combat its growing population.

In 1991–92, China went for major economic reforms, just as India did, ushering in a period of capitalism and westernization of its urban life. India, on the other hand, was still very cautious, and liberalization of Indian society happened in stages. 'So, our society did not change as much as China's had done in that period. Chinese growth and urbanization have been rapid, and the imbalance has therefore been even more acute.'[16]

Although rapid urbanization led to the creation of wealth and growth, thereby bringing down the poverty rate in urban as well as rural areas, it still had its drawbacks. China was emerging as a manufacturing hub for the West. Western manufacturing was shifted to China because of the cheap labour it provided as compared to western markets. On its part, China was more than willing to bring in western technology, create employment, improve urbanization, and create growth and wealth. 'Close to 200-300 million peasants were required now as workers, so the villages lost their young men and women to urban Shanghai, Beijing, the multiple coastal towns that were now the centres of export-led growth tied to the west.'[17] However, post Covid, China's growth story seems to be ending. After Covid restrictions were lifted, experts and policymakers in China expected a major jump in consumption. People flocked to travel agencies to make holiday bookings. But the euphoria ended once the Chinese youth were faced with the harsh reality of increasing unemployment. *The Guardian* reports that about 'one in five of China's 16- to 24-year-olds were unemployed in June'. As there are no professional jobs available, several university graduates are working as delivery associates.[18]

China's problems are not just economic but social as well, and they are too deep-seated. As per Chinese authorities, China's urbanization is now nearly 55–60 per cent, leaving 40–45 per cent as rural. Professor Dutta asserts China's middle class is confronted with three major issues: rapid urbanization, rapid economic empowerment, and impact of the one-child policy.

'Most of China was rural and worked as a commune under

Mao, from there it transformed into a traditional capitalist society structure, with about 55–60 per cent, according to Chinese officials, I would say roughly about 50 per cent urban dwellers. These are essentially broken families, where parents stay separately, and children go to different cities wherever they can find a job. Strict enforcement of the one-child norm meant one child in most families and none in many. As a result, children are getting pampered. The middle class value system is getting affected as children are growing up in either daycare or are being looked after by nannies.'[19]

Rapid economic empowerment has affected the Chinese family structure immensely. Though gender equality has taken place in a big way, it has not led to high representation of women at the top in Chinese organizations, which signifies that Chinese society remains highly patriarchal. 'In China, it is not easily done. It is not very common for a woman to head an organization. Even the political representation of women is extremely low. The Polit Bureau standing committee hardly has any women.'[20] In comparison, women in Indian organizations reach the top if they perform well, with Roshi Jain, a fund manager associated with HDFC Mutual Fund, and Sunaina Da Cunha, associated with Aditya Birla Sun Life Mutual Fund, being shining examples of that.

Comparing India with China, Dutta points out the rewards that the Indian middle class is reaping due to sustained development and urbanization. In India, the new middle class that is emerging has economic empowerment along with social and political empowerment. Here, women actively participate in elections, and more and more women stand for elections.

Thus, political, social, and economic empowerment of women in India is rising simultaneously. Whereas in the case of China, despite significant economic empowerment of women due to rapid urbanization, their political representation has been extremely low as in 'authoritarian China, women don't participate in elections'.[21] Not just women, but middle-class men, too, don't have any say in matters relating to the state. Only the ruling party is the decision-maker. This lopsided growth in society will, at some point of time, have an effect.

Thus, as per Dutta, the kind of authoritarian capitalism that took place in China post 1990, under Deng Xiaoping and later under the leadership of Xi Jinping has given rise to multiple issues. As China has grown, it has become wealthier and as a result, per capita incomes have risen. The Chinese middle class has more wealth, better housing, and better education, but their family structure is breaking down. 'The one-child policy has had an enormous effect on redefining Chinese families and the demographic decline. Also, economic empowerment is far higher than political empowerment, which remains at rock bottom.'[22]

There are other implications of the one-child policy, according to Dutta. First, the nature of socialization is vastly different. It creates a highly individualistic person, which is the epitome of capitalism; and second, children don't have any social responsibility.

'Although China today is a meritocratic society and merit is highly valued, yet the contradiction is that merit will not always win on its own, you have to be politically correct too. Otherwise, even if you are the brightest, you will not be rewarded. You'll not be promoted to the highest position...because you have to be politically loyal to the party. So, there's another element to it. On the one hand, there's talk of meritocracy, everyone wants to be number one, but at the same time, they know that unless they are loyal to the party they will not reach anywhere. The authoritarianism is sustained into the system.'[23] The pandemic has accentuated China's socio-economic problems. The slow development of the economy has upset the upward mobility curve of the middle class. Every year, thousands of Chinese students graduate, but the job market is saturated. According to a report, 'many potential middle class Chinese are unemployed or in low-paying jobs.'[24]

The effect of the economic downturn can be seen in society, too, as the class system in China is getting more and more rigid.

While new arrivals in the city are finding it difficult to enter the middle class, those already part of it are finding it tough to retain their middle-classness in the face of rising cost of living, lowering incomes, increasing costs of education and healthcare, etc. The Chinese middle class is also quite status conscious. Hence, moving to a medium-sized city is seen as a sign of failure. It is also not a very viable solution practically, as they provide limited career prospects, and the quality of education is also mediocre.

Mounting frustration and dissatisfaction among middle-class Chinese can be seen in the growing cultural movements in the past few years which reject constant competition and work pressure. As the report states, 'the "Lying Down" (Tangping) movement, advocates opting out of the rat race, working only as much as you need to survive, remaining single, not having children, and enjoying life. According to sociologist Sun Liping, those who adopt this lifestyle are children of parents who worked hard to build up substantial wealth; he condemns "lying down" as a luxury. Others see it as an expression of a deep malaise that society and the party must address. Why work "996"— 9am to 9pm, six days a week—if it doesn't enable you to climb the social ladder?'[25]

The dragon seems to be losing its fire. Still, it presents a case study for India to learn its lessons from.

Conclusion

The Way Forward

From the colonial times till today, the journey of the Indian middle class has been phenomenal. It has grown in size and aspirations; it has acquired new identities and behaviours; and it has become politically and economically powerful enough to bring transcendental changes in society.

At the crux of this change is the changing value system, which is highly influenced by economic factors. Every generation has had its own set of interests, ambitions, aspirations, and attitudes that collide and contrast with the next generation's, creating friction between the two.

A careful study of the generations would reveal that till the turn of the century, change was always from the third generation onwards. The impact of the first generation was so severe on the second that it was not able to come out of the stipulated social norms, as can be seen in the way women are positioned in society, or the continuing caste discrimination. It is only at the beginning of the twenty-first century that one begins to see a complete break from previous generations in attitudes, aspirations, and behaviour.

The Silent Generation/The Builders (Born before 1946): We have already talked about an existing middle class in India when the English arrived in India. This class, comprising small and big zamindars, landed peasants, artists, and craftsmen, was gradually replaced by the new middle class that emerged under the British.

The values of this new class differed from that of the old one. To start with, to quote sociologist Dhurjati Prasad Mukerji, Indian society 'was a "closed one", and remained so for a long time, with Buddhist, Hindu and Islamic philosophies intertwining with each other and, as a result, developing "ideational" traits of culture with more or less defined views on the nature of needs and ends and the means of their satisfaction, i.e. of social activity, with specific aesthetic, moral, and social values and systems, and with certain common notions of Truth, Knowledge, Self, and the Ultimate Reality'.[1]

The new generation of middle class was aspirational and attracted to power, and was becoming increasingly Western in mannerisms and outlook. The clash between the two was inevitable and became the central theme of most of the literary works produced during the time.

By 1925, the middle class had undergone a transformation. It had a political presence and was economically much stronger, with an emerging indigenous industrial and corporate sector. Western education had made this middle class self-aware and confident enough to demand representation in governance. But the biggest change that distinguished this 'silent generation', as it is called, from the earlier ones was that while, traditionally, the Indian culture was an amalgamation of different faiths, a true proponent of unity in diversity, this generation saw the rise of a polarized society led by the Muslim League on the one hand and the Hindu Mahasabha on the other.

The rise of nationalism was yet another factor influencing the educated middle class of this generation. It divided the middle class into the educated and aspirational upper-caste middle class nationalists and the upper-caste 'Indian in blood and colour but English in tastes, in opinions, morals and intellect', middle class salariat.

Scholars usually overlook one important aspect of Indian philosophy while studying or defining the middle class: 'aparigraha' or non-possession. Indian society has been highly influenced by the philosophy of 'ashtang yoga', and aparigraha is one of the ethical rules prescribed by mystic and philosopher Patanjali for an individual's personal growth. It teaches one to be content with what he/she has. Philosophically, the focus is more on being a better human being than a richer person. The silent generation middle class was largely influenced by this notion, and this mindset continued until the late eighties.

The Baby Boomers (1946–1964): The growing influence of socialism on the middle class, a result of Nehruvian politics, continued even after India's independence, though the RSS and the Hindu Mahasabha had also made their presence felt, and their brand of nationalism had started taking root among the educated middle class. Gandhi's assassination draws attention to the different versions of nationalism that were growing in Indian society.

Still, by and large, Indian society was socialistic by nature. The younger generation of the middle class was highly influenced by leftist ideology. One important distinction one can make between the old and the new generation is the increasing role of students in politics. A mixed economy presented limited job options to the youth, especially in the public sector, which was coveted the most by the middle class as it provided the much sought after job security and social status. But stagnating economic growth, impeded by continuous wars and border skirmishes with Pakistan and China, created great social upheaval in the seventies and eighties. Issues regarding exploitation of workers, political corruption, and rising inflation were taken up by communist leaders and backed by the youth. Middle class youths were increasingly becoming politically aware and were driven by the notion of equality.

Socially, this generation carried the same value system that the previous generation believed in. Core values of justice, morality, honesty, and truthfulness were generally adhered to.

Nevertheless, caste-consciousness and gender discrimination were still paramount and were taken as the stabilizing factors of society, despite a growing awareness about the social inequalities afflicting it.

Simplicity was a prominent feature of this generation, where frugality was considered an asset. Money was spent on essentials rather than luxuries. Even the rich refrained from flaunting their wealth. Caste distinctions mattered more than class distinctions, especially in urban areas. Rich, middle class, and lower class students would go to the same schools and colleges, and that in a way sensitized students about the less privileged. 'When I was in school or college,' says Sudhakar, 'I would have in my class students from the lower-middle class as well as from the upper-middle class.'[2]

Mohapatra has a different take on the generational change that happened in this period. 'Change is the law of nature. I will say that when I joined the university, my perception of myself was different from my father's, who was a school teacher. In the sense, during his time he belonged to the middle class, and during my time, I belonged to the middle class. But his perception of the middle class was different from mine.'[3]

Generations X (1965–1979) and Y (1980–1994): The biggest change that marked the next generation of the middle class was increasing participation of women in the country's economy. Despite rigid societal norms, which discouraged women from working, especially after marriage, these generations, especially Gen Y, saw a large number of middle-class women stepping out of their homes to work. However, financial independence did not really change the status of women in society. They were still bound by the rules of patriarchy, which meant that they had the dual responsibility of taking care of office as well as home.

The change started seeping in from 1980. There was a gradual shift towards luxury items. By the nineties, televisions, telephones, automobiles, mixer-grinders, refrigerators, etc. had become middle-class status symbols.

The liberalization in the 1990s created a consumerist middle class, which was competitive, career-oriented, and was materialistic by nature. As the market opened, new job opportunities became available to the younger generation. These were high-paying corporate jobs that required a professional approach, which was missing in the public sector. Increasing class consciousness brought significant changes to the middle class psyche, as was clear from its changing consumption pattern.

The added feature of this middle class was that it was gradually becoming brand conscious. The internet opened a channel for people to interact with one another, exchange ideas, research ideologies and arrive at conclusions that were not bound by community, region, or nation. It changed the way people viewed the world and helped break social barriers to a large extent, especially in urban areas.

Another major trend that caught the imagination of this generation, especially the middle class, was a heightened sense of religiosity. It was not so much about understanding religion, both among Hindus and Muslims, as about the various rituals associated with it. One point of view is that this overtly religious sentiment stemmed from the guilt that the middle class carried for being too Western in its outlook and mannerisms.

One finds a silent change taking over the younger generation, though it was still not rebellious enough to break away from the traditional mould. But chinks had started appearing in the armour of tradition. A clear indication of that was the crumbling joint family system in urban areas, which had started giving way to the nuclear family system.

However, some communities still prefer the joint family system; for example, the Gujarati middle class community. Says Dr Deepa Shah, a practicing dentist in suburban Mumbai, 'Even today, Gujaratis prefer the joint family system, and all major decisions, be it regarding marriage or business, are taken by the eldest brother in the family, and children are taught to respect the wishes of the head of the family. The joint family concept is very strong among Gujaratis. Also, but for a few exceptions, most Gujaratis don't discriminate between boys and girls. In fact, being a business community, they equate the birth of a girl child with the arrival of Goddess Lakshmi.

Generation Z (1995–2009): It is in the current generation that one can see the transformation that has taken over society. The economic, social, and political realities of the middle class today are far different from the previous generations. What were considered luxuries in the seventies and eighties are today's middle-class necessities. Back in the eighties, not everyone had a telephone connection or a car. Private schools were generally beyond the reach of the lower- and middle-middle classes. In contrast, this generation has grown up surrounded by technology. They can't imagine life without its trappings. And most middle-class children study in private schools, some even in elite schools, and colleges. Their interaction is mainly with children from similar or rich backgrounds. Given this background, one can analyse the psyche of this middle- class generation.

'With the kind of money which has come, there is a possibility they will never see poverty,' opines Sudhakar. 'All their classmates will be well-off so the sensitivity for the deprived to understand what poverty is, is missing. Secondly, if you look at the elite schools they also have a lot of homogeneity. Novelist Jerry Pinto once mentioned that he had gone to a school in Andheri where, in an entire class, there were just one Catholic and one Muslim student. He said children were growing up not knowing people of other religions, other communities and communities are also becoming insular.'[4]

Insularity is unhealthy for a country as diverse as India, still, one sees increasing ghettoization of Mumbai. The city is divided into Gujarati, Muslim, Sindhi, and Parsi neighbourhoods. Even gated communities ensure that there is minimum interaction between the middle and lower classes, and that leads to apathy.

Another, rather important, point raised by Sudhakar is extreme intolerance towards diversity of any kind. There is hardly any scope for criticism in society today, especially among the older generation. While students don't question their teachers fearing punishment for insubordination, teachers themselves hesitate to question the management fearing action. This suppression of independent voices has a huge fallout. First, it kills independent and nonpartisan thinking; and second, it stunts personal growth.

This is where the new generation of middle class, Generation Alpha (2010–2024), stands far apart from the earlier generations. Many youngsters today have started questioning the system, the teachers, the parents, and that is not all, they have started expressing themselves too, as was seen during the anti-CAA movement. Increasing globalization and exposure to different cultures have made this generation open to change in the urban centres of the city. They are candid about their preferences, be it material, social or sexual; and are aggressively vocal about it. The growing LGBTQA+ community is a reflection of that.

However, the most unusual characteristic of this generation, the upper-middle class in particular, is that unlike previous generations, it does not care for security as much. One reason could be that these youngsters have not seen the hardships of life and have not struggled for basic necessities of 'roti, kapda aur makan'. They are born with a roof over their heads, have never faced hunger, and have enough discretionary income to buy new, branded things every once in a while. These facilities are taken for granted, as is the fact that it is the parents' responsibility to avail them of such facilities, unlike in the West, where once the child becomes an adult, he has to fend for himself. Hence, the sense of achievement is not there, and neither is the fear of loss.

In the urban areas, this attitude extends to personal relationships too, where a live-in relationship takes precedence over marriage, at least for the initial couple of years. The compatibility factor, which was never talked of earlier, is a much discussed topic today. And this compatibility is both at the mental as well as physical levels.

Another defining change, according to Chaturvedi, is that material aspirations have gone down. The younger generation is not too keen on assets, they crave new experiences. So, among the upper-middle class, off-beat activities, like backpacking across the globe, or travelling to remote areas of the world are becoming more popular.

Mohapatra feels the current generation of middle class, while maintaining its cosmopolitan character, has not lost touch with its cultural grounding. He believes that there's no clash between generations because change implies that the whole society is changing. 'Society expects from a particular group of people to behave accordingly....'[5]

What he means is that every generation is conditioned by the society to behave in a certain manner. Society makes the demands on individuals who simply reciprocate. That being the case, it is natural for two generations living under one roof to have different perspectives, which means clash of perceptions is inevitable.

An analysis of the different generations of Indian middle class brings forth a few revelations. Foremost among them is that the current and upcoming generation is not bound by the social norms that were in effect until the recent past, the catalyst of change being Generation Z. This generation is global in its approach to life, and for them boundaries, physical or otherwise, don't matter.

There is a marginal increase in cases of inter-caste marriages. In 2014, only 5 per cent of marriages in India were inter-caste; however, by 2023, the number had doubled.[6] A report states that inter-caste marriages are becoming popular with youngsters, especially in North India. The report is based on a study by researchers from University of Michigan of data (313,000 profiles) gathered from major Indian matrimonial websites. The study found that 'younger generations are more open to inter-caste marriage, which is pointing to a shift in attitudes'. Inter-faith marriages, on the other hand, are limited to the metropolitan cities and are mostly a hushed affair. According to a 2021 PEW Research Center report, inter-faith marriages are just over 2.1 per cent in India.[7]

The other major shift that has happened is at the individual level. The current generation of middle- and upper-middle classes is very aware of its rights and does not believe in any form of compromise. Kathuria believes that empowerment has made people individualistic.

Last year, a girl in Gujarat married herself. It was probably the first case of sologamy in India. The case generated much curiosity and debate among scholars. Most people from the older generation called it an act of exhibitionism, which the current generation is accused of indulging in time and again. This generation lives on Instagram and X. Whether they are in a theatre, or shopping, or eating in a restaurant, or having a quiet moment at home, all their activity is fodder for social media. The pressure to be active on social media and to show how happy one is, however far removed from reality it may be, takes its toll on the mental health of the individual. Thus, the sologamy case was viewed by many as an act to generate views.

Psychoanalysts have a different take on this. They view it as a statement that reads, 'I am committed to myself'. Right from childhood, children are so conditioned by society to have a special someone in their lives that leading an independent life may seem daunting to some. Hence, the marriage rituals and the celebration were just the means to satisfy that notion of marriage. Still, it does point to the difference in perception that has crept in among the youth regarding social norms. They are now celebrating individualism.

It has been seventy-seven years since India attained independence, a long time for today's generation to even fathom the socio-political conditions that existed then. Gandhi, Nehru, Bose, Shastri, Patel, Radhakrishnan—they may be familiar with these names, but what they stood for is lost to them. And as reading as a habit has taken a beating with every passing generation, it is easy to misguide them with misinformation and half-truths. That being said, one cannot question their strong sense of justice that is displayed from time to time whenever the need arises.

ᔕ

Changing goal posts

The basic premise of development for any country, especially a country as diverse as India, is that to sustain growth, all its social groups need to be a part of its economic journey. This was the core idea behind bringing reservations in the first place. In the battle of majority vs minority and upper vs lower castes, it is this growth that gets compromised.

The reason why this change in the middle-class behaviour has happened can be attributed to the lack of a common goal.

In the pre-Independence period, despite the diversity, the goal of the middle class (excluding the section that supported the British) was clear: freedom. And to achieve that, people rose above their differences, whether regional, religious, caste, or gender.

After Independence came the phase when the nation-building process was going on and the entire focus was on developing national resources and international relations. In 1950, Shyama Prasad Mukherjee resigned from Nehru's cabinet to form Jan Sangh. The purpose was to create an alternative to the Congress and give a political voice to the rightists, especially since the RSS had been banned following Gandhi's assassination. Yet at the social level, it was the Nehruvian ideology that ruled. The goal before the rightists, centrists, and leftists was the same: nation-building. The middle class was inclusive and very much influenced by it.

This brings us to the contemporary middle class. The reason it has become so polarized, apart from its politization, is that, unlike the previous phases, it is not bound by any specific, common goal. Each group differs from the other in terms of interests and goals.

For example, for the Dalit middle class, the primary issue is to gain social equality. Their idea of nationalism does not correspond with the general perception, which talks of allegiance to an imagined abstract image of the nation, to signs and symbols and not the social relationships between the people constituting the nation. As Gopal Guru says, 'Social groups such as Dalits, who have been historically cast out of the framework of the public sphere and forced to remain passive objects of history, view nationalism as an opportunity to achieve self-realization as active subjects. Self-realization can also be defined in terms of the Dalit desire to matter, to have equal dignity in the different forms and spheres of nationalist articulation.'[8]

This holds true for minorities, too. For them, nationalism becomes a two-point agenda: first, to create a national identity for themselves, which is currently being undermined by the Hindutva forces; and second, to link their national identity with their religious identity. On the other end is the urban middle class youth, which believes in the concept of 'world citizens' where national identity becomes redundant.

Moreover, as Keshav Chaturvedi points out, the struggle for the middle-class youth today is not for survival, but for 'growth and self-expression'.[9] Hence, the aspirations and goals are as varied as the middle class itself, and often they are in conflict with each other. Even within the backward classes, there are differences between those who have progressed socially as well as economically through the years and are politically dominant, like the Yadavs; and the others who have been thoroughly neglected and remain at the bottom of the pyramid, having no voice at all, like the Kahars or the Kushvahas.

Thus, in the absence of a unified goal, social divisions have become more prominent. Vested interests and vote-bank politics have further polarized communities.

Along with religion, caste has become the centre of political discourse, especially in the 2024 Lok Sabha elections.

One reason could be that there is increasing class consciousness among Dalits, Scheduled Tribes, and Other Backward Castes, and there is also the emergence of new middle classes in these interest groups, which are not only class-conscious but have become politically aware and active too. In her doctoral research, *Dalits and Social Mobility: A Discussion on the Dalit Middle Class*, PhD Scholar Anshika Srivastava makes a rather critical observation regarding the Dalit middle class: 'Given that the middle class comprises different fractions, the Dalits have entered the lower middle class in significant numbers, while few have managed to reach the upper fractions (Hunt, 2014).'[10]

The sentiment is echoed by author Anand Teltumbde, whose book *Dalits: Past, Present and Future* deals with the history of Dalits in particular and the origin of castes and their progression with time in general. Teltumbde maintains that it is only in urban areas where Dalits have made significant progress and have managed to enter the lower- and middle-middle class brackets. Some of them have even made it to the 'higher echelons and senior management positions in the Public Sector Undertakings (PSUs)'. The reality is vastly different for those residing in the rural areas. And they constitute the majority. 'What appears impressive is confined to a miniscule section of urban Dalits whose visibility eclipses the existence of rural Dalits and makes them invisible. For them the decades have brought a little change but also added a huge burden to shoulder, paradoxically, the burden of the progress of their urban counterpart that precipitates into persisting humiliation and occasional atrocities.'[11]

Veteran journalist and author of *The Disruptor*, V. P. Singh's biography, Debashish Mukherji is of the opinion that the growth of urban middle class of SCs, STs, and OBCs is due to reservations.[12] He says that the purpose behind Mandalization was to increase representation of the OBCs in the bureaucracy. However, it ended up changing the politics of India, especially North India. Vehement opposition to Mandalization helped in creating caste-consciousness amongst the OBCs. 'It taught them how much they mattered and the sheer size (Mandal report put them at 52%. However, recent surveys say they constitute around 35–40% of the population), and they became aware of their strength and political identity as a group, and they began asserting it collectively.... They began voting as an OBC bloc.'[13]

However, there is also a psychological aspect linked to their class consciousness, as the change is only in the economic positioning of the Dalits, STs, and OBCs and not in their social status. For instance, despite being politically powerful and a dominating caste identity today, Yadavs feel that they have not been accepted by the upper castes as being socially equal. They view the 'purification' of the CM's residence, after Akhilesh Yadav vacated it, by CM Yogi as an insult.[14]

In her research, Srivastava also highlights the fact that there can be varied response from people of the Dalit community to their mobility, keeping in mind their inter-personal relations with others. 'One of the identified responses,' notes Srivastava, 'is that of "passing one's identity as non-Dalit" in public sphere. This practice of passing was noted not only in the early studies on Dalit middle classes like that of Isaacs (1965), Ram (1988) but even in the recent times. For instance, Pandey (2011) discusses how the Dalits may engage in adoption of neutral caste names, use of first names…in an attempt to hide their caste location and background.'

Challenges faced by the middle class

An expanding middle class, nevertheless, is also facing increasing challenges that stem from its social, political, and economic situations. Economic hardships, social divisions, inter-generational conflicts, communal tensions, politicization of the middle class—they have jeopardized the middle-class dream of upward social mobility and, in the process, compromised the future of India.

Of the many challenges facing the middle class today, perhaps the most critical is to get its voice back politically. Over the years, the middle class has almost surrendered itself to the whims of political parties and has become a pawn in their hands. One can say that elections in India are fought on emotions and sentiments rather than issues. Marathi pride or the Gujarati pride or, for that matter, the Rajasthani pride, gets more importance than employment, education, and healthcare.

'The reason,' says Keshav Chaturvedi, 'is that a lot of people came into the middle class in a short span of time. These people were attitudinally and educationally not ready to be in the middle class. It is just that the finances pushed them upward. They are seeking validation. And the political parties are giving them that. "We are Indians. We are at the top. China and Pakistan have been shown their places."'[15]

Such declarations do play on the sentiments of the middle class and appeal to their nationalistic pride, and create a false sense of achievement, especially when the mainstream media backs these official claims. In the past decade, such rhetoric has become quite the norm during election time, whether it is the general election, or the state election. In a political environment that projects a majoritarian view, it suits the middle class not to question authority.

Ivan John concurs with the view that freedom of speech has become a challenge for the middle class. Though there is more space to talk about contradictions and conflicts, one is aware that there are a lot more people watching what is being said or written or posted. And between the harassment and the living in fear, 'I fear, people will now not speak as much, or speak out more openly, as they will be more worried about lawsuits, sedition cases etc. We are seeing that in the real world. ...Everything's political and which side we stand depends on whether we are willing to put ourselves out there and fight against the system. And very often, sad to say, most of the middle class is sometimes not willing to do that.'[16]

Political awareness also makes the middle class react to situations according to their needs, and that creates conflicts in society. The middle class has interests to protect. As Habib rightly says, for all those who have nothing to protect, nothing to talk about, discuss, or be scared of, whether economically, socially, or educationally, there's no threat to their lives from any section; they don't get involved in any way. 'It is actually the middle class that has aspirations. When they have aspirations, they have threats from different sections, from the government, and from fellow citizens, so they become more politically aware and more conscious of what is happening around them.'[17]

However, he considers the greatest challenge to be irrationality. All other challenges are related to it. 'If you are rational, logical, if you behave or think rationally then everything follows from that. Then you will respect your fellow citizens. Middle class has more responsibility than lower classes or upper classes.'[18]

Changing social norms have broadly divided the middle class into two groups. One is of hard-core traditionalists, which include the older generations and some politically motivated youths, like the Bajrang Dal and the Vishwa Hindu Parishad activists, who claim to be the custodians of Hindu culture and play the role of vigilantes on Valentine's Day; and the other is of aspirational liberals, who want to break the shackles of caste and religion. They are upwardly mobile and subscribe to Western social ideals. The tussle between the old and the new generation over changing social norms has led to the breaking down of the old value system. The older generations find it difficult to attune themselves to the new values replacing them. The issue of one's sexual orientation, for instance, is still a hushed affair in middle-class homes.

Similarly, caste still plays a huge role in inter-community interactions, though Mohapatra believes there are changes in the boundaries of class and caste, especially in the urban areas, as the younger middle-class generation is exposed to world cultures through movies and internet. They move around the world and most of them are not really committed to 'religious sacred behaviour'. The biggest challenge, according to him, though, is economic. 'I will be putting one word for it—consumerist. The Indian middle class today, I call them the new middle class, is highly consumerist... it is also grounded. They are ambitious yet at the same time they are not ruthless.'[19]

Contradictions seem to be an essential part of middle-class life. Misra says, 'The middle class is in contradiction with its own corporate owners. It's in contradiction with its own old self (old middle class) as well as the owner and it is in contradiction with people who are working with it as labour, as it has to sometimes manage this labour class. So, if you see logically, there are multiple contradictions, and these are reflected in culture.'[20]

Sucheta Mahajan highlights another major issue that is plaguing the country, and specifically the middle class, today—that of brain drain. A recent report states that according to the latest Education Ministry data, 'more than 770,000 Indian students went abroad to study in 2022, a six-year high. Also, many Indian students find it tough to find jobs after returning home, which is why they apply for permanent residency in their country of study. More than 90 per cent of the students do not wish to come back to India, say estimates.'

This raises serious concerns on the subject of brain drain.[21]

'The desire for a very comfortable standard of living is very high. And post liberalization, the possibility of financing it is also there,' she says.

So, along with that has come the belief that our educational institutes are not good enough, which they are, and that the children should go abroad for studies.

This, according to the historian, has already eroded the base of India's institutions and democracy. She raises a very pertinent question: if the middle class is exiting at the top levels in the sciences, technology, even arts, economics especially, who is going to have a stake in the growth of the country in the near future?

The thought is seconded by Sudhakar who contends that we (the middle class) have become increasingly self-centred. Most parents want their child to go abroad and earn money. The nation doesn't figure in their scheme of things, 'unless you wear it on the sleeve to show that you are patriotic'. He believes contributing towards the nation is not something many people are thinking of.

One rising trend seen in the cities is of nuclear families. With corporate culture replacing bureaucracy culture, working middle class individuals find it difficult to find a work-life balance. Sadly, being a patriarchal society, the higher burden falls squarely on middle-class women in India, especially in tier-two and tier-three cities. Deepika maintains that women themselves are responsible for not asserting their authority as far as their child's social and educational development is concerned, especially in areas in and around Varanasi. As a result, they are not taken seriously either by their children or by their husbands.

However, for most people, the most critical problem faced by the middle class remains financial, especially after the Covid-19 pandemic. Given the aspirations and lifestyle it has, the middle class has been struggling with the financial strain in the wake of job cuts and lay-offs following the pandemic. Rising inflation has made matters worse, and it has increased the economic insecurity of the middle-income groups. Increasing costs of housing, healthcare, education, and other essential goods and services has put significant financial strain on the middle class.

Despite the exponential growth of the middle class in the past few decades, as per the World Bank categorization, India remains a lower-middle-income country with a per capita income of $2,388 in 2022.

The 'why' needs to be clearly understood. With a rapidly growing middle class, India has become one of the biggest consumer markets in the world. Yet, it is the same middle class that has emerged as the biggest hurdle in its path of development. And the reason is its diversity.

Diversity, in itself, is not a disadvantage. In fact, it makes people more aware and open to different cultural practices and faiths. We present India on the world stage with the catchphrase 'unity in diversity'. But as ethnic identities dominate over the national identity, unity seems to have taken a backseat. Each year, the number of hate crimes increases.

A country can progress only when all its stakeholders are on the path of progress. When the larger goal is national development, effort should be on collaboration rather than exclusivity. The European middle class slowly became civilizational on the nationalism platform. Instead of France and Germany, it went towards European Union, fighting for universal values and environmental issues. The Indian middle classes, on the other hand, moved towards decolonization and asserting their own identities, and in the process, they adopted several traditional identity principles in an uncritical way.

According to Anand Kumar, the Indian middle class needs to make the same connect with the Indian masses that existed during the freedom movement.

With the rise of the Hindutva forces over the past decades, the Indian middle class seems to have been plagued by the politics of majoritarianism. The resulting fragmentation, disharmony, and distrust have made the goal of making India a developed country, a distant dream. Trolling and threats on social media have heightened middle-class insecurities, especially in the minority communities who usually abstain from participating in discussions on such issues. The debate of majority versus minority has obliterated all talks of universal brotherhood from public platforms, including the media, although 'Vasudev Kutumbakam' remains the official government line. And that has had a serious impact on the socio-economic growth of the country.

There have been areas where the middle class has made tremendous progress. The economy of India, for instance, saw unprecedented growth till 2010, as evidenced by an expanding middle class. It is only since 2016–17 that the economy suffered a setback due to demonetization followed by a hastily implemented GST. The situation became worse during the pandemic years (2020–22), which saw scores of lower-middle-class people slipping back into the lower-class bracket as small businesses folded and manufacturing almost came to a standstill.

More concerning is the fact that there are specific areas where the middle class has seemingly regressed. The biggest example of that can be seen in the polarization of communities.

This raises pertinent questions about the future of the Indian middle class. Will it continue to be a political stooge or develop an independent thought process? Will it once again uphold the ideals of democracy and free speech? And, most importantly, will it remain narrow in its approach to social issues or become inclusive and work towards the overall growth of society?

To answer all these questions, and to wriggle out of the quandary it finds itself in today, the middle class needs to rethink its role in society, retrace its steps to modernization of thoughts, and recreate social harmony. Only then can it survive the vagaries of human nature which, more often than not, result in destruction. And only then can we attain the much-coveted developed nation tag.

Acknowledgements

Writing on the middle class has been the most exhaustive yet exhilarating experience for me till date. During the one and a half years of my research, I read scores of books, journals, articles, and blogs, met some amazing people, and learned a lot about the society I live in and, more importantly, about myself and where I stand on the issues plaguing us. So, my deepest gratitude to Aleph Book Company and my editor, Pujitha Krishnan, for trusting me with this mammoth project. I would also like to thank the editorial team of Aleph for their continued support.

This journey would not have been possible without a few kindred spirits who graciously shared with me their invaluable views and helped me connect with the right people. Thank you Madhukar Upadhyay and Keshav Chaturvedi. I am grateful to all the people who responded to my emails and phone calls and agreed to an interview despite their busy schedules. It was a pleasure knowing you all.

Finally, my sincere thanks to my spouse, sisters, and daughter for bearing with me whenever I forced my rough drafts on them to read; to my friends for listening to my monologues on the subject at our get-togethers; and, last but not the least, to my parents, to whom I dedicate this book.

Thank you all!

Notes

INTRODUCTION

1 Peden Doma Bhutia, 'Is the World Ready to Meet the Indian Middle Class?', Skift.com, 9 January 2024, <https://skift.com/2024/01/09/is-the-world-ready-to-meet-the-indian-middle-class-megatrends-2024/>.

2 Ibid.

3 PTI, 'India's Population Estimated At 1.44 Billion, 24% In 0-14 Age Bracket: UN Report', *NDTV*, 17 April 2024.

4 Chris Versace, Leonore Hawkins, Mark Abssy, 'World Reimagined: The Rise of the Global Middle Class', Nassdaq.com, 9 July 2021, <https:// www.nasdaq.com/articles/world-reimagined%3a-the-rise-of-the-global-middle-class-2021-07-09>.

5 Natalie Chun and Anil Deolalikar, 'Who are the Middle Class and What Values do They Hold? Evidence from the World Values Survey', Adb.org, October 2010, <https:// www.adb.org/publications/who-are-middle-class-and-what-values-do-they-hold-evidence-world-values-survey>.

6 Richard V. Reeves, Katherine Guyot, Eleanor Krause, 'Defining the middle class: Cash, credentials, or culture?', Brookings Institution, 7 May 2018, <https://www.brookings.edu/articles/defining-the-middle-class-cash-credentials-or-culture/>.

7 Joseph Lopreato, Lawrence E. Hazelrigg, *Class, Conflict, and Mobility: Theories and Studies of Class Structure*, San Francisco: Chandler Publishing Company, 1972, pp. 40–41.

8 James T. Duke, *Conflict and Power in Social Life*, Utah: Brigham Young University Press, 1976, p. 34.

9 Charles E. Hurst, *Social Inequality: Forms, Causes, and Consequences*, United Kingdom: Pearson/Allyn and Bacon, 2007, p. 198.

10 Ibid, p. 203.

11 Émile Durkheim, *The Division of Labor in Society*, United States: Free Press, 1960, p. 399.

12 Ibid.

13 Anna Tarkhnishvili, Levan Tarkhnishvili, 'Middle Class: Definition, Role and Development', *Global Journal of Human Social Science*, Vol. 13, No. 7, 2013.

14 Akshay Ramanlal Desai, *Social Background of Indian Nationalism*, Mumbai: Indian Branch, Oxford University Press, 1948, pp. 47–63.

15 Pavan K. Varma, *The Great Indian Middle Class*, New Delhi: Viking, 1998, p. 2.

16 Imtiaz Ahmad, Helmut Reifeld (eds.), *Middle Class Values in India and Western Europe*, New Delhi: Social Science Press, 2001.

17 Rajesh Misra in conversation with the author, Lucknow, 20 January 2023.

18 S. C. Mohapatra in conversation with the author, New Delhi, 11 November 2022.

19 Madhukar Upadhyay in conversation with the author, Noida, 23 January 2023.

20 Govind Sadashiv Ghurye, *Caste and Race in India*, London: K. Paul, Trench, Trubner & Company Limited, 1932, p. 2.

21 Rajesh Misra in conversation with the author, Lucknow, 20 January 2023.

22 'India's middle class: Despondent, ignored, irrelevant and dumped?', *Sunday Guardian*, 14 June 2020.
23 Astha Savyasachi, 'Communal Textbooks, Teachers Who Brought Down Babri: How RSS Schools Create Hindutva Foot Soldiers', *The Wire*, 22 May 2023.
24 Alex Von Tunzelmann, *Indian Summer: The Secret History of the End of an Empire*, London: Pocket, 2008, p. 11.

1. THE MIDDLE CLASS BEFORE THE BRITISH

1 R. C. Majumdar, *Corporate Life in Ancient India*, Poona: The Oriental Book Agency, 1922, p. 28-30.
2 Mark Cartwright, 'Trade in the Roman World', Worldhistory.org, 12 April 2018, <https://www.worldhistory.org/article/638/trade-in-the-roman-world/>.
3 B. B. Misra, *The Indian Middle Classes: Their Growth in Modern Times*, London: Oxford University Press, 1961, p. 8.
4 Max Weber, Don Martindale (ed.), *The Religion of India: The Sociology of Hinduism and Buddhism*, Hans H. Gerth (tr.), Illinois: The Free Press, Glencoe, 1958, p. 113.
5 William Wilson Hunter, *The Indian Empire*, London: W. H. Ellen & Co. Ltd., 1886, p. 245.
6 K. M. Panikkar, *Hindu Society at Cross Roads*, Bombay: Popular Press Private, 1955, p. 9.
7 Ibid, p. 8.
8 'Unit-30 Social Mobility in Caste and Class', Block 8 Social Mobility, New Delhi: IGNOU, 2017, <https://egyankosh.ac.in/bitstream/123456789/21628/1/Unit-30.pdf>.
9 Sucheta Mahajan in conversation with the author, New Delhi, 22 March 2023.
10 A. Ghosh, *The City in Early Historical India*, Shimla: Indian Institute of Advanced Study, 1973, p. 35.
11 Weber, *The Religion of India*.
12 Misra, *The Indian Middle Classes*, p. 152.
13 S. K. Das, *The Economic History of Ancient India*, 1925, p. 65.
14 Robert Wilde, 'Effects of the Hundred Years War', ThoughtCo.com, 31 July 2019, <https://www.thoughtco.com/aftermath-of-the-hundred-years-war-1221904>.
15 Misra, *The Indian Middle Classes*, p. 4.
16 K. K. Thaplyal, *Guilds in Ancient India: A Study of Guild Organization in Northern Indian and Western Deccan from Circa 600 BC to Circa 600 AD*, India: New Age International, 1996.
17 Ibid.
18 W. W. Hunter, *Imperial Gazetteer of India,* (New ed.), Volume 1, London: Clarendon Press, 1907.
19 Ibid, Vol. 6, Edinburgh: Morrison and Gibb, 1886.
20 Tapan Ray Chaudhary, Irfan Habib (eds.), *Cambridge Economic History of India*, Vol. 1, c. 1200–c. 1750, Cambridge: Cambridge University Press, 1982, p. 190.
21 V. P. S. Raghuvanshi, *Indian Society in the Eighteenth Century*, New Delhi: Associated Publishing House, 1969.
22 H. G. Briggs, *The Cities of Gujaráshtra: Their Topography and History Illustrated in the Journal of a Recent Tour, with Accompanying Documents*, India: 'Times' Press by James Chesson, 1849, p. 17.

23 Hunter, *The Indian Empire*, p. 183.
24 S. C. Mohapatra in conversation with the author, New Delhi, 11 November 2022.
25 Roland R. Renne, *Land Economics*, New York: Harper & Brothers, 1947.
26 Ivan John in conversation with the author, Mumbai, 13 August 2022.
27 Madhukar Upadhyay in conversation with the author, Noida, 23 February 2023.
28 Chaudhary and Habib, *Cambridge Economic History of India*, p. 181.
29 Rajesh Misra in conversation with the author, Lucknow, 20 January 2023.
30 Sucheta Mahajan in conversation with the author, 22 March 2023.
31 Anand Kumar in conversation with the author, 1 April 2023.

2. PLASSEY, BUXAR, AND THE BRITISH

1 Hunter, *Imperial Gazetteer of India*, Vol. 6.
2 Brooks Adams, *The Law of Civilization and Decay: An Essay on History*, United Kingdom: Swan Sonnenschein, 1895, p. 313.
3 Suki Haider, 'Hero and villain: Robert Clive of the East India Company', Open University, OpenLearn.edu, 9 November 2020, <https://www.open.edu/openlearn/history-the-arts/history/hero-and-villain-robert-clive-the-east-india-company>.
4 L. S. S. O'Malley, *Bengal District Gazetteers, Midnapore*, Calcutta: The Bengal Secretariat Book Depot, 1911, p. 40.
5 John Malcolm, *A Memoir of Central India*, Vol. II, United Kingdom: Parbury & Allen, 1832, p. 434.
6 Anand Kumar in conversation with the author, 1 April 2023.
7 S. C. Mohapatra in conversation with the author, 11 November 2022.
8 Jon Wilson, *The Chaos of Empire: The British Raj and the Conquest of India*, London: Simon and Schuster UK Ltd, 2016, pp. 5–6.
9 Raghuvanshi, *Indian Society in the Eighteenth Century*, p. 4.

3. BENGAL RENAISSANCE AND THE REVOLT OF 1857

1 Misra, *The Indian Middle Classes*, p. 10.
2 J. W. Kaye, *Administration of the East India Company: A History of India Progress*, United Kingdom: R. Bentley, 1853, p. 78.
3 Ibid.
4 Sucheta Mahajan in conversation with the author, New Delhi, 22 March 2023.
5 A. R. Desai, *Social Background of Indian Nationalism*, London: Oxford University Press, 1948, p. 25.
6 Lord William Bentinck, Speech on 8 November 1829, Reprinted in A. B. Keith, *Speeches and Documents on Indian Policy 1750-1921*, Volume 1, London: Oxford University Press, 1985, p. 215.
7 Ibid, p. 62.
8 Suresh Chandra Ghosh, *The History of Education in Modern India*, India: Orient Blackswan, 2000, p. 18.
9 Misra, *The Indian Middle Classes*, p. 10.
10 Ibid, p. 9.
11 A. R. Desai, *Social Background of Indian Nationalism*, New Delhi: Popular Book Depot, 1948, p. 10.
12 Dharma Kumar (ed.), *Cambridge Economic History of India*, Vol. II, c.1757–c. 1970, India: Cambridge University Press, 1983, p. 24.

13 Rabindranath Tagore, C. F. Andrews (ed.), *Letters to a Friend*, India: George Allen & Unwin, 1931, p. 167.
14 David Kopf, *British Orientalism and the Bengal Renaissance: The Dynamics of Indian Modernization 1773–1835*, United States: University of California Press, 2023.
15 P. L. Rawat, *History of Indian Education*, India: Ram Prasad and Sons, 1956, pp. 18, 21.
16 Ibid, p. 39.
17 William Ward, *A View of the History, Literature, and Mythology of the Hindoos: Including a Minute Description of Their Manners and Customs, and Translations from Their Principal Works*, United Kingdom: Kingsbury, Parbury and Allen, 1822.
18 Reginald Heber, *Narrative of a Journey Through the Upper Provinces of India*, Vol. II, London, 1828, p. 291; Misra, *The Indian Middle Classes*, p. 153.
19 Misra, *The Indian Middle Classes*, p. 154.
20 Ghosh, *The History of Education in Modern India*.
21 Ibid, p. 25.
22 Ramchandra Guha, 'First Liberals', Makers of Modern India.
23 J. C. Ghosh (ed.), *The English Works of Raja Ram Mohun Roy*, Vol. II, Bhowanipore: Oriental Press, 1887.
24 Sophia Dobson Collet, *The Life and Letters of Raja Rammohun Roy*, Calcutta, 1914.
25 Modhumita Roy, 'Englishing India: Reinstituting Class and Social Privilege', *Academia.edu*, 1994.
26 'Impact on Society', BrahmoSamaj.net, <www.thebrahmosamaj.net/impact/socialimpact.html>.
27 Sucheta Mahajan in conversation with the author, New Delhi, 22 March 2023.
28 Thirthankar Roy, 'The Mutiny and the Merchants', *The Historical Journal*, 59, Vol. 2, 2016, pp. 393–416.
29 J. W. Kaye, G. B. Malleson, *History of the Indian Mutiny, 1857-1858: Commencing from the Close of the Second Volume of Sir John Kaye's History of the Sepoy War*, Vol. VI, United Kingdom: Allen, 1880, p. 127.
30 British Parliamentary Papers, *Appendix (A) to Further Papers (no. 5)*, p. 299.
31 L. E. Ruutz Rees, *A Personal Narrative of the Siege of Lucknow: From Its Commencement to Its Relief by Sir Colin Campbell*, United Kingdom: Longman, Brown, Green, Longmans, & Roberts, 1858, p. 34.
32 Ibid, p. 26.
33 Ibid, p. 28.
34 Charles Ball, *The History of the Indian Mutiny: Giving a Detailed Account of the Sepoy Insurrection in India: And a Concise History of the Great Military Events Which Have Tended to Consolidate British Empire in Hindostan*, Vol. II, United Kingdom: London Printing and Publishing Company, 1858, p. 572.
35 R. C. Majumdar, *The Sepoy Mutiny and the Revolt of 1857*, India: K. L. Mukhopadhyay, 1957, p. 57.
36 P. C. Joshi (ed.), *Rebellion, 1857: A Symposium*, India: People's Publishing House, 1957, p. 112.
37 Ibid.
38 William Forbes-Mitchell, *Reminiscences of the Great Mutiny 1857-59: Including the Relief, Siege, and Capture of Lucknow, and the Campaigns in Rohilcund and Oude*, New York: The Macmillan Company, 1897, pp. 57–58.
39 Lata Singh, 'Making the "Margin" Visible', peoplesdemocracy.in, 23 September

2007, <https://archives.peoplesdemocracy.in/2007/0923/09232007_1857.html>.

4. IMPACT OF THE REVOLT AND THE SWADESHI MOVEMENT

1 Rajesh Misra in conversation with the author, Lucknow, 20 January 2023.

2 Sucheta Mahajan in conversation with the author, 22 March 2023.

3 Bipin Chandra, Mridula Mukherjee, K. N. Panikkar, et al., *India's Struggle for Independence*, India: Penguin Random House India Private Limited, 2016.

4 B. R. Ambedkar, *Dr. Babasaheb Ambedkar: Writings and Speeches*, India: Education Department, Government of Maharashtra, 1992.

5 Surendranath Banerjea, *A Nation in Making: Being the Reminiscences of Fifty Years of Public Life*, India: Oxford University Press, 1927, p. 191.

6 The text of this speech, delivered at the Field and Academy Club meeting of 10 Agrahayan 1312, is given in Kedarnath Dasgupta's *Shiksharandolan* (1905), Part III. Source: The Swadeshi Movement in Bengal 1903-08 by Sumit Sarkar, People's Publishing House, New Delhi, 1973.

7 Chandra, et al., *India's Struggle for Independence*, p. 104.

8 Rajat Kanta Ray, *Social Conflict and Political Unrest in Bengal, 1875–1927*, India: Oxford University Press, 1984, p. 32.

9 Ibid, p. 33.

10 Sumit Sarkar, *The Swadeshi Movement in Bengal (1903-1908)*, New Delhi: People's Publishing House, 1973, p. 27.

11 Ranjit Roy, 'Swadeshi Movement', Banglapedia.org, <https://en.banglapedia.org/index.php/Swadeshi_Movement>.

12 Anand Kumar in conversation with the author, 1 April 2023.

5. THE NATIONAL MOVEMENT (1920–1947)

1 D. Chakrabarty, C. Bhattacharyya (eds.), *Congress in Evolution: A Collection of Congress Resolutions from 1885–1934 and Other Important Documents*, Kolkata: Book Company Limited, 1935, p. xxiii.

2 Chakrabarty, *Subhas Chandra Bose and Middle Class Radicalism*, p. 38.

3 Madhukar Upadhyay in conversation with the author, Noida, 27 February 2023.

4 B. R. Khan, 'Sixth Quinquennial Report on the Progress of Education in Bengal', *Aspects of Society and Politics in Bengal, 1927-36*, pp. 172–73.

5 Ajay Konwar, *The Non-Cooperation Movement in the Erstwhile District of Errang*, Jorhat: Jengraimukh College; 'Boycott of Government Schools in Ahmedabad', Digital District Depository Detail, 15 March 2023, <https://amritmahotsav.nic.in/district-reopsitory-detail.htm?14650>.

6 'Jalandhar Charkha Club', IndianCulture.gov.in, <https://indianculture.gov.in/node/2816155>.

7 'Report of Progress of Non-Cooperation Movement in Amritsar, Punjab', [online facsimile], <https://nvli.in/archives/report-progress-non-cooperation-movement-amritsar-punjab>.

8 *Bombay Chronicle*, 14 November 1921, <https://www.granthsanjeevani.com/ jspui/handle/123456789/6773>.

9 John Last, '"The Prince of Wales" 1921 Trip to India Was a Royal Disaster', *JSTOR Daily*, 2 February 2022.

10 Mahatma Gandhi, *Young India: 1919-1922*, India: S. Ganesan, 1924, p. 1019.

11 Chandra, et al., *India's Struggle for Independence,* p. 155.
12 Amitabha Gupta, 'A Great Robbery that shook the Raj', *Peepul Tree Stories,* 7 September 2019.
13 Bhagat Singh, 'To Young Political Workers', 2 February 1931, shahidbhagatsingh.org, <http://www.shahidbhagatsingh.org/index.asp?link=political_workers>.
14 Webb Miller, 'Gandhi's Salt March Campaign: Contemporary Dispatches (1/2)', Satyagraha Foundation for Nonviolence Studies, satyagrahafoundation.org, <https://www.satyagrahafoundation.org/gandhis-salt-march-campaign-contemporary-dispatches-12/>.
15 D. G. Tendulkar, *Mahatma Volume 1: Life of Mohandas Karamchand Gandhi,* New Delhi: Publications Division Ministry of Information & Broadcasting, Government of India, 1915, p. 49.
16 Rajesh Misra in conversation with the author, Lucknow, 20 January 2023.
17 Ibid.

6. FEMINIST MOVEMENT IN PRE-INDEPENDENT INDIA

1 Shakuntala Rao Shastri, *Women in the Vedic Age,* Bombay: Bharatiya Vidya Bhawan, 1954, pp. 25–26.
2 *Manusmriti,* Shlokas 17–18.
3 Dr Angbin Yasmin, '"Middle Class" Women in Mughal India', *Academia.edu.*
4 Yasmin Angbin, *Proceedings of the Indian National Congress,* Vol. 75, Platinum Jubilee, India: Indian National Congress, 2014, pp. 295–306.
5 Margrit Pernau, *Ashraf into Middle Classes: Muslims in Nineteenth-Century Delhi,* India: Oxford University Press, 2013, pp. 148–151.
6 Nawab Shaikh Mohammed Qutb-ud-Din, *A Gift to Husband and Wife,* 1851, p. 170.
7 Zeeshan Hussain, 'Position of women in Medieval India', GroundXero.in, 24 October 2019, <ref. https://www.groundxero.in/2019/10/24/position-of-women-in-medieval-india/>.
8 S. C. Mohaptra in conversation with the author, New Delhi, 11 November 2022.
9 Radha Kumar, *The History of Doing: An Illustrated Account of Movements for Women's Rights and Feminism in India 1800-1990,* India: Kali for Women, 1993, p. 2.
10 Sanchari Pal, 'Remembering Madam Bhikaji Cama, the Brave Lady to First Hoist India's Flag on Foreign Soil', TheBetterIndia.com, 24 September 2016.
11 Madhukar Upadhyay in conversation with the author, Noida, 23 February 2023.
12 Kumar, *The History of Doing,* p. 2.

7. GANDHI, NEHRU, AND THE MIDDLE CLASS

1 Tara Chand, *History of the Freedom Movement in India,* Vol. IV, India: Publications Division, Ministry of Information and Broadcasting, 1972, p. 3.
2 Madhukar Upadhyay in conversation with the author, Noida, 23 February 2023.
3 'The Curse of Industrialisation', MKGandhi.org, <https://www.mkgandhi.org/momgandhi/chap49.htm>.
4 Geoffrey Ashe, *Gandhi: A Biography,* United States: Cooper Square Publishing, LLC, 2000, p. 217.
5 Chand, *History of the Freedom Movement in India,* p. 3.
6 Jawaharlal Nehru, *An Autobiography,* New Delhi: Penguin Books Limited, 2004, p. 532.

7 Ibid, p. 54.
8 'The End at The Beginning: Gandhi and Nehru Letters', TheBeacon.in, 29 March 2019, <https://www.thebeacon.in/2019/03/29/the-end-at-the-beginning-gandhi-and-nehru-letters/>.
9 Ibid.

8. MIDDLE CLASS SHIFT TO THE RIGHT

1 Ajaz Ashraf, 'Opinion: Why it's essential for school students to learn about religious violence in ancient India', *Scroll.in*, 1 May 2018.
2 Pratharma Banerjee, 'Are communal riots a new thing in India? Yes, and it started with the British', *The Print*, 3 March 2020; Rajat Ghai, 'The peasant rebels of the Satnami Rebellion', DownToEarth.org, 15 October 2019, <https://www.downtoearth.org.in/reviews/the-peasant-rebels-of-the-satnami-rebellion-67044>.
3 Manmath Nath Das, *India Under Morley and Minto: Politics Behind Revolution, Repression and Reforms*, London: G. Allen and Unwin, 1964, p. 13.
4 Ibid, p. 33.
5 *Minto Papers, Letters and Telegrams*, Vol. I, No. 87, Minto to J. B. Leslie-Rogers, March 15, 1909, p. 18; Das, *India Under Morley and Minto*.
6 Ibid, p. 147.
7 Chandra, *India's Struggle for Independence*, pp. 121–122.
8 Sudheendra Kulkarni, 'The Tilak-Jinnah pact embodied communal harmony that is much needed in modern-day India', *Scroll.in*, 3 August 2020.
9 Madhukar Upadhyay in conversation with the author, Noida, 23 February 2023.
10 Ibid.

9. THE MIDDLE CLASSES OF THE WORLD

1 Marc Bloch, *Feudal Society*, Vols. I and II, United States: University of Chicago Press, 1966.
2 'French Revolution', Britannica.com, <https://www.britannica.com/event/French-Revolution>.
3 Dr Darius von Güttner, 'The French Revolution and Europe – Its Echoes, Its Influence, Its Impact', ResearchGate.net, Vol. 51, No. 1, January 2016, pp. 34–42.
4 Mark Philp, 'Britain and the French Revolution', *BBC*, 17 February 2011.
5 Kathryn Hughes, 'The Middle Classes: Etiquette and Upward Mobility', The British Library, 2014, <www.bl.uk/romantics-and-victorians/articles/the-middle-classes-etiquette-and-upward-mobility>.
6 Pamela M. Pilbeam, *The Middle Classes in Europe 1789 –1914: France, Germany, Italy and Russia*, Chicago: Lyceum Books, 1990.
7 Ibid, p. 9.
8 Jürgen Kocka, 'The Middle Classes in Europe', *The Journal of Modern History*, Vol. 67, No. 4, 1995, pp. 783–806.
9 Ibid, p. 787.
10 Rajesh Misra in conversation with the author, Lucknow, 20 January 2023.
11 Rowan Allen and Denny Rose, *History of Europe*, Waltham Abbey: EDTECH Press, 2018.
12 Ibid.
13 Elisabetta Cassina Wolff, 'Both Mussolini's and Hitler's rise to power followed the

rules of democracy', University of Oslo, 21 March 2022, <https://www.hf.uio.no/iakh/english/research/news-and-events/news/2022/both-mussolinis-and-hitlers-rise-to-power>.

10. 1947: INDEPENDENCE AND SOCIAL MOVEMENTS

1 Constitution of India, 1950, Preamble.

2 S. Irfan Habib (ed.), *Indian Nationalism: The Essential Writings*, India: Aleph Book Company, 2017, p. 4.

3 Lucien Febvre, Peter Burke (ed.), *A New Kind of History: From the Writings of Febvre*, United Kingdom: Routledge and Kegan Paul, 1973, p. 14.

4 Rajesh Misra in conversation with the author, Lucknow, 20 January 2023.

5 Barbara H. Rosenwein, 'Worrying about Emotions in History', *American Historical Review*, 2002, p. 842.

6 Rajesh Misra in conversation with the author, Lucknow, 20 January 2023.

7 Rajesh Misra in conversation with the author, Lucknow, 23 January 2023.

8 S. K. Jain, Alok Sarin, 'Setting the Stage: The Partition of India and the Silences of Psychiatry', *The Psychological Impact of the Partition of India*, India: SAGE Publications India, 2018.

9 Ibid.

10 Ibid.

11 Deepra Dandekar, 'Refugees in India after 1947', *Academia.edu*, 2018.

12 WildFilmsIndia, 'Candid interview on the Partition, history and present-day Delhi | Khushwant Singh', YouTube, 13 November 2019, <https://www.youtube. com/watch?v=8g38TFg8IGo>.

13 Shyamal Kataria and Muhamed Ali, 'Sindh: The Partition that Never Happened', *Migration Letters*, Vol. 20, 2023, pp. 288–98.

14 Chanda Kathuria in conversation with the author, Mumbai, 12 December 2022.

15 Researcmaarket19, 'How Sindhi's became the fastest growing rich community in India: Characteristics of their entrepreneurship', Issuu.com, 25 July 2019, <https://issuu.com/researchmarket19/docs/how_sindhi_s_became_the_fastest_ gro>.

16 Ved Mehta, *Mahatma Gandhi and His Apostles*, India: Penguin Books Limited, 1977, p. 59.

17 Paul John, 'Bapu's first ashram was shunned for letting in a Dalit', *Times of India*, 20 May 2013.

18 Rajesh Misra in conversation with the author, Lucknow, 20 January 2023.

19 'Why February 21 Is International Mother Language Day—All About 'Ekushe', Bangladesh Bhasha Andolan History', *ABP News*, 21 February 2022.

20 Uttara Shahani, 'LANGUAGE WITHOUT A LAND: PARTITION, SINDHI REFUGEES, AND THE EIGHTH SCHEDULE OF THE INDIAN CONSTITUTION.', *Asian Affairs*, 2022.

21 M Christhu Doss, 'What History Tells Us About Discussions Around Hindi as 'Rashtra Bhasha', *The Wire*, 25 September 2019.

22 Meeting of the Parliamentary Official Language Committee, New Delhi, April 2022.

23 'T.N. BJP won't allow imposition of Hindi, says Annamalai', *The Hindu*, 12 April 2022.

24 J Sam Daniel Stalin, 'Order To Rename 'Curd' Withdrawn As Move Leaves Sour Taste In Tamil Nadu', *NDTV*, 30 March 2023.

25 Adrija Roychowdhury, 'There are 600 potentially endangered languages in India… each dead language takes away a culture system', *Indian Express*, 3 May 2020.

26 Rajesh Misra in conversation with the author, Lucknow, 20 January 2023.

27 'India can't have parallel legal systems for rich and poor: SC', *Economic Times*, 22 July 2021.

28 Sambuddha Mitra Mustafi, 'India Ink - Notes on the World's Largest Democracy Search India Ink SEARCH Why Indian Elites Like to Call Themselves 'Middle Class', *New York Times*, 17 May 2013.

29 Arun Kumar, 'Is Redistribution of Wealth in India a 'Jumla' or a Necessity?', *The Wire*, 26 April 2024.

30 '1973: Chipko movement starts ', *Frontline*, 14 August 2022.

31 Amit Mitra, 'Chipko: an unfinished mission', DownToEarth.org, 30 April 1993, <https://www.downtoearth.org.in/coverage/chipko-an-unfinished-mission-30883>.

32 Ibid.

33 S. Gopikrishna Warrier, 'Silent Valley: A controversy that focused global attention on a rainforest 40 years ago', Mongabay.com, 1 February 2018, <https://india.mongabay.com/2018/02/silent-valley-a-controversy-that-focused-global-attention-on-a-rainforest-40-years-ago/>.

34 '1985: Narmada Bachao Andolan', *Frontline*, 15 August 2022.

35 K. M. Aarif, A. Nefla, S. B. Muzaffar, et al., 'Traditional fishing activities enhance the abundance of selected waterbird species in a wetland in India', Avian Research, Vol. 8, Article 16, 2017.

36 G. S. Ghurye, *Caste, Class, and Occupation*, Mumbai: Popular Book Depot, 1961.

37 Kancha Ilaiah Shepherd, 'How the Brahmin Conception of Leather as "Untouchable" Segregated Dalits and Weakened India', *The Wire*, 20 December 2021.

38 'The Dalit Panther Movement: An Inspiring Era Of India's Dalit Rights Movement', AmbedkariteToday.com, <https://www.ambedkaritetoday.com/2019/04/the-dalit-panther-movement-history.html>.

11. CASTE IN EDUCATION: MANDAL COMMISSION

1 Bhimrao Ramji Ambedkar, Vasant Moon, *Dr. Babasaheb Ambedkar, Writings and Speeches*, India: Dr. Ambedkar Foundation, Government of Maharashtra, January 2014, p. 38.

2 Romila Thapar, 'The culture of discrimination', Indian Cultural Forum, 26 April 2018, <https://indianculturalforum.in/2018/04/26/the-culture-of-discrimination/>.

3 Surinder S. Jodhka, Niraja Jayal, Pratap Bhanu (eds.), 'Caste and Politics', *The Oxford Companion to Politics in India*, India: Oxford University Press, 2010.

4 S. C. Mohaptra in conversation with the author, New Delhi, 11 November 2022.

5 'Social Backwardness and Caste', Mandal Commission Report, 1980, p. 16.

6 Ibid.

7 Pragya Kaushika, '25 years of Mandal protests- His struggle changed India's politics: Rajeev Goswami's daughter', *Indian Express*, 6 October 2015.

8 'Mandal report touches a peculiar chord among youth', *India Today*, 31 October 1990.

9 Ibid.

10 Ibid.

11 Ibid.
12 Irena Akbar, '25 years of Mandal protests- I had no idea what reservation was: Self-immolation survivor Atul Aggarwal', *Indian Express*, 4 October 2015.
13 'Mandal report touches a peculiar chord among youth'.
14 Ibid.
15 S. P. Singh, A. Avasthi, P. Kulhara, 'A psychosocial study of "self-immolation" in India', *Acta Psychiatrica Scandinavica*, 1998, pp. 71–75.
16 Rajesh Misra in conversation with the author, Lucknow, 20 January 2023.
17 Ibid.
18 Ibid.
19 'Storm created by Mandal Commission poses serious threat to V.P. Singh's political survival', *India Today*, 15 October 1990.
20 Ibid.; Farzand Ahmed, 'Violent anti-Mandal protests threaten to escalate into no-holds-barred war in Bihar', *India Today,* 15 November 1990

12. MIDDLE CLASS WOMEN AND THE FEMINIST MOVEMENT

1 Madhukar Upadhyay in conversation with the author, Noida, 23 February 2023.
2 Dwijendra Nath Thakur, 'Feminism and Women Movement in India', *Research Journal of Humanities and Social Sciences*, Vol. 4, Issue 4, 2012, pp. 458–464.
3 Ivan John in conversation with the author, 13 August 2022.
4 Srila Ray, '#MeToo Is A Crucial Moment to Revisit the History of Indian Feminism', *Economic and Political Weekly*, Vol. 53, Issue 42, 20 October 2018.
5 Thakur, 'Feminism and Women Movement in India'.
6 Usha Mehta, Usha Thakkar, 'The Anti-Price-Rise Movement in Bombay', *Canadian Woman Studies*, Vol. 13, No. 1, 1992.
7 Radha Kumar, *The History of Doing: An Illustrated Account of Movements for Women's Rights and Feminism in India 1800-1990*, India: Kali for Women, 1993.
8 Nishtha Shanti, 'The Mathura Rape Case Of 1972: A Watershed Moment in India's Rape Laws', Feminism in India, 2 September 2021, <https://feminisminindia.com/2021/09/02/mathura-rape-case-1972-watershed-moment-india-rape-laws/#>.
9 Ray, '"#MeToo Is A Crucial Moment to Revisit the History of Indian Feminism', *Economic and Political Weekly*.
10 Ivan John in conversation with the author, 13 August 2022.

13. MIDDLE CLASS POLITICS FROM 1947–91

1 Madhukar Upadhyay in conversation with the author on 23 February 2023, Noida.
2 Ibid.
3 'Nehru's Presidential Address at the Lahore Congress, 1929', TheNehru.org, <https://www.thenehru.org/2023/06/nehrus-presidential-address-at-lahore.html>.
4 Madhavan K. Palat, 'Nehru's socialism was evolutionary, inclusive, and not based on class', *The Hindu*, 12 February 2022; H. Venkatasubbiah, 'Nehru's economic philosophy', *The Hindu*, 29 May 1964.
5 Savya Sachi, 'Nehru's Conception of Socialism', *The Economic Weekly*, July 1964.
6 S. Irfan Habib in conversation with the author, New Delhi, 26 June 2023.
7 Ibid.

8 Sachi, 'Nehru's Conception of Socialism'.

9 Lancy Lobo and Jayesh Shah (eds.), 'The Indian Middle Class and its Politics', *The Trajectory of India's Middle Class: Economy, Ethics, and Etiquette*, 6 March 2015.

10 P. G. Altbach, 'Student Politics and Higher Education in India', *Deadalus*, Vol. 97, No. 1, 1968, pp. 254–73.

11 Ibid.

12 Ibid.

13 Professor Sudhakar in conversation with the author, Mumbai, 26 September 2023.

14 Adrija Roychowdhury, 'Naxalbari: How a peasant uprising triggered a pan-India political movement', *Indian Express*, 25 May 2018.

15 Professor Sudhakar in conversation with the author, Mumbai, 26 September 2023.

16 Amrita Shah, 'Protests by the privileged? Gujarat has a long history', *Times of India*, 30 August 2015.

17 'TOI Archives: The failure of a system; JP movement', *Economic Times*, 28 August, 2011.

18 Arun Kumar, 'The 1970s Indian Economy: A Period of Growing Strains and the Nation's Fight Against Poverty', *The Wire*, 10 March 2021.

19 Inder Malhota, *Indira Gandhi: A Personal and Political Biography*, Boston: Northeastern University Press, 1991.

20 Ayush Ranka, 'The Middle-Class Supported the Emergency When it Was Declared', *The Wire*, 25 June 2021.

21 Rajesh Misra in conversation with the author, Lucknow, 20 January 2023.

22 William Mazzarella, Rachel Dwyer (ed.), 'Middle Class', *South Asia Keywords*, 2005.

23 Professor Sudhakar in conversation with the author, Mumbai, 26 September 2023.

24 Anand Kumar in conversation with the author, 1 April 2023.

25 Professor Sudhakar in conversation with the author, Mumbai, 26 September 2023.

14. NEW ECONOMIC POLICY: CRISIS, MANAGEMENT, AND IMPACT

1 S. B. Kumar, 'P.V. Narasimha Rao: The Precursor of the Era of Economic Reforms in India', *Indian Journal of Public Administration*, Vol. 63, No. 4, pp. 616–30.

2 Reserve Bank of India, *The Reserve Bank of India (Part A and Part B) - Vol. 4: 1981-1997*, New Delhi: Academic Foundation, 2013, pp. 443–91.

3 Vinay K. Srivastava, 'Reliving the landmark 1991 economic reforms', *The Hindu BusinessLine*, 26 July 2021.

4 'Ideas of India: The 1991 Project', The 1991 Project.com, 19 August 2021, <https://the1991project.com/podcasts/the1991project>.

5 Vinay Sitapati, 'Rescuing the Economy, 1991–92', *Half - Lion: How P.V. Narasimha Rao Transformed India*, India: Penguin Random House India Private Limited, 27 June 2016.

6 Express Web Desk, 'Road ahead is more daunting than 1991 crisis: Manmohan Singh', *Indian Express*, 23 July 2021.

7 Reserve Bank of India, 'Management and Resolution of the 1991 Crisis', *The Reserve Bank of India, 1967-1981*, Volume 4, India: RBI Central Office, 2005, pp. 462–463.

8 'Saurabh Dwivedi dks Premchand ds D;k fdLls lquk xbZ iksrh Sara Rai? Kitabwala|Premchand hindi stories', YouTube, 7 March 2023, <https://www.

youtube.com/watch?v=EsN0hy593Ow>.

9 Anand Subramanian in conversation with the author, Mumbai, 17 December 2022.

10 Laura Copley, 'Hierarchy of Needs: A 2024 Take on Maslow's Findings', PositivePsychology.com, 8 January 2024, <https://positivepsychology.com/hierarchy-of-needs/>.

11 Chandra R. Srikanth, 'In 1990, there was an offer to buy us out for ₹2 crore. Infosys has ₹6.5 lakh crore m-cap now: NR Narayana Murthy on 1991 reforms', Moneycontrol.com, 21 July 2021, <https://www.moneycontrol.com/news/business/nr-narayana-murthy-1991-reforms-impact-economic-liberalisation-infosys-7194741.html>.

12 Ibid.

13 Subir Roy, 'Nilekani reveals Infosys's winning formula', Rediff.com, 18 August 2006, <https://www.rediff.com/money/2006/aug/18inter.htm>.

14 Shanglio Sun, 'Number of people employed by Infosys from financial year 2010 to 2023', Statista.com, 28 August 2023, <https://www.statista.com/statistics/328288/employees-at-infosys/>.

15 Roy, 'Nilekani reveals Infosys's winning formula'.

16 Srikanth, 'In 1990, there was an offer to buy us out for ₹2 crore. Infosys has ₹6.5 lakh crore m-cap now: NR Narayana Murthy on 1991 reforms'.

17 Ambuj Gupta, 'A Critique's View of Employee Stock Options in India: Re-Assessment and Perspectives', *SSRN*, 10 August 2010, <https://papers.ssrn.com/sol3/Delivery.cfm/SSRN_ID1692057_code913456.pdf?abstractid=1692057&mirid=1>.

18 Malini Goyal, 'Indian middle-class moves from functional living to a lifestyle of fulfilment', *India Today*, 9 June 2003.

19 Leela Fernandes, *India's New Middle Class: Democratic Politics in an Era of Economic Reform*, Minnesota: University of Minnesota Press, 29 November 2006, p. 72.

20 Ibid.

21 'The changing landscape of India's credit industry', PWC.in, August 2021, <https://www.pwc.in/industries/financial-services/fintech/dp/the-changing-landscape-of-indias-credit-industry.html>.

22 'What is striking in India is the indifference of the privileged', Chomsky.info, 6 July 2013, <https://chomsky.info/20130706/>.

23 Harsh Mander, 'In Feeble Light', *Looking Away: Inequality, Prejudice and Indifference in New India*, India: Speaking Tiger, 2015, p. 11.

24 Chanda Kathuria in conversation with the author, Mumbai, 12 December 2022.

25 Rakesh Kocchar, 'In the pandemic, India's middle class shrinks and poverty spreads while China sees smaller changes', Pew Research Center, 18 March 2021, <https://www.pewresearch.org/short-reads/2021/03/18/in-the-pandemic-indias-middle-class-shrinks-and-poverty-spreads-while-china-sees-smaller-changes/>.

26 Bhartendu Sood, 'Impact of Covid has not been same on the middle class', *Reader's Blog*, 27 June 2021, <https://timesofindia.indiatimes.com/readersblog/my-contemplations/impact-of-covid-has-not-been-same-on-the-middle-class-34279/>.

27 Nilanjan Banik, 'A Knotty Affair: India's Burgeoning Population and Stagnating Middle-Income', *The Wire*, 26 April 2023.

28 Ibid.

15. STRUCTURE AND COMPOSITION OF THE MIDDLE CLASS

1 'Tragedy of those "who must not be touched": All you need to know about the Dalit situation in India', *India Today*, 11 March 2016.; Darpan Singh, 'Who is Dalit or Savarna? Why caste system must go in totality', *India Today*, 18 August 2022.

2 Fernandes, *India's New Middle Class*, p. xviii.

3 Ibid.

4 Leela Fernandes, 'India's Middle Classes in Contemporary India', *Routledge Handbook of Contemporary India*, 2015, p. 237.

5 Sandhya Krishnan, Neeraj Hatekar, 'Rise of the New Middle Class in India and Its Changing Structure', *Economic and Political Weekly*, Volume 52, Issue 22, 3 June 2017, pp. 40–48.

6 Ibid.

7 Swati Ramanathan and Ramesh Ramanathan, 'Many layers within India's middle class', *Hindustan Times*, 16 April 2019.

8 E. Sridharan, 'The Growth and Sectoral Composition of India's Middle Class: Its Impact on the Politics of Economic Liberalization', *India Review*, Volume 4, October 2004, pp. 405–428.

9 Ramanathan, Ramanathan, 'Many layers within India's middle class', 16 April 2019.

10 Anirudh Krishna and Devendra Bajpai, 'Layers in Globalising Society and the New Middle Class in India', *Economic and Political Weekly*, Vol. 50, No. 5, January 2015,

11 Ibid.

12 'What is Dalit Middle Class?', NewsClick.in, 13 July 2017, <https://www.newsclick.in/what-dalit-middle-class>.

13 Dr Y. Srinivasa Rao, 'Problematic Dalit Middle Class', RoundTableIndia.co.in, 3 November 2017, <https://www.roundtableindia.co.in/problematic-dalit-middle-class/>.

14 'Dr. Ambedkar's Historical Speech At Agra', Countercurrents.org, 26 August 2016, <https://countercurrents.org/2016/08/dr-ambedkars-historical-speech-at-agra/>.

15 Ashwaq Masoodi, 'Joining the India story: Rise of the Muslim middle',

16 Hilal Ahmed, 'New Indian Muslim middle class is privately religious, barely political', *The Print*, 29 September 2018.

17 Christopher Jaffrelot, 'The Class Element in the 2014 Indian Election and the BJP's Success with Special Reference to the Hindi Belt', *Studies in Indian Politics*, Vol. 3, No. 1, pp. 19–38.

18 'The History of the LGBTQ+ Movement in India', *Fine Print*, No. 6,

19 Milanka Chaudhury, 'LGBTQ Pride Month: In the end, equality has to be served', *Wionews.com*, 9 June 2023, <https://www.wionews.com/opinions-blogs/ lgbtq-pride-month-in-the-end-equality-has-to-be-served-599473>.

20 Pushpesh Kumar, 'Queering Indian Sociology: A Critical Engagement', *Queering Indian Sociology: A Critical Engagement*, Volume 2, Issue 1, April 2018, p. 72.

21 Ibid, pp. 70–71.

22 Prabhash K. Dutta, 'Homosexuality in ancient India: 10 instances', *India Today*, 10 July 2018.

23 Ivan John in conversation with the author, Mumbai, 13 August 2022.

24 Payal Dhar, '"I have sacrificed a lot": Growing up LGBTQ+ in India', *Al Jazeera*, 21 June 2021.

25 Riya Gangwal, 'Deconstructing Queer Representation in Indian Politics', 16 December 2021, <https://www.cgapsouthasia.org/post/deconstructing-queer-representation-in-indian-politics>.

26 Zoya Mateen, 'Lok Sabha elections: LGBTQ Indians are more accepted than ever - but politics hasn't caught up', *BBC*, 27 May 2024.

16. CHARACTERISTICS AND BEHAVIOUR

1 Anand Kumar in conversation with the author, 28 February 2023.

2 Rajesh Misra in conversation with the author, Lucknow, 20 January 2023.

3 Anand Kumar in conversation with the author, 1 April 2023.

4 M. Rajivlochan, 'Why India's youth is chasing the sarkari naukri', *Indian Express*, 29 February 2024.

5 Ivan John in conversation with the author, Mumbai, 13 August 2022.

6 Ibid.

7 PTI, 'NCW received nearly 31,000 complaints of crimes against women in 2022', *Business Standard*, 1 January 2023.

8 Malavika Murali, 'Around 3,400 communal riots took place from 2016-2020: Centre', *Hindustan Times*, 30 March 2022.

9 Padmakshi Sharma, 'Mainstream News Channels Ran Programs With Anti-Muslim Prejudice While Reporting CAA Protests: Citizen's Committee Report', Livelaw.in, 10 October 2022.

10 Concerned Citizens Tribunal, 'Genocide in Gujarat: Patterns of violence', Humanrightsasia.com, <http://www.humanrights.asia/resources/journals-magazines/article2/focus-the-international-criminal-court/genocide-in-gujarat-patterns-of-violence/>.

11 Urvashi Bahuguna, '"If we want to reduce violence in this country, we need to change how power works": Revati Laul', *Scroll.in*, 30 March 2019.

12 Damayantee Dhar, 'Gujarat: SIT Says No Rape, NO Murder in Modasa Dalit Rape Case', *Newsclick*, 18 March 2020.

13 Harshita Rathore, 'Rape, Caste, Double Standards, and India's Middle Class', *The Diplomat*, 20 February 2020.

14 Katie Bohn, 'People often avoid feeling compassion for others, feel it's a lot of effort', Psu.edu, 31 August 2021, <https://www.psu.edu/news/research/story/people-often-avoid-feeling-compassion-others-feel-its-lot-effort/>.

15 '2022 Corruption Perceptions Index reveals neglect of anti-corruption efforts in Asia Pacific', Transparency.org, 31 January 2023, <https://www.transparency.org/en/press/2022-corruption-perceptions-index-neglect-anti-corruption-efforts-asia-pacific>.

16 Rajesh Misra in conversation with the author, Lucknow, 20 January 2023.

17 Ivan John in conversation with the author, 13 August 2022.

18 Anand Vardhan, 'Dear Media, Bihar doesn't need IAS or IIT toppers as role models', Newslaundry.com, 6 July 2017, <https://www.newslaundry.com/2017/07/06/dear-media-bihar-doesnt-need-ias-or-iit-toppers-as-role-models>.

19 Manjesh Rana, 'Behind the Veil: How prevalent is the practice of purdah across women in India?', *India Today*, 12 May 2022.

20 Milan Vaishnav, Neelanjan Sircar, and Devesh Kapur, 'Three economists went around India asking: do you call yourself middle class?', *The Print*, 24 November 2017.

21 Amin Maalouf, *In the Name of Identity: Violence and the Need to Belong*, United Kingdom: Arcade Pub., 2001.
22 Dr Vipul Mudgal in conversation with the author, 10 November 2023.

17. POLITICS AND THE MIDDLE CLASS

1 Nagesh Prabhu, 'Why the Indian middle class gravitates towards Modi', *The Hindu*, 7 December 2020.
2 Sabyasachi Basu Ray Chaudhury, 'How India's Economy and Hindutva Rise Together', *The Wire*, 26 August 2023.
3 S. Irfan Habib in conversation with the author, 26 June 2023.
4 Sravasti Dasgupta, 'Narendra Modi and the Question of Invoking Religion in Poll Speeches', *The Wire*, 15 April 2024; 'What promises did the BJP make in its 2014 manifesto', *Business Today*, 7 April 2019; Omar Rashid, 'Food, Clothes, Prayers, Population: You Name it, the BJP Has Communalised it', *The Wire*, 16 May 2024.
5 Abhishek Hari, 'Explainer: How the Sedition Law Has Been Used in the Modi Era', *The Wire*, 11 May 2022.
6 Anand Kumar in conversation with the author, 1 April 2023.
7 Varishtha Singh, 'The Unconstitutionality of 'Bulldozer Justice', *The Wire*, 23 November 2023.
8 Swati Shikha, Anisha Reddy, 'Delhi Burning: A Timeline Of Anti-CAA Protests And Northeast Delhi Violence', *Outlook India*, 24 February 2023.
9. 'Shaheen Bagh: Anurag Thakur, Parvesh Varma penalised for comments', *BBC*, 29 January 2020.
10 Prabhash K. Dutta, 'What happened at Bhima Koregaon', *India Today*, 29 August 2018.
11 Ranjan Roy, 'The Necessity for Delinking Democracy From Majoritarianism', *The Wire*, 25 February 2020.
12 S. Irfan Habib in conversation with the author, 26 June 2023.
13 Astha Rajvanshi, 'How Modi's Supporters Used Social Media to Spread Disinformation During the Elections', *Time*, 3 June 2024.
14 Harsh Mander, 'Lynching, the scourge of new India', *The Hindu*, 16 October 2019; Kanishka Singh, 'Anti-Muslim hate speech soars in India, research group says', Reuters, 26 February 2024; Neel Madhav, Alishan Jafri, 'Why India is witnessing spike in attacks on Christians, churches', *Al Jazeera*, 2 December 2021.
15 '"Shoot the traitors" slogan raised at Union Minister Anurag Thakur's rally, Delhi CEO seeks report', *Indian Express*, 28 January 2020.
16 Professor Sudhakar in conversation with the author, Mumbai, 16 December 2022.
17 Ibid.
18 Keshav Chaturvedi in conversation with the author, New Delhi, 6 March 2023.
19 Milan Vaishnav (ed.), 'The BJP in Power: Indian Democracy and Religious Nationalism', carnegieendowment.org, 4 April 2019, <https://carnegie-production-assets.s3.amazonaws.com/static/files/BJP_In_Power_final.pdf>; Rizwan Ahmad, 'Renaming India: Saffronisation of public spaces', *Al Jazeera*, 12 October 2018; Kathleen Kavanaugh, 'The Politics of Identity: State-building and Erasure in Modi's 'New' India', georgetown.edu, 2 December 2023, <https://gjia.georgetown.edu/2023/12/02/the-politics-of-identity-state-building-and-erasure-in-modis-new-india/>.

20 Aditi Bhatia, 'Saffronisation of India: A Critical Source Analysis of Contemporary Political Ideology', *World Englishes*, Volume 39, Issue 2, May 2020, pp. 568–580.
21 S. Irfan Habib in conversation with the author, 26 June 2023.
22 Madhukar Upadhyay in conversation with the author, Noida, 23 February 2023.
23 S. Irfan Habib in conversation with the author, 26 June 2023.
24 Sucheta Mahajan in conversation with the author, 22 March 2023.
25 Anjani Thomas, 'Dara Shikoh has become modern-India's symbol of unity—it's also why he lost to Aurangzeb', *The Print*, 20 March 2023.
26 'Mughal rulers were plunderers, history will be re-written, says Uttar Pradesh deputy chief minister', *Wion*, 13 September 2017.
27 Dr Vipul Mudgal in conversation with the author, 10 November 2023.
28 Ibid.

18. EDUCATING THE MIDDLE CLASS

1 Jotirao Phule, *Shetkaryaca Asud* (Cultivator's Whipcord), Gail Omvedt and Bharat Patankar (trs.), [online facsimile], <https://drambedkarbooks.com/wp-content/uploads/2009/03/phule.pdf>.
2 Saptarshi Bhattacharya, 'India has not taken education seriously since independence: Prof. Krishna Kumar', *HinduCentre.com*, 1 December 2017.
3 Nikhil Rampal, 'China has 20-year edge but NEP can help India improve education quality—UN University paper', *The Print*, 10 July 2022.
4 'Nehru's approach to primary education lamentable: Amartya', *Economic Times*, 4 July 2011.
5 Dr. Tara Chand, P. C. Sanyal, Snehamoy Durtta, Kamta Prasad et al., 'Report of the Committee on Secondary Education in India', [online facsimile], 1948, <https://archive.org/details/dli.ministry.20265>.
6 H. B. Wood, 'Education in India under the Five-Year Plan', *The Elementary School Journal*, Volume 55, Issue 9, p. 522.
7 Sukanya Shantha, 'Source: Dalit Student's Suicide Points to Well-Known–But Ignored–Caste Discrimination in IITs', *The Wire*, 15 February 2023.
8 Muhammad Rafi, 'Dalit aaya, dalit aaya': Overwhelming evidence of Darshan Solanki facing caste discrimination at IIT-Bombay, claims family', *Mid-day*, 11 May 2023.
9 Abha Goradia, 'Aniket Ambhore suicide report: 'SC/ST students could face difficulties due to hardened attitudes against quota policy', *Indian Express*, 20 November 2019.
10 Irina Cozma, 'Values, Passion, or Purpose—Which Should Guide Your Career?', *Harvard Business Review*, 23 October 2023.
11 Saptarishi Bhattacharya, 'India has not taken education seriously since independence: Prof. Krishna Kumar'.
12 Navtan Kumar, 'Demand for uniform education system rises', *Sunday Guardian*, 20 June 2020.
13 Ibid.
14 Ministry of Human Resource Development, *National Education Policy*, Government of India, 2020.
15 'Vinay Kumar Rao IIT Director talks about the coaching industry in India and its future', *Deccan Herald*, 17 July 2023.

16 S. Irfan Habib in conversation with the author, 26 June 2023.
17 Akshat Josh in conversation with the author, 1 January 2023.
18 Nidhi Hebbar, 'India's education market: the Elite, the Pyramid Base, and everyone in between.', *Medium.com,* 12 December 2019, <https://medium.com/@nidhihebbar/indiaseducation-market-the-elite-the-pyramid-base-and-everyone-in-between-a1383aa6a6e8>.

19. STRUGGLES OF MIDDLE-CLASS WOMEN

1 'Manusmriti: The Ultimate Guide To Becoming A "Good Woman"', FeminisminIndia.com, 11 January 2018.
2 Ish Mishra, 'Woman's Question in Communal Ideologies in India: A Study into the Ideologies of RSS and Jamat-e-Islami', *Mainstream,* Volume LXI, No. 50, 27 November 2021.
3 Prabhash K. Dutta, 'When media was muzzled: History retold', *India Today,* 3 August 2018; 'Indira Gandhi death anniversary: Remembering her political journey through some of her quotes', *Mirror Online,* 31 October 2020.
4 'India Report Volume 1', *National Family Health Survey (NFHS-5), 2019-21,* Mumbai: International Institute for Population Sciences, March 2022.
5 'Chapter 3 Literacy and Education', mospi.gov.in, < https://mospi.gov.in/sites/default/files/reports_and_publication/statistical_publication/social_statistics/WM16Chapter3.pdf>.
6 'Female employment rate declines in India', Lawstreet.co, 31 July 2018, <https://lawstreet.co/executive/female-employment-rate-declines-in-india#google_vignette>.
7 'White-collar job openings for women witness 35% growth in February: Report', *Economic Times,* 6 March 2023.
8 Nilanjana Bhowmick, *Lies Our Mothers Told Us: The Indian Woman's Burden,* New Delhi: Aleph Book Company, 2022.
9 'Cruelty by husbands and their relatives makes up one-third of crimes against women in India: MoSP', *Al Jazeera,* 26 March 2023; Neeraj Chauhan, 'Crimes against women, children rose by 4%, 8.7% in 2022: NCRB report', *Hindustan Times,* 4 December 2023.
10 Anamika Prasad in conversation with the author, 30 July 2024.
11 Ibid.
12 Ibid.
13 Vandana Shah in conversation with the author, 6 January 2023.
14 Zoya (name changed on request) in conversation with the author, 30 July 2024.
15 'About 4.6 crore females 'missing' in India due to son preference: UNFPA report', *The Week,* 1 July 2020.
16 Sujatha Gidla, *Ants Among Elephants: An Untouchable Family and the Making of Modern* India, United States: Farrar, Straus and Giroux, 2017.
17 Ghazala Wahab in conversation with the author, 6 March 2023.
18 Ibid.
19 Vandana Shah in conversation with the author, Mumbai, 6 January 2023.
20 Martin Rew, Geetanjali Gangoli, Aisha K. Gill, 'Violence between Female In-laws in India', *Journal of International Women's Studies:* Vol. 14: No. 1.

20. INTERACTION WITH OTHER CLASSES

1 R. M. Maciver and Charles R. Page, *Society: An Introductory Analysis*, London: Macmillan, 1950.
2 Anand Kumar in conversation with the author, 1 April 2023.
3 S. C. Mohapatra in conversation with the author, New Delhi, 11 November 2022.
4 Snehal Shingavi, 'Austerity, neoliberalism, and the Indian working class', *International Socialist Review*, Issue 103, Winter 2016–17.
5 Rajesh Misra in conversation with the author, Lucknow, 23 January 2023.
6 Ibid.
7 Thorstein Veblen, *The Theory of the Leisure Class: An Economic Study of Institutions*, New York: Macmillan Company, 1915, p. 74.
8 Deepanshu Mohan, 'Are India's elite abandoning the country's poor and vulnerable?', *Scroll.in*, 15 February 2022, <https://scroll.in/article/1016930/are-indias-elite-abandoningthe-countrys-poor-and-vulnerable>.
9 Tanya Chaitanya, 'Nita Ambani: I Gave My Kids Rs.5 As Pocket Money', iDiva.com, 7 October 2011, <https://www.idiva.com/career/money/nita-ambani-i-gave-my-kids-rs5-as-pocket-money/8216>.
10 S. C. Mohapatra in conversation with the author, New Delhi, 11 November 2022.

21. MIDDLE CLASSES AROUND THE WORLD

1 Luiz Carlos Bresser-Pereira, 'The Golden Age of Capitalism', Bresserpereira.org.br, <https://www.bresserpereira.org.br/index.php/academic-papers/11503-8013>.
2 Kei Koizumi, 'The Evolution of Public Funding of Science in the United States From World War II to the Present', *Oxford Research Encyclopedias*, 31 March 2020.
3 Anand Kumar in conversation with the author, 1 April 2023.
4 Selin Sayek Böke, 'Socio-economic inequalities in Europe: time to restore social trust by strengthening social rights', Parliamentary Assembly of the Council of Europe, 9 September 2021, <https://assembly.coe.int/LifeRay/SOC/Pdf/TextesProvisoires/2021/20210909-SocialInequalities-EN.pdf>.
5 Ibid.
6 Homi Kharas, 'How a Growing Global Middle Class Could Save the World's Economy', Pewresearch.org, 5 July 2016.
7 Álvaro Leandro, 'United States: Challenges Faced by the Middle Class', *Oecdecoscope*, 12 October 2022.
8 Rakesh Kochhar, 'The Pandemic Stalls Growth in the Global Middle Class, Pushes Poverty up Sharply; by Rakesh Kochhar', Pewresearch.org, 18 March 2021.
9 Jad Moawad, Daniel Oesch, 'The Myth of the Middle-Class Squeeze: Employment and Western Countries, 1980-2020, European Commission, Seville, 2023, JRC131515)
10 Louis Chauvel, Eyal Bar Haim, Anne Hartung, Emily Murphy, 'Rewealthization in twenty-first century Western countries: the defining trend of the socioeconomic squeeze of the middle class', *The Journal of Chinese Sociology*, Volume 8, 11 January 2021.
11 Ibid.
12 Caroline Zientek, 'Examining Japan's Middle Class', *Borgen Project*, 10 September 2022, <https://borgenproject.org/japans-middle-class/>.
13 Chris Versace, Lenore Elle Hawkins, and Mark Abssy, 'World Reimagined: The

Rise of the Global Middle Class', Nasdaq.com, 9 July 2021, <https://www.324nasdaq.com/articles/world-reimagined%3A-the-rise-of-the-global-middle-class-2021-07-09>.

14 Rana Mitter, 'China's race for growth is fading. So too is its dream of middle-class security', *The Guardian*, 23 July 2018.

15 Sujit Dutta in conversation with the author, New Delhi, 28 February 2023.

16 Ibid.

17 Ibid.

18 Mitter, 'China's race for growth is fading. So too is its dream of middle-class security'.

19 Ibid.

20 Ibid.

21 Ibid.

22 Sujit Dutta in conversation with the author, New Delhi, 28 February 2023.

23 Ibid.

24 Jean-Louis Rocca, 'China's frustrated middle class', *Le Monde diplomatique*, November 2022.

25 Ibid.

CONCLUSION: THE WAY FORWARD

1 Dhurjati Prasad Mukherji, *Modern Indian Culture: A Sociological Study*, India: Hind Kitabs, 1948, p. 2.

2 Professor Sudhakar in conversation with the author, Mumbai, 16 December 2022.

3 S. C. Mohapatra in conversation with the author, New Delhi, 11 November 2022.

4 Professor Sudhakar in conversation with the author, Mumbai, 16 December 2022.

5 S. C. Mohapatra in conversation with the author, New Delhi, 11 November 2023.

6 Kumudin Das, K. C. Das, T. K. Roy and P. K. Tripathy, 'Dynamics of inter-religious and inter-caste marriages in India', *Population Association*, <https://paa2011.populationassociation.org/papers/111281#:~:text=Table%201%20shows%20that%20in,husbands%20belong%20to%20higher%20castes

7 'Are people becoming more open to intercaste marriages', *Times of India*, 24 June 2019.; Zenaira Bakhsh, 'When India's right wing comes for interfaith marriage: 'Love jihad,' a right-wing conspiracy theory, is putting the lives of Muslim-Hindu couples at risk', Codastory.com, 9 January 2023.

8 Gopal Guru, 'Nationalism as the Framework for Dalit Self-realization', *The Brown Journal of World Affairs*, Volume 23, Issue 1, *JSTOR Daily*, 2016, pp. 239–252.

9 Keshav Chaturvedi in conversation with the author, New Delhi, 6 March 2023.

10 Anshika Srivastava, 'Dalits and Social Mobility: A Discussion on the Dalit Middle Class', *Asian Journal of Multidisciplinary Studies*, Volume 3, Issue 2, January 2015.

11 Anand Teltumbde, *Dalits: Past, Present and Future*, New Delhi: Routledge, 2020, pp. 8–9.

12 'Reservations have created an urban middle class of SCs, STs, OBCs', AllIndiansMatter.in, 7 September 2022, <https://www.allindiansmatter.in/reservations-have-created-an-urban-middle-class-of-scs-sts-obcs/>.

13 Ibid.

14 Shivam Vij, 'In Uttar Pradesh, Dalits and Yadavs pretend they never hated each other', *The Print*, 13 May 2019.

15 Keshav Chaturvedi in conversation with the author, New Delhi, 6 March 2023.
16 Ivan John in conversation with the author, Mumbai, 13 August 2022.
17 S. Irfan Habib in conversation with the author, 26 June 2023.
18 Ibid.
19 S. C. Mohapatra in conversation with the author, New Delhi, 11 November 2023.
20 Rajesh Misra in conversation with the author, Lucknow, 20 January 2023.
21 'Why Indians don't want to be Indian citizens anymore', *Economic Times*, 1 July 2023.

Index